THE ANNOTATED ALICE

The ANNOTATED Alice

ALICE'S ADVENTURES IN WONDERLAND
&
THROUGH THE LOOKING GLASS

BY

LEWIS CARROLL

ILLUSTRATED BY
JOHN TENNIEL

With an Introduction and Notes by
MARTIN GARDNER

A MERIDIAN BOOK

MARTIN GARDNER was born in Tulsa, Oklahoma. He attended the University of Chicago, where he majored in philosophy, and began his writing career as a reporter on the Tulsa *Tribune*. He is well known for his regular monthly column on recreational mathematics in *Scientific American,* and a recently published collection of these under the title *The Scientific American Book of Mathematical Puzzles & Diversions* has proved very popular. Among Mr. Gardner's other books are *Fads and Fallacies in the Name of Science* and *Logic Machines and Diagrams.* In 1962 he brought out *The Annotated Snark* and *Relativity for the Millions.*

First Printing/World Publishing Company, October, 1963
First Printing/New American Library, May, 1974
             12   13   14   15   16   17
PRINTED IN THE UNITED STATES OF AMERICA

For Brother Jim and Sister Judy

"Wipe your glosses with what you know"

JAMES JOYCE

Introduction

Let it be said at once that there is something preposterous about an annotated ALICE. Writing in 1932, on the hundred-year anniversary of Lewis Carroll's birth, Gilbert K. Chesterton voiced his "dreadful fear" that Alice's story had already fallen under the heavy hands of the scholars and was becoming "cold and monumental like a classic tomb."

"Poor, poor, little Alice!" bemoaned G.K. "She has not only been caught and made to do lessons; she has been forced to inflict lessons on others. Alice is now not only a schoolgirl but a schoolmistress. The holiday is over and Dodgson is again a don. There will be lots and lots of examination papers, with questions like: (1) What do you know of the following; mimsy, gimble, haddocks' eyes, treacle-wells, beautiful soup? (2) Record all the moves in the chess game in *Through the Looking-Glass*, and give diagram. (3) Outline the practical policy of the White Knight for dealing with the social problem of green whiskers. (4) Distinguish between Tweedledum and Tweedledee."

There is much to be said for Chesterton's plea not to take ALICE too seriously. But no joke is funny unless you see the point of it, and sometimes a point has to be explained. In the case of ALICE we are dealing with a very curious, complicated kind of nonsense, written for British readers of another century, and we need to know a great many things that are not part of the text if we wish to capture its full wit and flavor. It is even worse than that, for some of Carroll's jokes could be understood only by residents of Oxford, and other jokes, still more private, could be understood only by the lovely daughters of Dean Liddell.

The fact is that Carroll's nonsense is not nearly as random and point-less as it seems to a modern American child who tries to read the ALICE books. One says "tries" because the time is past when a child under fifteen, even in England, can read ALICE with the same delight as gained from, say, *The Wind in the Willows* or *The Wizard of Oz*. Children today are bewildered and sometimes frightened by the nightmarish atmosphere of Alice's dreams. It is only because adults—scientists and mathematicians in particular—continue to relish the ALICE books that they are assured of immortality. It is only to such adults that the notes of this volume are addressed.

There are two types of notes I have done my best to avoid, not because they are difficult to do or should not be done, but because they are so exceedingly easy to do that any clever reader can write them out for himself. I refer to allegorical and psychoanalytic exegesis. Like Homer, the Bible, and all other great works of fantasy, the ALICE books lend themselves readily to any type of symbolic interpretation—political, metaphysical, or Freudian. Some learned commentaries of this sort are hilarious. Shane Leslie, for instance, writing on "Lewis Carroll and the Oxford Movement" (in the *London Mercury*, July 1933), finds in ALICE a secret history of the religious controversies of Victorian England. The jar of orange marmalade, for example, is a symbol of Protestantism (William of Orange; get it?). The battle of the White and Red Knights is the famous clash of Thomas Huxley and Bishop Samuel Wilberforce. The blue Caterpillar is Benjamin Jowett, the White Queen is Cardinal John Henry Newman, the Red Queen is Cardinal Henry Manning, the Cheshire Cat is Cardinal Nicholas Wiseman, and the Jabberwock "can only be a fearsome representation of the British view of the Papacy . . ."

In recent years the trend has naturally been toward psychoanalytic interpretations. Alexander Woollcott once expressed relief that the Freudians had left Alice's dreams unexplored; but that was twenty years ago and now, alas, we are all amateur head-shrinkers. We do not have to be told what it means to tumble down a rabbit hole or curl up inside a tiny house with one foot up the chimney. The rub is that any work of nonsense abounds with so many inviting symbols that you can start with any assumption you please about the author and easily build up an impressive case for it. Consider, for example, the scene in which Alice seizes the end of the White King's pencil and begins scribbling for him. In five minutes one can invent six different interpretations. Whether Carroll's unconscious had any of them in mind, however, is an altogether dubious matter. More pertinent is the fact that Carroll was interested in psychic phenomena and automatic writing, and the hypothesis must not be ruled out that it is only by accident that a pencil in this scene is shaped the way it is.

We must remember also that many characters and episodes in

ALICE are a direct result of puns and other linguistic jokes, and would have taken quite different forms if Carroll had been writing, say, in French. One does not need to look for an involved explanation of the Mock Turtle; his melancholy presence is quite adequately explained by mock-turtle soup. Are the many references to eating in ALICE a sign of Carroll's "oral aggression," or did Carroll recognize that small children are obsessed by eating and like to read about it in their books? A similar question mark applies to the sadistic elements in ALICE, which are quite mild compared with those of animated cartoons for the past thirty years. It seems unreasonable to suppose that all the makers of animated cartoons are sado-masochists; more reasonable to assume that they all made the same discovery about what children like to see on the screen. Carroll was a skillful storyteller, and we should give him credit for the ability to make a similar discovery. The point here is not that Carroll was not neurotic (we all know he was), but that books of nonsense fantasy for children are not such fruitful sources of psychoanalytic insight as one might suppose them to be. They are much too rich in symbols. The symbols have too many explanations.

Readers who care to explore the various conflicting analytic interpretations that have been made of ALICE will find useful the references cited in the bibliography at the back of this book. Phyllis Greenacre, a New York psychoanalyst, has made the best and most detailed study of Carroll from this point of view. Her arguments are most ingenious, possibly true, but one wishes that she were less sure of herself. There is a letter in which Carroll speaks of his father's death as "the greatest blow that has ever fallen on my life." In the Alice books the most obvious mother symbols, the Queen of Hearts and the Red Queen, are heartless creatures, whereas the King of Hearts and the White King, both likely candidates for father symbols, are amiable fellows. Suppose, however, we give all this a looking-glass reversal and decide that Carroll had an unresolved Oedipus complex. Perhaps he identified little girls with his mother so that Alice herself is the real mother symbol. This is Dr. Greenacre's view. She points out that the age difference between Carroll and Alice was about the same as the age difference between Carroll and his mother, and she assures us that this "reversal of the unresolved Oedipal attachment is quite common." According to Dr. Greenacre, the Jabberwock and Snark are screen memories of what analysts still persist in calling the "primal scene." Maybe so; but one wonders.

The inner springs of the Rev. Charles Lutwidge Dodgson's eccentricities may be obscure, but the outer facts about his life are well known. For almost half a century he was a resident of Christ Church, the Oxford college that was his alma mater. For more than half that period he was a teacher of mathematics. His lectures were humorless and boring. He made no significant contributions to mathematics, though two of his logical paradoxes, published in the journal *Mind*, touch on difficult problems involving what is now called metalogic. His books on logic and mathematics are written quaintly, with many amusing problems, but their level is elementary and they are seldom read today.

In appearance Carroll was handsome and asymmetric—two facts that may have contributed to his interest in mirror reflections. One shoulder was higher than the other, his smile was slightly askew, and the level of his blue eyes not quite the same. He was of moderate height, thin, carrying himself stiffly erect and walking with a peculiar jerky gait. He was afflicted with one deaf ear and a stammer that trembled his upper lip. Although ordained a deacon (by Bishop Wilberforce) he seldom preached because of his speech defect and he never went on to holy orders. There is no doubt about the depth and sincerity of his Church of England views. He was orthodox in all respects save his inability to believe in eternal damnation.

In politics he was a Tory, awed by lords and ladies and inclined to be snobbish toward inferiors. He objected strongly to profanity and suggestive dialogue on the stage, and one of his many unfinished projects was to bowdlerize Bowdler by editing an edition of Shakespeare suitable for young girls. He planned to do this by taking out certain passages that even Bowdler had found inoffensive. He was so shy that he could sit for hours at a social gathering and contribute nothing to the conversation, but his shyness and stammering "softly and suddenly vanished away" when he was alone with a child. He was a fussy, prim, fastidious, cranky, kind, gentle bachelor whose life was sexless, uneventful and happy. "My life is so strangely free from all trial and trouble," he once wrote, "that I cannot doubt my own happiness is one of the talents entrusted to me to 'occupy' with, till the Master shall return, by doing something to make other lives happy."

So far so dull. We begin to catch glimpses of a more colorful personality when we turn to Charles Dodgson's hobbies. As a child he dabbled in puppetry and sleight of hand, and throughout his life enjoyed doing magic tricks, especially for children. He liked to form a mouse with his handkerchief then make it jump mysteriously out of his hand. He taught children how to fold paper boats and paper pistols that popped when swung through the air. He took up photography when the art was just beginning, specializing in portraits of children and famous people, and composing his pictures with remarkable skill and good taste. He enjoyed games of all sorts, especially chess, croquet, backgammon and billiards. He invented a great many mathematical and word puzzles, games, cipher methods, and a system for memorizing numbers (in his diary he mentions using his mnemonic system for memorizing *pi* to seventy-one decimal places). He was an enthusiastic patron of opera and the theater at a time when this was frowned upon by church officials. The famous actress Ellen Terry was one of his lifelong friends.

Ellen Terry was an exception. Carroll's principal hobby—the hobby that aroused his greatest joys—was entertaining little girls. "I am fond of children (except boys)," he once wrote. He professed a horror of little boys, and in later life avoided them as much as possible. Adopting the Roman symbol for a day of good fortune, he would write in his diary, "I mark this day with a white stone" whenever he felt it to be specially memorable. In almost every case his white-stone days were days on which he entertained a child-friend or made the acquaintance of a new one. He thought the naked bodies of little girls (unlike the bodies of boys) extremely beautiful. Upon occasion he sketched or photographed them in the nude, with the mother's permission, of course. "If I had the loveliest child in the world, to draw or photograph," he wrote, "and found she had a modest shrinking (however slight, and however easily overcome) from being taken nude, I should feel it was a solemn duty owed to God to drop the request *altogether*." Lest these undraped pictures later embarrass the girls, he requested that after his death they be destroyed or returned to the children or their parents. None seems to have survived.

In *Sylvie and Bruno Concluded* there is a passage that expresses poignantly Carroll's fixation upon little girls of all the passion of which he was capable. The narrator of the story, a thinly disguised Charles Dodgson, recalls that only once in his life did he ever see perfection. ". . . it was in a London exhibition, where, in making my way through a crowd, I suddenly met, face to face, a child of quite unearthly beauty." Carroll never ceased looking for such a child. He became adept at meeting little girls in railway carriages and on public beaches. A black bag that he always took with him on these seaside trips contained wire puzzles and other unusual gifts to stimulate their interest. He even carried a supply of safety pins for pinning up the skirts of little girls when they wished to wade in the surf. Opening gambits could be amusing. Once when he was sketching near the sea a little girl who had fallen into the water walked by with dripping clothes. Carroll tore a corner from a piece of blotting paper and said, "May I offer you this to blot yourself up?"

A long procession of charming little girls (we know they were charming from their photographs) skipped through Carroll's life, but none ever quite took the place of his first love, Alice Liddell. "I have had scores of child-friends since your time," he wrote to her after her marriage, "but they have been quite a different thing." Alice was the daughter of Henry George Liddell (the name rhymes with fiddle), the dean of Christ Church. Some notion of how attractive Alice must have been can be gained from a passage in *Praeterita,* a fragmentary autobiography by John Ruskin. Florence Becker Lennon reprints the passage in her biography of Carroll, and it is from her book that I shall quote.

Ruskin was at that time teaching at Oxford and he had given Alice drawing lessons. One snowy winter evening when Dean and Mrs. Liddell were dining out, Alice invited Ruskin over for a cup of tea. "I think Alice must have sent me a little note," he writes, "when the eastern coast of Tom Quad was clear." Ruskin had settled in an armchair by a roaring fire when the door burst open and "there was a sudden sense of some stars having been blown out by the wind." Dean and Mrs. Liddell had returned, having found the roads blocked with snow.

"How sorry you must be to see us, Mr. Ruskin!" said Mrs. Liddell.

"I was never more so," Ruskin replied.

The dean suggested that they go back to their tea. "And so we did," Ruskin continues, "but we couldn't keep papa and mamma out of the drawing-room when they had done dinner, and I went back to Corpus, disconsolate."

And now for the most significant part of the story. Ruskin *thinks* that Alice's sisters, Edith and Rhoda, were also present, but he isn't sure. "It is all so like a dream now," he writes. Yes, Alice must have been quite an attractive little girl.

There has been much argumentation about whether Carroll was in love with Alice Liddell. If this is taken to mean that he wanted to marry her or make love to her, there is not the slightest evidence for it. On the other hand, his attitude toward her was the attitude of a man in love. We do know that Mrs. Liddell sensed something unusual, took steps to discourage Carroll's attention, and later burned all of his early letters to Alice. There is a cryptic reference in Carroll's diary on October 28, 1862, to his being out of Mrs. Liddell's good graces "ever since Lord Newry's business." What business Lord Newry has in Carroll's diary remains to this day a tantalizing mystery.

There is no indication that Carroll was conscious of anything but the purest innocence in his relations with little girls, nor is there a hint of impropriety in any of the fond recollections that dozens of them later wrote about him. There was a tendency in Victorian England, reflected in the literature of the time, to idealize the beauty and virginal purity of little girls. No doubt this made it easier for Carroll to suppose that his fondness for them was on a high spiritual level, though of course this hardly is a sufficient explanation for that fondness. Of late Carroll has been compared with Humbert Humbert, the narrator of Vladimir Nabokov's novel *Lolita*. It is true that both had a passion for little girls, but their goals were exactly opposite. Humbert Humbert's "nymphets" were creatures to be used carnally. Carroll's little girls appealed to him precisely because he felt sexually safe with them. The thing that distinguishes Carroll from other writers who lived sexless lives (Thoreau, Henry James . . .) and from writers who were strongly drawn to little girls (Poe, Ernest Dowson . . .) was his curious combination, almost unique in literary history, of complete sexual innocence with a passion that can only be described as thoroughly heterosexual.

Carroll enjoyed kissing his child-friends and closing letters by sending them 10,000,000 kisses, or $4\frac{3}{4}$, or a two-millionth part of a kiss. He would have been horrified at the suggestion that a sexual element might be involved. There is one amusing record in his diary of his having kissed one little girl, only to discover later that she was seventeen. Carroll promptly wrote a mock apology to her mother, assuring her that it would never happen again, but the mother was not amused.

On one occasion a pretty fifteen-year-old actress named Irene Barnes (she later played the roles of White Queen and Knave of Hearts in the stage musical of ALICE) spent a week with Charles Dodgson at a seaside resort. "As I remember him now," Irene recalls in her autobiography, *To Tell My Story* (the passage is quoted by Roger Green in Vol. 2, page 454, of Carroll's *Diary*), "he was very slight, a little under six foot, with a fresh, youngish face, white hair, and an impression of extreme cleanliness. . . . He had a deep love for children, though I am inclined to think not such a great understanding of them. . . . His great delight was to teach me his Game of Logic [this was a method of solving syllogisms by placing black and red counters on a diagram of Carroll's own invention]. Dare I say this made the evening rather long, when the band was playing outside on the parade, and the moon shining on the sea?"

It is easy to say that Carroll found an outlet for his repressions in the unrestrained, whimsically violent visions of his ALICE books. Victorian children no doubt enjoyed similar release. They were delighted to have at last some books without a pious moral, but Carroll grew more and more restive with the thought that he had not yet written a book for youngsters that would convey some sort of evangelistic Christian message. His effort in this direction was *Sylvie and Bruno,* a long, fantastic novel that appeared in two separately published parts. It contains some splendid comic scenes, and the Gardener's song, which runs like a demented fugue through the tale, is Carroll at his best. Here is the final verse, sung by the Gardener with tears streaming down his cheeks.

> He thought he saw an Argument
> That proved he was the Pope:
> He looked again, and found it was
> A Bar of Mottled Soap.
> "A fact so dread," he faintly said,
> "Extinguishes all hope!"

But the superb nonsense songs were not the features Carroll most admired about this story. He preferred a song sung by the two fairy children, Sylvie and her brother Bruno, the refrain of which went:

> For I think it is Love,
> For I feel it is Love,
> For I'm sure it is nothing but Love!

Carroll considered this the finest poem he had ever written. Even those who may agree with the sentiment behind it, and behind other portions of the novel that are heavily sugared with piety, find it difficult to read these portions today without embarrassment for the author. They seem to have been written at the bottom of treacle wells. Sadly one must conclude that, on the whole, *Sylvie and Bruno* is both an artistic and rhetorical failure. Surely few Victorian children, for whom the story was intended, were ever moved, amused, or elevated by it.

Ironically, it is Carroll's earlier and pagan nonsense that has, at least for a few modern readers, a more effective religious message than *Sylvie and Bruno.* For nonsense, as Chesterton liked to tell us, is a way of looking at existence that is akin to religious humility and wonder. The Unicorn thought Alice a fabulous monster. It is part of the philosophic dullness of our time that there are millions of rational monsters walking about on their hind legs, observing the world through pairs of flexible little lenses, periodically supplying themselves with energy by pushing organic substances through holes in their faces, who see nothing fabulous whatever about themselves. Occasionally the noses of these creatures are shaken by momentary paroxysms. Kierkegaard once imagined a philosopher sneezing while recording one of his profound sentences. How could such a man, Kierkegaard wondered, take his metaphysics seriously?

The last level of metaphor in the ALICE books is this: that life, viewed rationally and without illusion, appears to be a nonsense tale told by an idiot mathematician. At the heart of things science finds only a mad, never-ending quadrille of Mock Turtle Waves and Gryphon Particles. For a moment the waves and particles dance in grotesque, inconceivably complex patterns capable of reflecting on their own absurdity. We all live slapstick lives, under an inexplicable sentence of death, and when we try to find out what the Castle authorities want us to do, we are shifted from one bumbling bureaucrat to another. We are not even sure that Count West-West, the owner of the Castle, really exists. More than one critic has commented on the similarities between Kafka's *Trial* and the trial of the Jack of Hearts; between Kafka's *Castle* and a chess game in which living pieces are ignorant of the game's plan and cannot tell if they move of their own wills or are being pushed by invisible fingers.

This vision of the monstrous mindlessness of the cosmos ("Off with its head!") can be grim and disturbing, as it is in Kafka and the Book of Job, or lighthearted comedy, as in ALICE or Chesterton's *The Man Who Was Thursday*. When Sunday, the symbol of God in Chesterton's metaphysical nightmare, flings little messages to his pursuers, they turn out to be nonsense messages. One of them is even signed Snowdrop, the name of Alice's White Kitten. It is a vision that can lead to despair and suicide, to the laughter that closes Jean Paul Sartre's story "The Wall," to the humanist's resolve to carry on bravely in the face of ultimate darkness. Curiously, it can also suggest the wild hypothesis that there may be a light behind the darkness.

Laughter, declares Reinhold Niebuhr in one of his finest sermons, is a kind of no man's land between faith and despair. We preserve our sanity by laughing at life's surface absurdities, but the laughter turns to bitterness and derision if directed toward the deeper irrationalities of evil and death. "That is why," he concludes, "there is laughter in the vestibule of the temple, the echo of laughter in the temple itself, but only faith and prayer, and no laughter, in the holy of holies."

Lord Dunsany said the same thing this way in *The Gods of Pagana*. The speaker is Limpang-Tung, the god of mirth and melodious minstrels.

"I will send jests into the world and a little mirth. And while Death seems to thee as far away as the purple rim of hills, or sorrow as far off as rain in the blue days of summer, then pray to Limpang-Tung. But when thou growest old, or ere thou diest, pray not to Limpang-Tung, for thou becomest part of a scheme that he doth not understand.

"Go out into the starry night, and Limpang-Tung will dance with thee . . . Or offer up a jest to Limpang-Tung; only pray not in thy sorrow to Limpang-Tung, for he saith of sorrow: 'It may be very clever of the gods, but he doth not understand.' "

ALICE'S ADVENTURES IN WONDERLAND and THROUGH THE LOOKING-GLASS are two incomparable jests that the Reverend C. L. Dodgson, on a mental holiday from Christ Church chores, once offered up to Limpang-Tung.

Alice's
ADVENTURES
IN WONDERLAND

CHAPTER

All in the golden afternoon[1]
  Full leisurely we glide;
For both our oars, with little skill,
  By little arms are plied,
While little hands make vain pretence
  Our wanderings to guide.

Ah, cruel Three! In such an hour,
  Beneath such dreamy weather,
To beg a tale of breath too weak
  To stir the tiniest feather!
Yet what can one poor voice avail
  Against three tongues together?

Imperious Prima flashes forth
  Her edict "to begin it":
In gentler tones Secunda hopes
  "There will be nonsense in it."
While Tertia interrupts the tale
  Not *more* than once a minute.

1. In these prefatory verses Carroll recalls that "golden afternoon" in 1862 when he and his friend the Reverend Robinson Duckworth (then a fellow of Trinity College, Oxford, later canon of Westminster) took the three charming Liddell sisters on a rowing expedition up the Thames. "Prima" was the eldest sister, Lorina Charlotte, age thirteen. Alice Pleasance, age ten, was "Secunda," and the youngest sister, Edith, age eight, was "Tertia." Carroll was then thirty. The date was Friday, July 4, "as memorable a day in the history of literature," W. H. Auden has observed, "as it is in American history."

The trip was about three miles, beginning at Folly Bridge, near Oxford, and ending at the village of Godstow. "We had tea on the bank there," Carroll recorded in his diary, "and did not reach Christ Church again till quarter past eight, when we took them on to my rooms to see my collection of micro-photographs, and restored them to the Deanery just before nine." Seven months later he added to this entry the following note: "On which occasion I told them the fairy-tale of Alice's adventures underground . . ."

Twenty-five years later (in his article "Alice on the Stage," *The Theatre,* April 1887) Carroll wrote:

Many a day had we rowed together on that quiet stream — the three little maidens and I—and many a fairy tale had been extemporised for their benefit — whether it were at times when the narrator was "i' the vein,"

21

and fancies unsought came crowding thick upon him, or at times when the jaded Muse was goaded into action, and plodded meekly on, more because she had to say something than that she had something to say— yet none of these many tales got written down: they lived and died, like summer midges, each in its own golden afternoon until there came a day when, as it chanced, one of my little listeners petitioned that the tale might be written out for her. That was many a year ago, but I distinctly remember, now as I write, how, in a desperate attempt to strike out some new line of fairy-lore, I had sent my heroine straight down a rabbit-hole, to begin with, without the least idea what was to happen afterwards. And so, to please a child I loved (I don't remember any other motive), I printed in manuscript, and illustrated with my own crude designs — designs that rebelled against every law of Anatomy or Art (for I had never had a lesson in drawing) — the book which I have just had published in facsimile. In writing it out, I added many fresh ideas, which seemed to grow of themselves upon the original stock; and many more added themselves when, years afterwards, I wrote it all over again for publication. . . .
Stand forth, then, from the shadowy past, "Alice," the child of my dreams. Full many a year has slipped away, since that "golden afternoon" that gave thee birth, but I can call it up almost as clearly as if it were yesterday — the cloudless blue above, the watery mirror below, the boat drifting idly on its way, the tinkle of the drops that fell from the oars, as they waved so sleepily to and fro, and (the one bright gleam of life in all the slumberous scene) the three eager faces, hungry for news of fairy-land, and who would not be said "nay" to: from whose lips "Tell us a story, please," had all the stern immutability of Fate!

Alice twice recorded her memories of the occasion. The following lines are quoted by Stuart Collingwood in *The Life and Letters of Lewis Carroll:*

Most of Mr. Dodgson's stories were told to us on river expeditions to Nuneham or Godstow, near Oxford. My eldest sister, now Mrs. Skene, was 'Prima', I was 'Secunda', and 'Tertia' was my sister Edith. I believe the beginning of Alice was told one summer afternoon when the sun was so burning that we had landed in the meadows down the river, deserting the boat to take refuge in the only bit of shade to be found, which was under a new-made hayrick. Here from all three came the old petition of 'Tell us a story', and so began the ever-delightful tale. Sometimes to tease us — and perhaps being really tired — Mr. Dodgson would stop suddenly and say, 'And that's all till next time.' 'Ah, but it is next time,' would be the exclamation from all three; and after some persuasion the story would start afresh. Another day, perhaps the story would begin in the boat, and Mr. Dodgson, in the middle of telling a thrilling adventure, would pretend to go fast asleep, to our great dismay.

Alice's son, Caryl Hargreaves, writing in the *Cornhill Magazine,* July 1932, quotes his mother as follows:

Nearly all of *Alice's Adventures Underground* was told on that blazing summer afternoon with the heat haze shimmering over the meadows where the party landed to shelter for a while in the shadow cast by the haycocks near Godstow. I think the stories he told us that afternoon must have been better than usual, because I have such a distinct recollection of the expedition, and also, on the next day I started to pester him to write down the story for me, which I had never done before. It was due to my 'going on, going on' and importunity that, after saying he would think about it, he eventually gave the hesitating promise which started him writing it down at all.

And finally we have Reverend Duckworth's account, to be found in Collingwood's *The Lewis Carroll Picture Book:*

I rowed *stroke* and he rowed *bow* in the famous Long Vacation voyage to

All in the Golden Afternoon

Anon, to sudden silence won,
  In fancy they pursue
The dream-child moving through a land
  Of wonders wild and new,
In friendly chat with bird or beast—
  And half believe it true.

And ever, as the story drained
  The wells of fancy dry,
And faintly strove that weary one
  To put the subject by,
"The rest next time—" "It *is* next time!"
  The happy voices cry.

Thus grew the tale of Wonderland:
  Thus slowly, one by one,
Its quaint events were hammered out—
  And now the tale is done,
And home we steer, a merry crew,
  Beneath the setting sun.

Alice! A childish story take,
  And with a gentle hand
Lay it where Childhood's dreams are
  twined
  In Memory's mystic band,
Like pilgrim's withered wreath of
  flowers[2]
  Pluck'd in a far-off land.

Godstow, when the three Miss Liddells were our passengers, and the
story was actually composed and
spoken *over my shoulder* for the
benefit of Alice Liddell, who was
acting as 'cox' of our gig. I remember
turning round and saying, 'Dodgson,
is this an extempore romance of
yours?' And he replied, 'Yes, I'm inventing as we go along.' I also well
remember how, when we had conducted the three children back to the
Deanery, Alice said, as she bade us
good-night, 'Oh, Mr. Dodgson, I wish
you would write out Alice's adventures for me.' He said he should try,
and he afterwards told me that he sat
up nearly the whole night, commit-
ting to a MS. book his recollections
of the drolleries with which he had
enlivened the afternoon. He added
illustrations of his own, and presented the volume, which used often
to be seen on the drawing-room table
at the Deanery.

It is with sadness I add that
when a check was made in 1950
with the London meteorological
office (as reported in Helmut Gernsheim's *Lewis Carroll: Photographer*) records indicated that the
weather near Oxford on July 4,
1862, was "cool and rather wet."
There is little likelihood that this
is wrong. Nor is it possible that
Carroll incorrectly dated his entry
about the trip to Godstow, for his
diary has an entry for every day of
the week in question. The most
probable explanation of these de-
pressing facts is that Carroll, and
later both Duckworth and Alice,
confused the memorable day with
sunnier occasions on which similar
boating trips were made and similar tales told. No matter. The day
was golden enough.

2. It was a common practice of
early pilgrims to wear wreaths of
flowers on their heads.

CHAPTER I

Down the Rabbit-Hole

Alice[1] was beginning to get very tired of sitting by her sister on the bank, and of having nothing to do: once or twice she had peeped into the book her sister was reading, but it had no pictures or conversations in it, "and what is the use of a book," thought Alice, "without pictures or conversations?"

So she was considering, in her own mind (as well as she could, for the hot day made her feel very sleepy and stupid), whether the pleasure of making a daisy-chain would be worth the trouble of getting up and picking the daisies, when suddenly a white rabbit with pink eyes ran close by her.

There was nothing so *very* remarkable in that; nor did Alice think it so *very* much out of the way to hear the Rabbit say to itself, "Oh dear! Oh dear! I

[1].Tenniel's pictures of Alice are not pictures of Alice Liddell, who had dark hair cut short with straight bangs across her forehead. Carroll sent Tenniel a photograph of Mary Hilton Badcock, another child-friend, recommending that he use her for a model, but whether Tenniel accepted this advice is a matter of dispute. That he did not is strongly suggested by these lines from a letter Carroll wrote some time after both *Alice* books had been published (the letter is quoted by Mrs. Lennon in her book on Carroll):

> Mr. Tenniel is the only artist, who has drawn for me, who has resolutely refused to use a model, and declared he no more needed one than I should need a multiplication table to work a mathematical problem! I venture to think that he was mistaken and that for want of a model, he drew several pictures of "Alice" entirely out of proportion — head decidedly too large and feet decidedly too small.

In "Alice on the Stage," an article cited in a previous note, Carroll gave the following description of his heroine's personality:

What wert thou, dream-Alice, in thy foster-father's eyes? How shall he picture thee? Loving, first, loving and gentle: loving as a dog (forgive the prosaic simile, but I know no earthly love so pure and perfect), and gentle as a fawn: then courteous—courteous to *all*, high or low, grand or grotesque, King or Caterpillar, even as though she were herself a King's daughter, and her clothing of wrought gold: then trustful, ready to accept the wildest impossibilities with all that utter trust that only dreamers know; and lastly, curious— wildly curious, and with the eager enjoyment of Life that comes only in the happy hours of childhood, when all is new and fair, and when Sin and Sorrow are but names — empty words signifying nothing!

shall be too late!" (when she thought it over afterwards, it occurred to her that she ought to have wondered at this, but at the time it all seemed quite natural); but when the Rabbit actually *took a watch out of its waistcoat-pocket,* and looked at it, and then hurried on, Alice started to her feet, for it flashed across her mind that she had never before seen a rabbit with either a waistcoat-pocket, or a watch to take out of it, and, burning with curiosity, she ran across the field after it, and was just in time to see it pop down a large rabbit-hole under the hedge.

In another moment down went Alice after it, never once considering how in the world she was to get out again.

The rabbit-hole went straight on like a tunnel for some way, and then dipped suddenly down, so suddenly that Alice had not a moment to think about stopping herself before she found herself falling down what seemed to be a very deep well.

Either the well was very deep, or she fell very slowly, for she had plenty of time as she went down to look about her, and to wonder what was going to happen next. First, she tried to look down and make out what she was coming to, but it was too dark to see anything: then she looked at the sides of the well, and noticed that they were filled with cupboards and bookshelves: here and there she saw maps and pictures hung upon pegs. She took down a jar from one of the shelves as she passed: it was labeled "ORANGE MARMA-LADE," but to her great disappointment it was empty: she did not like to drop the jar, for fear of killing somebody underneath, so managed to put it into one of the cupboards as she fell past it.**2**

"Well!" thought Alice to herself, "after such a fall as this, I shall think nothing of tumbling down stairs! How brave they'll all think me at home! Why, I wouldn't say anything about it, even if I fell off the top of the house!" (which was very likely true.)**3**

Down, down, down. Would the fall *never* come to an end? "I wonder how many miles I've fallen by this time?" she said aloud. "I must be getting somewhere near the centre of the earth. Let me see: that would be four thousand miles down, I think—" (for, you see, Alice had learnt several things of this sort in her lessons in the schoolroom, and though this was not a *very* good opportunity for showing off her knowledge, as there was no one to listen to her, still it was good practice to say it over) "—yes, that's about the right distance—but then I wonder what Latitude or Longitude I've got to?" (Alice had not the slightest idea what Latitude was, or Longitude either, but she thought they were nice grand words to say.)

Presently she began again. "I wonder

2. Carroll was aware, of course, that in a normal state of free fall Alice could neither drop the jar (it would remain suspended in front of her) nor replace it on a shelf (her speed would be too great). It is interesting to note that in his novel *Sylvie and Bruno*, Chapter 8, Carroll describes the difficulty of having tea inside a falling house, as well as in a house being pulled downward at an even faster acceleration; anticipating in some respects the famous "thought experiment" in which Einstein used an imaginary falling elevator to explain certain aspects of relativity theory.

3. William Empson has pointed out (in the section on Lewis Carroll in his *Some Aspects of Pastoral*) that this is the first death joke in the Alice books. There are many more to come.

4. In Carroll's day there was considerable popular speculation about what would happen if one fell through a hole that went straight through the center of the earth. Plutarch had asked the question and many famous thinkers, including Francis Bacon and Voltaire, had argued about it. Galileo (*Dialogo dei Massimi Sistemi, Giornata Seconda*, Florence edition of 1842, Vol. 1, pages 251–52) gave the correct answer: the object would fall with increasing speed but decreasing acceleration until it reached the center of the earth, at which spot its acceleration would be zero. Thereafter it would slow down in speed, with increasing deceleration, until it reached the opening at the other end. Then it would fall back again. By ignoring air resistance and the coriolis force resulting from the earth's rotation (unless the hole ran from pole to pole), the object would oscillate back and forth forever. Air resistance of course would eventually bring it to rest at the earth's center. The interested reader should consult "A Hole through the Earth," by the French astronomer Camille Flammarion, in *The Strand Magazine*, Vol. 37, page 348, 1909, if only to look at the lurid illustrations.

Carroll's interest in the matter is indicated by the fact that in chapter 7 of his *Sylvie and Bruno*, a German professor describes (in addition to a Moebius strip, a projective plane, and other whimsical scientific and mathematical devices) a remarkable method of running trains with gravity as the sole power source. The track runs through a perfectly straight tunnel from one town to another. Since the middle of the tunnel is necessarily nearer the earth's center than its ends, the train runs downhill to the center, acquiring enough momentum to carry it up the other half of the tunnel. Curiously, such a train would make the trip (ignoring air resistance and friction of the wheels) in exactly the same time that it would take an object to fall through the center of the earth — a little more than forty-two minutes. This time is constant regardless of the tunnel's length.

The fall into the earth as a device for entering a wonderland has been used by many other writers of children's fantasy, notably by L. Frank Baum in *Dorothy and the Wizard in Oz,* and Ruth Plumly Thompson in *The Royal Book of Oz*. Baum also used the tube through the earth as an effective plot gimmick in *Tik-Tok of Oz*.

5. Dinah was the name of a cat that belonged to the Liddell children. We meet her again, with her kittens, in the first chapter of *Through the Looking-Glass.*

if I shall fall right *through* the earth![4] How funny it'll seem to come out among the people that walk with their heads downwards! The Antipathies, I think—" (she was rather glad there *was* no one listening, this time, as it didn't sound at all the right word) "—but I shall have to ask them what the name of the country is, you know. Please, Ma'am, is this New Zealand or Australia?" (and she tried to curtsey as she spoke—fancy, *curtseying* as you're falling through the air! Do you think you could manage it?) "And what an ignorant little girl she'll think me for asking! No, it'll never do to ask: perhaps I shall see it written up somewhere."

Down, down, down. There was nothing else to do, so Alice soon began talking again. "Dinah'll miss me very much to-night, I should think!" (Dinah was the cat.)[5] "I hope they'll remember her saucer of milk at tea-time. Dinah, my dear! I wish you were down here with me! There are no mice in the air, I'm afraid, but you might catch a bat, and that's very like a mouse, you know. But do cats eat bats, I wonder?" And here Alice began to get rather sleepy, and went on saying to herself, in a dreamy sort of way, "Do cats eat bats? Do cats eat bats?" and sometimes, "Do bats eat cats?" for, you see, as she couldn't answer either question, it didn't much matter which way she put it. She felt that she was dozing off, and had

just begun to dream that she was walking
hand in hand with Dinah, and was saying to her, very earnestly, "Now, Dinah,
tell me the truth: did you ever eat a bat?"
when suddenly, thump! thump! down she
came upon a heap of sticks and dry leaves,
and the fall was over.

Alice was not a bit hurt, and she
jumped up on to her feet in a moment:
she looked up, but it was all dark overhead: before her was another long passage, and the White Rabbit was still in
sight, hurrying down it. There was not a
moment to be lost: away went Alice like
the wind, and was just in time to hear it
say, as it turned a corner, "Oh my ears
and whiskers, how late it's getting!" She
was close behind it when she turned the
corner, but the Rabbit was no longer to
be seen: she found herself in a long, low
hall, which was lit up by a row of lamps
hanging from the roof.

There were doors all round the hall,
but they were all locked; and when Alice
had been all the way down one side and
up the other, trying every door, she
walked sadly down the middle, wondering how she was ever to get out again.

Suddenly she came upon a little three-
legged table, all made of solid glass: there
was nothing on it but a tiny golden key,
and Alice's first idea was that this might
belong to one of the doors of the hall;
but, alas! either the locks were too large,

or the key was too small, but at any rate it would not open any of them. However, on the second time round, she came upon a low curtain she had not noticed before, and behind it was a little door about fifteen inches high: she tried the little golden key in the lock, and to her great delight it fitted!

Alice opened the door and found that it led into a small passage, not much larger than a rat-hole: she knelt down and looked along the passage into the loveliest garden you ever saw. How she longed to get out of that dark hall, and wander about among those beds of bright flowers and those cool fountains,[6] but she could not even get her head through the doorway; "and even if my head *would* go through," thought poor Alice, "it would be of very little use without my shoulders. Oh, how I wish I could shut up like a telescope! I think I could, if I only knew how to begin." For, you see, so many out-of-the-way things had happened lately that Alice had begun to think that very few things indeed were really impossible.

There seemed to be no use in waiting by the little door, so she went back to the table, half hoping she might find another key on it, or at any rate a book of rules for shutting people up like telescopes: this time she found a little bottle on it ("which certainly was not here before," said Alice), and tied round the neck of the

6. As sublibrarian of Christ Church, Carroll used a small room overlooking the deanery garden where the Liddell children played croquet. How often he must have watched them, longing to escape from the dark halls of Oxford into the bright flowers and cool fountains of childhood's Eden!

bottle was a paper label with the words "DRINK ME" beautifully printed on it in large letters.

It was all very well to say "Drink me," but the wise little Alice was not going to do *that* in a hurry. "No, I'll look first," she said, "and see whether it's marked *'poison'* or not": for she had read several nice little stories about children who had got burnt, and eaten up by wild beasts, and other unpleasant things, all because they *would* not remember the simple rules their friends had taught them: such as, that a red-hot poker will burn you if you hold it too long; and that, if you cut your finger *very* deeply with a knife, it usually bleeds; and she had never forgotten that, if you drink much from a bottle marked "poison," it is almost certain to disagree with you, sooner or later.

However, this bottle was *not* marked "poison," so Alice ventured to taste it, and, finding it very nice (it had, in fact, a sort of mixed flavour of cherry-tart, custard, pine-apple, roast turkey, toffy, and hot buttered toast), she very soon finished it off.

* * * * *
* * * * *
* * * * *

"What a curious feeling!" said Alice, "I must be shutting up like a telescope!"

And so it was indeed: she was now only ten inches high, and her face brightened up at the thought that she was now the right size for going through the little door into that lovely garden. First, however, she waited for a few minutes to see if she was going to shrink any further: she felt a little nervous about this; "for it might end, you know," said Alice to herself, "in my going out altogether, like a candle. I wonder what I should be like then?" And she tried to fancy what the flame of a candle looks like after the candle is blown out, for she could not remember ever having seen such a thing.

After a while, finding that nothing more happened, she decided on going into the garden at once; but, alas for poor Alice! when she got to the door, she found she had forgotten the little golden key, and when she went back to the table for it, she found she could not possibly reach it: she could see it quite plainly through the glass, and she tried her best to climb up one of the legs of the table, but it was too slippery; and when she had tired herself out with trying, the poor little thing sat down and cried.

"Come, there's no use in crying like that!" said Alice to herself, rather sharply. "I advise you to leave off this minute!" She generally gave herself very good advice (though she very seldom followed it), and sometimes she scolded herself so severely as to bring tears into her eyes; and once she remembered trying to box her own ears for having cheated herself in a game of croquet she was playing against herself, for this curious child was very fond of pretending to be two people. "But it's no use now," thought poor Alice, "to pretend to be two people! Why, there's hardly enough of me left to make *one* respectable person!"

Soon her eye fell on a little glass box that was lying under the table: she opened it, and found in it a very small cake, on which the words "EAT ME" were beautifully marked in currants. "Well, I'll eat it," said Alice, "and if it makes me grow larger, I can reach the key; and if it makes me grow smaller, I can creep under the door: so either way I'll get into the garden, and I don't care which happens!"

She ate a little bit, and said anxiously to herself "Which way? Which way?" holding her hand on the top of her head to feel which way it was growing; and she was quite surprised to find that she remained the same size. To be sure, this is what generally happens when one eats cake; but Alice had got so much into the way of expecting nothing but out-of-the-way things to happen, that it seemed quite dull and stupid for life to go on in the common way.

So she set to work, and very soon finished off the cake.

    *   *   *   *   *
      *   *   *   *   *
   *   *   *   *   *

CHAPTER II

The Pool of Tears

"Curiouser and curiouser!" cried Alice (she was so much surprised, that for the moment she quite forgot how to speak good English). "Now I'm opening out like the largest telescope that ever was! Good-bye, feet!" (for when she looked down at her feet, they seemed to be almost out of sight, they were getting so far off). "Oh, my poor little feet, I wonder who will put on your shoes and stockings for you now, dears? I'm sure *I* shan't be able! I shall be a great deal too far off to trouble myself about you: you must manage the best way you can—but I must be kind to them," thought Alice, "or perhaps they won't walk the way I want to go! Let me see. I'll give them a new pair of boots every Christmas."

And she went on planning to herself how she would manage it. "They must

1. A fender is a low metal frame or screen, sometimes ornamental, between the hearthrug and an open fireplace.

go by the carrier," she thought; "and how funny it'll seem, sending presents to one's own feet! And how odd the directions will look!

> Alice's Right Foot, Esq.,
> Hearthrug,
> near the Fender.[1]
> (with Alice's love).

Oh dear, what nonsense I'm talking!"

Just at this moment her head struck against the roof of the hall: in fact she was now rather more than nine feet high, and she at once took up the little golden key and hurried off to the garden door.

Poor Alice! It was as much as she could do, lying down on one side, to look through into the garden with one eye; but to get through was more hopeless than ever: she sat down and began to cry again.

"You ought to be ashamed of yourself," said Alice, "a great girl like you," (she might well say this), "to go on crying in this way! Stop this moment, I tell you!" But she went on all the same, shedding gallons of tears, until there was a large pool all round her, about four inches deep and reaching half down the hall.

After a time she heard a little pattering of feet in the distance, and she hastily dried her eyes to see what was coming. It was the White Rabbit returning, splendidly dressed, with a pair of white kid gloves in one hand and a large fan in the other: he came trotting along in a great hurry, muttering to himself, as he came, "Oh! the Duchess, the Duchess! Oh! *won't* she be savage if I've kept her waiting!" Alice felt so desperate that she was ready to ask help of any one: so, when the Rabbit came near her, she began, in a low, timid voice, "If you please, sir—" The Rabbit started violently, dropped the white kid gloves and the fan, and scurried away into the darkness as hard as he could go.**2**

Alice took up the fan and gloves, and, as the hall was very hot, she kept fanning herself all the time she went on talking. "Dear, dear! How queer everything is to-day! And yesterday things went on just as usual. I wonder if I've been changed in the night? Let me think: *was* I the same when I got up this morning? I almost think I can remember feeling a little different. But if I'm not the same, the next question is, 'Who in the world am I?' Ah, *that's* the great puzzle!" And she began thinking over all the children she knew that were of the same age as herself, to see if she could have been changed for any of them.

"I'm sure I'm not Ada," she said, "for her hair goes in such long ringlets, and mine doesn't go in ringlets at all; and I'm sure I can't be Mabel, for I know all sorts of things, and she, oh, she knows such a very little! Besides, *she's* she, and

2. In his article "Alice on the Stage" (cited in the first note on the book's prefatory poem) Carroll wrote:

> And the White Rabbit, what of *him?* Was *he* framed on the "Alice" lines, or meant as a contrast? As a contrast, distinctly. For *her* "youth," "audacity," "vigour," and "swift directness of purpose," read "elderly," "timid," "feeble," and "nervously shilly-shallying," and you will get *something* of what I meant him to be. I *think* the White Rabbit should wear spectacles. I am sure his voice should quaver, and his knees quiver, and his whole air suggest a total inability to say "Bo" to a goose!

In *Alice's Adventures Underground,* the original manuscript, the rabbit drops a nosegay instead of a fan. Alice's subsequent shrinking is the result of smelling these flowers.

3. The simplest explanation of why Alice will never get to 20 is this: the multiplication table traditionally stops with the twelves, so if you continue this nonsense progression — 4 times 5 is 12, 4 times 6 is 13, 4 times 7 is 14, and so on — you end with 4 times 12 (the highest she can go) is 19 — just one short of 20.

A. L. Taylor, in his book *The White Knight,* advances an interesting but more complicated theory. Four times 5 actually is 12 in a number system using a base of 18. Four times 6 is 13 in a system with a base of 21. If we continue this progression, always increasing the base by 3, our products keep increasing by one until we reach 20, where for the first time the scheme breaks down. Four times 13 is not 20 (in a number system with a base of 42), but "1" followed by whatever symbol is adopted for "10."

4. Most of the poems in the two Alice books are parodies of poems or popular songs that were well known to Carroll's contemporary readers. With few exceptions the originals have now been forgotten, their titles kept alive only by the fact that Carroll chose to poke fun at them. Because much of the wit of a burlesque is missed if one is not familiar with what is being caricatured, all the originals will be reprinted in this edition. Here we have a skillful parody of the best-known poem of Isaac Watts (1674-1748), English theologian and writer of such well-known hymns as "O God, our help in ages past." Watts's poem, "Against Idleness and Mischief" (from his *Divine Songs for Children,* 1715), is reprinted below in its entirety.

> How doth the little busy bee
> Improve each shining hour,
> And gather honey all the day
> From every opening flower!

I'm I, and—oh dear, how puzzling it all is! I'll try if I know all the things I used to know. Let me see: four times five is twelve, and four times six is thirteen, and four times seven is—oh dear! I shall never get to twenty at that rate![3] However, the Multiplication Table doesn't signify: let's try Geography. London is the capital of Paris, and Paris is the capital of Rome, and Rome—no, *that's* all wrong, I'm certain! I must have been changed for Mabel! I'll try and say '*How doth the little*—' " and she crossed her hands on her lap, as if she were saying lessons, and began to repeat it, but her voice sounded hoarse and strange, and the words did not come the same as they used to do:—[4]

> "How doth the little crocodile
> Improve his shining tail,
> And pour the waters of the Nile
> On every golden scale!

> "How cheerfully he seems to grin,
> How neatly spreads his claws,
> And welcomes little fishes in,
> With gently smiling jaws!"

"I'm sure those are not the right words," said poor Alice, and her eyes filled with tears again as she went on, "I must be Mabel after all, and I shall have to go and live in that poky little house, and have next to no toys to play with, and oh, ever so many lessons to learn! No, I've made up my mind about it: if I'm Mabel,

I'll stay down here! It'll be no use their putting their heads down and saying, 'Come up again, dear!' I shall only look up and say, 'Who am I, then? Tell me that first, and then, if I like being that person, I'll come up: if not, I'll stay down here till I'm somebody else'—but, oh dear!" cried Alice, with a sudden burst of tears, "I do wish they *would* put their heads down! I am so *very* tired of being all alone here!"

As she said this, she looked down at her hands, and was surprised to see that she had put on one of the Rabbit's little white kid gloves while she was talking. "How *can* I have done that?" she thought. "I must be growing small again." She got up and went to the table to measure herself by it, and found that, as nearly as she could guess, she was now about two feet high, and was going on shrinking rapidly: she soon found out that the cause of this was the fan she was holding, and she dropped it hastily, just in time to save herself from shrinking away altogether.

"That *was* a narrow escape!" said Alice, a good deal frightened at the sudden change, but very glad to find herself still in existence.[5] "And now for the garden!" And she ran with all speed back to the little door; but, alas! the little door was shut again, and the little golden key was lying on the glass table as before, "and things are worse than ever," thought the

How skillfully she builds her cell!
How neat she spreads the wax!
And labours hard to store it well
With the sweet food she makes.

In works of labour or of skill,
I would be busy too;
For Satan finds some mischief still
For idle hands to do.

In books, or work, or healthful play,
Let my first years be passed,
That I may give for every day
Some good account at last.

5. Alice's earlier expansions have been cited by cosmologists to illustrate aspects of the expanding-universe theory. Her narrow escape in this passage calls to mind a *diminishing*-universe theory once advanced in Carrollian jest by the eminent mathematician Sir Edmund Whittaker. Perhaps the total amount of matter in the universe is continually growing smaller, and eventually the entire universe will fade away into nothing at all. "This would have the recommendation," Whittaker said, "of supplying a very simple picture of the final destiny of the universe." (*Eddington's Principle in the Philosophy of Science,* a lecture by Whittaker published in 1951 by the Cambridge University Press.)

6. Bathing machines were small individual locker rooms on wheels. They were drawn into the sea by horses to the depth desired by the bather, who then emerged modestly through a door facing the sea. A huge umbrella in back of the machine concealed the bather from public view. On the beach the machines were of course used for privacy in dressing and undressing. This quaint Victorian contraption was invented about 1750 by Benjamin Beale, a Quaker who lived at Margate, and was first used on the Margate beach. The machines were later introduced at Weymouth by Ralph Allen, the original of Mr. Allworthy in Fielding's *Tom Jones.* In Smollett's *Humphry Clinker,* 1771, a letter of Matt Bramble's describes a bathing machine at Scarborough. (See *Notes and Queries,* August 13, 1904, Series 10, Vol. 2, pages 130–31.)

The second "fit" of Carroll's great nonsense poem, *The Hunting of the Snark* (subtitled: *An Agony in Eight Fits*) tells us that a fondness for bathing machines is one of the "five unmistakable marks" by which a genuine snark can be recognized.

> *The fourth is its fondness for bathing-machines,*
> *Which it constantly carries about,*
> *And believes that they add to the beauty of scenes —*
> *A sentiment open to doubt.*

poor child, "for I never was so small as this before, never! And I declare it's too bad, that it is!"

As she said these words her foot slipped, and in another moment, splash! she was up to her chin in salt water. Her first idea was that she had somehow fallen into the

sea, "and in that case I can go back by railway," she said to herself. (Alice had been to the seaside once in her life, and had come to the general conclusion that, wherever you go to on the English coast, you find a number of bathing machines[6] in the sea, some children digging in the sand with wooden spades, then a row of lodging houses, and behind them a railway station.) However, she soon made out that she was in the pool of tears which she had wept when she was nine feet high.

"I wish I hadn't cried so much!" said Alice, as she swam about, trying to find her way out. "I shall be punished for it now,

I suppose, by being drowned in my own tears! That *will* be a queer thing, to be sure! However, everything is queer to-day."

Just then she heard something splashing about in the pool a little way off, and she swam nearer to make out what it was: at first she thought it must be a walrus or hippopotamus, but then she remembered how small she was now, and she soon made out that it was only a mouse, that had slipped in like herself.

"Would it be of any use, now," thought Alice, "to speak to this mouse? Everything is so out-of-the-way down here, that I should think very likely it can talk: at any rate, there's no harm in trying." So she began: "O Mouse, do you know the way out of this pool? I am very tired of swimming about here, O Mouse!" (Alice thought this must be the right way of speaking to a mouse: she had never done such a thing before, but she remembered having seen, in her brother's Latin Grammar, "A mouse—of a mouse—to a mouse—a mouse—O mouse!" The mouse looked at her rather inquisitively, and seemed to her to wink with one of its little eyes, but it said nothing.

"Perhaps it doesn't understand English," thought Alice. "I daresay it's a French mouse, come over with William the Conqueror." (For, with all her knowledge of history, Alice had no very clear notion how long ago anything had happened.) So she began again: "Où est ma chatte?" which was the first sentence in her French lesson-book. The Mouse gave a sudden leap out of the water, and seemed to quiver all over with fright. "Oh, I beg your pardon!" cried Alice hastily, afraid that she had hurt the poor animal's feelings. "I quite forgot you didn't like cats."

"Not like cats!" cried the Mouse, in a shrill, passionate voice. "Would *you* like cats if you were me?"

"Well, perhaps not," said Alice in a soothing tone: "don't be angry about it. And yet I wish I could show you our cat Dinah. I think you'd take a fancy to cats, if you could only see her. She is such a dear quiet thing," Alice went on, half to herself, as she swam lazily about in the pool, "and she sits purring so nicely by the fire, licking her paws and washing her face—and she is such a nice soft thing to nurse—and she's such a capital one for catching mice—oh, I beg your pardon!" cried Alice again, for this time the Mouse was bristling all over, and she felt certain it must be really offended. "We won't talk about her any more if you'd rather not."

"We, indeed!" cried the Mouse, who was trembling down to the end of its tail. "As if *I* would talk on such a subject! Our family always *hated* cats: nasty, low, vulgar things! Don't let me hear the name again!"

"I won't indeed!" said Alice, in a great hurry to change the subject of conversation. "Are you—are you fond—of—of dogs?" The Mouse did not answer, so Alice went on eagerly: "There is such a nice little dog, near our house, I should like to show you! A little bright-eyed terrier, you know, with oh, such long curly brown hair! And it'll fetch things when you throw them, and it'll sit up and beg for its dinner, and all sorts of things—I can't remember half of them—and it belongs to a farmer, you know, and he says it's so useful, it's worth a hundred pounds! He says it kills all the rats and— oh dear!" cried Alice in a sorrowful tone. "I'm afraid I've offended it again!" For the Mouse was swimming away from her

7. The Duck is Reverend Duckworth; the Lory (an Australian parrot) is Lorina Liddell; Edith Liddell is the Eaglet; and the Dodo is Lewis Carroll himself. When Carroll stammered he pronounced his name "Do-Do-Dodgson," and it is amusing to note that when his biography entered the *Encyclopaedia Britannica* it was inserted just before the entry on the Dodo. The individuals in this "queer-looking party" represent the participants in an episode entered in Carroll's diary on June 17, 1862. Carroll took his sisters, Fanny and Elizabeth, and his Aunt Lucy Lutwidge (the "other curious creatures"?) on a boating expedition, accompanied by Reverend Duckworth and the three Liddell girls.

June 17 (Tu). Expedition to Nuneham. Duckworth (of Trinity) and Ina, Alice and Edith came with us. We set out about 12.30 and got to Nuneham about 2: dined there, then walked in the park and set off for home about 4.30. About a mile above Nuneham heavy rain came on, and after bearing it a short time I settled that we had better leave the boat and walk: three miles of this drenched us all pretty well. I went on first with the children, as they could walk much faster than Elizabeth, and took them to the only house I knew in Sandford, Mrs. Broughton's, where Ranken lodges. I left them with her to get their clothes dried, and went off to find a vehicle, but none was to be had there, so on the others arriving, Duckworth and I walked on to Iffley, whence we sent them a fly.

In the original manuscript, *Alice's Adventures Underground,* appear a number of details relating to this experience that Carroll later deleted because he thought they would have little interest to anyone outside the circle of individuals involved. When the facsimile edition of the manuscript was published in 1886, Duckworth received a copy inscribed, "The Duck from the Dodo."

as hard as it could go, and making quite a commotion in the pool as it went.

So she called softly after it, "Mouse dear! Do come back again, and we won't talk about cats, or dogs either, if you don't like them!" When the Mouse heard this, it turned round and swam slowly back to her: its face was quite pale (with passion, Alice thought), and it said, in a low, trembling voice, "Let us get to the shore, and then I'll tell you my history, and you'll understand why it is I hate cats and dogs."

It was high time to go, for the pool was getting quite crowded with the birds and animals that had fallen into it: there was a Duck and a Dodo, a Lory and an Eaglet, and several other curious creatures.[7] Alice led the way, and the whole party swam to the shore.

CHAPTER III

A Caucus-Race and a Long Tale

They were indeed a queer-looking party that assembled on the bank—the birds with draggled feathers, the animals with their fur clinging close to them, and all dripping wet, cross, and uncomfortable.

The first question of course was, how to get dry again: they had a consultation about this, and after a few minutes it seemed quite natural to Alice to find herself talking familiarly with them, as if she had known them all her life. Indeed, she had quite a long argument with the Lory, who at last turned sulky, and would only say, "I'm older than you, and must know better." And this Alice would not allow, without knowing how old it was, and, as the Lory positively refused to tell its age, there was no more to be said.

At last the Mouse, who seemed to be a person of some authority among them,

1. Roger Lancelyn Green, editor of Carroll's diary, identifies this dusty passage as an actual quotation from Havilland Chepmell's *Short Course of History*, 1862, pages 143–44. Carroll was distantly related to the earls Edwin and Morcar, but Green thinks it unlikely that Carroll knew this. (See *The Diaries of Lewis Carroll*, Vol. I, page 2.)

Chepmell's book was one of the lesson-books studied by the Liddell children. Green elsewhere suggests that Carroll may have intended the Mouse to represent Miss Prickett, the children's governess.

called out, "Sit down, all of you, and listen to me! *I'll* soon make you dry enough!" They all sat down at once, in a large ring, with the Mouse in the middle. Alice kept her eyes anxiously fixed on it, for she felt sure she would catch a bad cold if she did not get dry very soon.

"Ahem!" said the Mouse with an important air. "Are you all ready? This is the driest thing I know. Silence all round, if you please! 'William the Conqueror, whose cause was favoured by the pope, was soon submitted to by the English, who wanted leaders, and had been of late much accustomed to usurpation and conquest. Edwin and Morcar, the earls of Mercia and Northumbria—' " **1**

"Ugh!" said the Lory, with a shiver.

"I beg your pardon!" said the Mouse, frowning, but very politely. "Did you speak?"

"Not I!" said the Lory, hastily.

"I thought you did," said the Mouse.

"I proceed. 'Edwin and Morcar, the earls of Mercia and Northumbria, declared for him; and even Stigand, the patriotic archbishop of Canterbury, found it advisable—' "

"Found *what?*" said the Duck.

"Found *it,*" the Mouse replied rather crossly: "of course you know what 'it' means."

"I know what 'it' means well enough, when *I* find a thing," said the Duck: "it's generally a frog or a worm. The question is, what did the archbishop find?"

The Mouse did not notice this question, but hurriedly went on, " '—found it advisable to go with Edgar Atheling to meet William and offer him the crown. William's conduct at first was moderate. But the insolence of his Normans—' How are you getting on now, my dear?" it continued, turning to Alice as it spoke.

"As wet as ever," said Alice in a melancholy tone: "it doesn't seem to dry me at all."

"In that case," said the Dodo solemnly, rising to its feet, "I move that the meeting adjourn, for the immediate adoption of more energetic remedies—"

"Speak English!" said the Eaglet. "I don't know the meaning of half those long words, and, what's more, I don't believe you do either!" And the Eaglet bent down its head to hide a smile: some of the other birds tittered audibly.

2. The term "caucus" originated in the United States in reference to a meeting of the leaders of a faction to decide on a candidate or policy. It was adopted in England with a slightly different meaning, referring to a system of highly disciplined party organization by committees. It was generally used by one party as an abusive term for the organization of an opposing party. Carroll may have intended his caucus-race to symbolize the fact that committee members generally do a lot of running around in circles, getting nowhere, and with everybody wanting a political plum. It has been suggested that he was influenced by the caucus of crows in Chapter 7 of *Water Babies,* a scene that Charles Kingsley obviously intended as barbed political satire, but the two scenes have little in common.

The caucus-race does not appear in the original manuscript, *Alice's Adventures Underground.* It replaces the following deleted passage, based on the episode cited in Note 7 of the previous chapter.

'I only meant to say,' said the Dodo in rather an offended tone, 'that I know of a house near here, where we could get the young lady and the rest of the party dried, and then we could listen comfortably to the story which I think you were good enough to promise to tell us,' bowing gravely to the mouse.

The mouse made no objection to this, and the whole party moved along the river bank, (for the pool had by this time begun to flow out of the hall, and the edge of it was fringed with rushes and forget-me-nots,) in a slow procession, the Dodo leading the way. After a time the Dodo became impatient, and, leaving the Duck to bring up the rest of the party, moved on at a quicker pace with Alice, the Lory and the Eaglet, and soon brought them to a little cottage, and there they sat snugly by the fire, wrapped up in blankets, until the rest of the party had arrived, and they were all dry again.

"What I was going to say," said the Dodo in an offended tone, "was, that the best thing to get us dry would be a Caucus-race."**2**

"What *is* a Caucus-race?" said Alice; not that she much wanted to know, but the Dodo had paused as if it thought that *somebody* ought to speak, and no one else seemed inclined to say anything.

"Why," said the Dodo, "the best way to explain it is to do it." (And, as you might like to try the thing yourself, some winter day, I will tell you how the Dodo managed it.)

First it marked out a race-course, in a sort of circle, ("the exact shape doesn't matter," it said,) and then all the party were placed along the course, here and there. There was no "One, two, three, and away!" but they began running when they liked, and left off when they liked, so that it was not easy to know when the race was over. However, when they had been running half-an-hour or so, and were quite dry again, the Dodo suddenly called out, "The race is over!" and they all crowded round it, panting, and asking, "But who has won?"

This question the Dodo could not answer without a great deal of thought, and it stood for a long time with one finger pressed upon its forehead, (the position in which you usually see Shakespeare, in the pictures of him), while the rest waited in silence. At last the Dodo said *"Every-body* has won, and *all* must have prizes."

"But who is to give the prizes?" quite a chorus of voices asked.

"Why, *she,* of course," said the Dodo, pointing to Alice with one finger; and the whole party at once crowded round her, calling out, in a confused way, "Prizes! Prizes!"

Alice had no idea what to do, and in despair she put her hand in her pocket, and pulled out a box of comfits[3] (luckily the salt water had not got into it), and handed them round as prizes. There was exactly one a-piece, all round.

"But she must have a prize herself, you know," said the Mouse.

"Of course," the Dodo replied very gravely. "What else have you got in your pocket?" it went on, turning to Alice.

"Only a thimble," said Alice sadly.

3. Comfits are hard sweetmeats made by preserving dried fruits or seeds with sugar and covering them with a thin coating of syrup.

4. The mouse's tale is perhaps the best-known example in English of emblematic, or figured, verse: poems printed in such a way that they resemble something related to their subject matter. The affectation goes back to ancient Greece. Practitioners have included such distinguished bards as Robert Herrick, George Herbert, Stéphane Mallarmé, Dylan Thomas, e. e. cummings, and the modern French poet Guillaume Apollinaire. For a spirited if not convincing defense of emblematic verse as a serious art form, see Charles Boultenhouse's article, "Poems in the Shapes of Things," in the *Art News Annual*, 1959. Other examples of the form will be found in *Portfolio* magazine, summer 1950; C. C. Bombaugh's *Gleanings for the Curious*, 1867 (revised); William S. Walsh's *Handy-Book of Literary Curiosities*, 1892; and Carolyn Wells's *A Whimsey Anthology*, 1906.

Tennyson once told Carroll that he had dreamed a lengthy poem about fairies, which began with very long lines, then the lines got shorter and shorter until the poem ended with fifty or sixty lines of two syllables each. (Tennyson thought highly of the poem in his sleep, but forgot it completely when he awoke.) The opinion has been expressed *(The Diaries of Lewis Carroll,* Vol. I, page 146) that this may have given Carroll the idea for his mouse's tale.

In the original manuscript of the book, an entirely different poem appears as the tale; in a way a more appropriate one, for it fulfills the mouse's promise to explain why he dislikes cats and dogs, whereas the tale as it appears here contains no reference to cats. The original tale as Carroll hand-lettered it, reads as follows:

> We lived beneath the mat,
> Warm and snug and fat.
> But one woe, and that
> Was the cat!

"Hand it over here," said the Dodo.

Then they all crowded round her once more, while the Dodo solemnly presented the thimble, saying, "We beg your acceptance of this elegant thimble"; and, when it had finished this short speech, they all cheered.

Alice thought the whole thing very absurd, but they all looked so grave that she did not dare to laugh; and, as she could not think of anything to say, she simply bowed, and took the thimble, looking as solemn as she could.

The next thing was to eat the comfits: this caused some noise and confusion, as the large birds complained that they could not taste theirs, and the small ones choked and had to be patted on the back. However, it was over at last, and they sat down again in a ring, and begged the Mouse to tell them something more.

"You promised to tell me your history, you know," said Alice, "and why it is you hate—C and D," she added in a whisper, half afraid that it would be offended again.

"Mine is a long and a sad tale!" said the Mouse, turning to Alice, and sighing.

"It *is* a long tail, certainly," said Alice, looking down with wonder at the Mouse's tail; "but why do you call it sad?" And she kept on puzzling about it while the Mouse was speaking, so that her idea of the tale was something like this:—**4**

5
Fury said to
  a mouse, That
      he met
        in the
          house,
          'Let us
          both go
          to law:
          I will
          prosecute
          you.—
            Come, I'll
            take no
              denial;
                We must
                  have a
                    trial:
                        For
                        really
                        this
                        morning
                          I've
                          nothing
                          to do.'
                    Said the
                    mouse to
                    the cur,
                    'Such a
                        trial,
                        dear sir,
                  With no
                jury or
                judge,
                would be
                  wasting
                    our breath.'
                      'I'll be
                      judge,
                      I'll be
                    jury,'
                  Said
                    cunning
                      old Fury;
                        'I'll try
                          the whole
                            cause,
                            and
                          condemn
                            you
                              to
                              death.' "

To our joys a clog.
In our eyes a fog.
On our hearts a log
Was the dog!

When the cat's away,
Then the mice will play.
But, alas! one day;
(So they say)

Came the dog and cat,
Hunting for a rat,
Crushed the mice all flat,
Each one as he sat,
Underneath the mat,
Warm and snug and fat.
Think of that!

The American logician and philosopher Charles Peirce was much interested in the visual analogue of poetic onomatopoeia. Among his unpublished papers there is a copy of Poe's *The Raven,* written with a technique that Peirce called "art chirography," the words formed so as to convey a visual impression of the poem's ideas. This is not as absurd as it seems. The technique is employed frequently today in the lettering of advertisements, book jackets, titles of magazine stories and articles, cinema and TV titles, and so on.

5. Cf. The Barrister's Dream (Fit 6 of *The Hunting of the Snark*), in which the Snark serves as judge and jury as well as counsel for the defense.

"You are not attending!" said the Mouse to Alice, severely. "What are you thinking of?"

"I beg your pardon," said Alice very

6. This line was later quoted by Carroll himself to head the answers for a series of ten mathematical brain-teasers (he called them "knots") that he contributed to *The Monthly Packet* in 1880. In 1885 they appeared in book form as *A Tangled Tale*.

humbly: "you had got to the fifth bend, I think?"

"I had *not!*" cried the Mouse, sharply and very angrily.

"A knot!" said Alice, already to make herself useful, and looking anxiously about her. "Oh, do let me help to undo it!" **6**

"I shall do nothing of the sort," said the Mouse, getting up and walking away. "You insult me by talking such nonsense!"

"I didn't mean it!" pleaded poor Alice. "But you're so easily offended, you know!"

The Mouse only growled in reply.

"Please come back, and finish your story!" Alice called after it. And the others all joined in chorus "Yes, please do!" But the Mouse only shook its head impatiently, and walked a little quicker.

"What a pity it wouldn't stay!" sighed the Lory, as soon as it was quite out of sight. And an old Crab took the opportunity of saying to her daughter, "Ah, my dear! Let this be a lesson to you never to lose *your* temper!" "Hold your tongue, Ma!" said the young Crab, a little snappishly. "You're enough to try the patience of an oyster!"

"I wish I had our Dinah here, I know I do!" said Alice aloud, addressing nobody in particular. "*She'd* soon fetch it back!"

"And who is Dinah, if I might venture to ask the question?" said the Lory.

Alice replied eagerly, for she was always ready to talk about her pet: "Dinah's our cat. And she's such a capital one for catching mice, you can't think! And oh, I wish you could see her after the birds! Why, she'll eat a little bird as soon as look at it!"

This speech caused a remarkable sensation among the party. Some of the birds hurried off at once: one old Magpie began wrapping itself up very carefully, remarking, "I really must be getting home: the night-air doesn't suit my throat!" and a Canary called out in a trembling voice, to its children, "Come away, my dears! It's high time you were all in bed!" On various pretexts they all moved off, and Alice was soon left alone.

"I wish I hadn't mentioned Dinah!" she said to herself in a melancholy tone. "Nobody seems to like her, down here, and I'm sure she's the best cat in the world! Oh, my dear Dinah! I wonder if I shall ever see you any more!" And here poor Alice began to cry again, for she felt very lonely and low-spirited. In a little while, however, she again heard a little pattering of footsteps in the distance, and she looked up eagerly, half hoping that the Mouse had changed his mind, and was coming back to finish his story.

CHAPTER IV

The Rabbit Sends in a Little Bill

It was the White Rabbit, trotting slowly back again, and looking anxiously about as it went, as if it had lost something; and she heard it muttering to itself, "The Duchess! The Duchess! Oh my dear paws! Oh my fur and whiskers! She'll get me executed, as sure as ferrets are ferrets! Where *can* I have dropped them, I wonder?" Alice guessed in a moment that it was looking for the fan and the pair of white kid gloves, and she very good-naturedly began hunting about for them, but they were nowhere to be seen—everything seemed to have changed since her swim in the pool, and the great hall, with the glass table and the little door, had vanished completely.

Very soon the Rabbit noticed Alice, as she went hunting about, and called out to her, in an angry tone, "Why, Mary Ann,

1. Note how the White Rabbit's angry ordering about of his servants, here and elsewhere in the chapter, is in keeping with his timid character as described by Carroll in the passage quoted in Note 2 of Chapter 2.

2. "Going messages" is a phrase still used in England. It means "running errands."

what *are* you doing out here? Run home this moment, and fetch me a pair of gloves and a fan! Quick, now!"**1** And Alice was so much frightened that she ran off at once in the direction it pointed to, without trying to explain the mistake that it had made.

"He took me for his housemaid," she said to herself as she ran. "How surprised he'll be when he finds out who I am! But I'd better take him his fan and gloves—that is, if I can find them." As she said this, she came upon a neat little house, on the door of which was a bright brass plate with the name "W. RABBIT," engraved upon it. She went in without knocking, and hurried upstairs, in great fear lest she should meet the real Mary Ann, and be turned out of the house before she had found the fan and gloves.

"How queer it seems," Alice said to herself, "to be going messages for a rabbit!**2** I suppose Dinah'll be sending me on messages next!" And she began fancying the sort of thing that would happen: " 'Miss Alice! Come here directly, and get ready for your walk!' 'Coming in a minute, nurse! But I've got to watch this mouse-hole till Dinah comes back, and see that the mouse doesn't get out.' Only I don't think," Alice went on, "that they'd let Dinah stop in the house if it began ordering people about like that!"

By this time she had found her way

into a tidy little room with a table in the window, and on it (as she had hoped) a fan and two or three pairs of tiny white kid gloves: she took up the fan and a pair of the gloves, and was just going to leave the room, when her eye fell upon a little bottle that stood near the looking-glass. There was no label this time with the words "DRINK ME," but nevertheless she uncorked it and put it to her lips. "I know *something* interesting is sure to happen," she said to herself, "whenever I eat or drink anything: so I'll just see what this bottle does. I do hope it'll make me grow large again, for really I'm quite tired of being such a tiny little thing!"

It did so indeed, and much sooner than she had expected: before she had drunk half the bottle, she found her head pressing against the ceiling, and had to stoop to save her neck from being broken. She hastily put down the bottle, saying to herself, "That's quite enough—I hope I shan't grow any more—As it is, I can't get out at the door—I do wish I hadn't drunk quite so much!"

Alas! It was too late to wish that! She went on growing and growing, and very soon had to kneel down on the floor: in another minute there was not even room for this, and she tried the effect of lying down with one elbow against the door, and the other arm curled round her head. Still she went on growing, and, as a last re-

source, she put one arm out of the window, and one foot up the chimney, and said to herself, "Now I can do no more, whatever happens. What *will* become of me?"

Luckily for Alice, the little magic bottle had now had its full effect, and she grew no larger: still it was very uncomfortable, and, as there seemed to be no sort of chance of her ever getting out of the room again, no wonder she felt unhappy.

"It was much pleasanter at home," thought poor Alice, "when one wasn't always growing larger and smaller, and being ordered about by mice and rabbits. I almost wish I hadn't gone down that rabbit-hole — and yet — and yet — it's rather curious, you know, this sort of life! I do wonder what *can* have happened to me! When I used to read fairy tales, I fancied that kind of thing never happened, and now here I am in the middle of one! There ought to be a book written about me, that there ought! And when I grow up, I'll write one—but I'm grown up now," she added in a sorrowful tone: "at least there's no room to grow up any more *here*."

"But then," thought Alice, "shall I *never* get any older than I am now? That'll be a comfort, one way—never to be an old woman—but then—always to have lessons to learn! Oh, I shouldn't like *that!*"

"Oh, you foolish Alice!" she answered herself. "How can you learn lessons in here? Why, there's hardly room for *you,* and no room at all for any lesson-books!"

And so she went on, taking first one side and then the other, and making quite a conversation of it altogether; but after a few minutes she heard a voice outside, and stopped to listen.

"Mary Ann! Mary Ann!" said the voice. "Fetch me my gloves this moment!" Then came a little pattering of feet on the stairs. Alice knew it was the Rabbit coming to look for her, and she trembled till she shook the house, quite forgetting that she was now about a thousand times as large as the Rabbit, and had no reason to be afraid of it.

Presently the Rabbit came up to the

3. A cucumber-frame is a glass frame that provides heat for growing cucumbers by trapping solar radiation.

door, and tried to open it; but, as the door opened inwards, and Alice's elbow was pressed hard against it, that attempt proved a failure. Alice heard it say to itself, "Then I'll go round and get in at the window."

"*That* you won't!" thought Alice, and, after waiting till she fancied she heard the Rabbit just under the window, she suddenly spread out her hand, and made a snatch in the air. She did not get hold of anything, but she heard a little shriek and a fall, and a crash of broken glass, from which she concluded that it was just possible it had fallen into a cucumber-frame,**3** or something of the sort.

Next came an angry voice—the Rabbit's—"Pat! Pat! Where are you?" And then a voice she had never heard before, "Sure then I'm here! Digging for apples, yer honour!"

"Digging for apples, indeed!" said the Rabbit angrily. "Here! Come and help me out of *this!*" (Sounds of more broken glass.)

"Now tell me, Pat, what's that in the window?"

"Sure, it's an arm, yer honour!" (He pronounced it "arrum.")

"An arm, you goose! Who ever saw one that size? Why, it fills the whole window!"

"Sure, it does, yer honour: but it's an arm for all that."

"Well, it's got no business there, at any rate: go and take it away!"

There was a long silence after this, and Alice could only hear whispers now and then; such as "Sure, I don't like it, yer honour, at all, at all!" "Do as I tell you, you coward!" and at last she spread out her hand again and made another snatch in the air. This time there were *two* little shrieks, and more sounds of broken glass. "What a number of cucumber-frames there must be!" thought Alice. "I wonder what they'll do next! As for pulling me out of the window, I only wish they *could!* I'm sure *I* don't want to stay in here any longer!"

She waited for some time without hearing anything more: at last came a rumbling of little cart-wheels, and the sound of a good many voices all talking together: she made out the words: "Where's the other ladder?—Why, I hadn't to bring but one. Bill's got the other— Bill! Fetch it here, lad!—Here, put 'em up at this corner—No, tie 'em together first—they don't reach half high enough yet—Oh, they'll do well enough. Don't be particular—Here, Bill! Catch hold of this rope—Will the roof bear?—Mind that loose slate—Oh, it's coming down! Heads below!" (a loud crash)—"Now, who did that?—It was Bill, I fancy—Who's to go down the chimney?—Nay, *I* shan't! *You* do it!—*That* I won't, then!—Bill's got to go down—Here, Bill! The master says you've got to go down the chimney!"

"Oh! So Bill's got to come down the chimney, has he?" said Alice to herself. "Why, they seem to put everything upon Bill! I wouldn't be in Bill's place for a good deal; this fireplace is narrow, to be sure; but I *think* I can kick a little!"

She drew her foot as far down the chimney as she could, and waited till she heard a little animal (she couldn't guess of what sort it was) scratching and scrambling about in the chimney close above her: then, saying to herself "This is Bill," she gave one sharp kick, and waited to see what would happen next.

The first thing she heard was a general chorus of "There goes Bill!" then the Rabbit's voice alone—"Catch him, you by the hedge!" then silence, and then another confusion of voices—"Hold up his head—Brandy now—Don't choke him—How was it, old fellow? What happened to you? Tell us all about it!"

Last came a little feeble, squeaking voice. ("That's Bill," thought Alice), "Well, I hardly know — No more, thank ye; I'm better now—but I'm a deal too flustered to tell you—all I know is, something comes at me like a Jack-in-the-box, and up I goes like a sky-rocket!"

"So you did, old fellow!" said the others.

"We must burn the house down!" said

the Rabbit's voice, and Alice called out as
loud as she could, "If you do, I'll set
Dinah at you!"

There was a dead silence instantly, and
Alice thought to herself, "I wonder what
they *will* do next! If they had any sense,
they'd take the roof off." After a minute
or two, they began moving about again,
and Alice heard the Rabbit say, "A barrowful will do, to begin with."

"A barrowful of *what?*" thought Alice.
But she had not long to doubt, for the
next moment a shower of little pebbles
came rattling in at the window, and some
of them hit her in the face. "I'll put a
stop to this," she said to herself and
shouted out, "You'd better not do that
again!" which produced another dead silence.

Alice noticed, with some surprise, that
the pebbles were all turning into little
cakes as they lay on the floor, and a bright
idea came into her head. "If I eat one of
these cakes," she thought, "it's sure to
make some change in my size; and, as it
can't possibly make me larger, it must
make me smaller, I suppose."

So she swallowed one of the cakes, and
was delighted to find that she began
shrinking directly. As soon as she was
small enough to get through the door,
she ran out of the house, and found quite
a crowd of little animals and birds waiting
outside. The poor little Lizard, Bill, was

in the middle, being held up by two
guinea-pigs, who were giving it something out of a bottle. They all made a
rush at Alice the moment she appeared;
but she ran off as hard as she could, and
soon found herself safe in a thick wood.

"The first thing I've got to do," said
Alice to herself, as she wandered about in
the wood, "is to grow to my right size
again; and the second thing is to find my
way into that lovely garden. I think that
will be the best plan."

It sounded an excellent plan, no doubt,
and very neatly and simply arranged: the
only difficulty was, that she had not the
smallest idea how to set about it; and
while she was peering about anxiously
among the trees, a little sharp bark just
over her head made her look up in a
great hurry.

An enormous puppy was looking down
at her with large round eyes, and feebly
stretching out one paw, trying to touch
her. "Poor little thing!" said Alice, in a
coaxing tone, and she tried hard to
whistle to it; but she was terribly frightened all the time at the thought that it
might be hungry, in which case it would
be very likely to eat her up in spite of all
her coaxing.

Hardly knowing what she did, she
picked up a little bit of stick, and held it
out to the puppy: whereupon the puppy
jumped into the air off all its feet at once,

with a yelp of delight, and rushed at the stick, and made believe to worry it: then Alice dodged behind a great thistle, to keep herself from being run over; and, the moment she appeared on the other side, the puppy made another rush at the stick, and tumbled head over heels in its hurry to get hold of it: then Alice, thinking it was very like having a game of play with a cart-horse, and expecting every moment to be trampled under its feet, ran round the thistle again: then the puppy began a series of short charges at the stick, running a very little way forwards each time and a long way back, and barking hoarsely all the while, till at last it sat down a good way off, panting, with its tongue hanging out of its mouth, and its great eyes half shut.

This seemed to Alice a good oppor-

tunity for making her escape: so she set off at once, and ran till she was quite tired and out of breath, and till the puppy's bark sounded quite faint in the distance.

"And yet what a dear little puppy it was!" said Alice, as she leant against a buttercup to rest herself, and fanned herself with one of the leaves. "I should have liked teaching it tricks very much, if—if I'd only been the right size to do it! Oh dear! I'd nearly forgotten that I've got to grow up again! Let me see—how *is* it to be managed? I suppose I ought to eat or drink something or other; but the great question is, 'What'?"

The great question certainly was, "What?" Alice looked all round her at the flowers and the blades of grass, but she could not see anything that looked like the right thing to eat or drink under the circumstances. There was a large mushroom growing near her, about the same height as herself: and, when she had looked under it, and on both sides of it, and behind it, it occurred to her that she might as well look and see what was on the top of it.

She stretched herself up on tiptoe, and peeped over the edge of the mushroom, and her eyes immediately met those of a large blue caterpillar, that was sitting on the top, with its arms folded, quietly smoking a long hookah, and taking not the smallest notice of her or of anything else.

CHAPTER V

Advice from a Caterpillar

The Caterpillar[1] and Alice looked at each other for some time in silence: at last the Caterpillar took the hookah out of its mouth, and addressed her in a languid, sleepy voice.

"Who are *You?*" said the Caterpillar.

This was not an encouraging opening for a conversation. Alice replied, rather shyly, "I—I hardly know, Sir, just at present—at least I know who I *was* when I got up this morning, but I think I must have been changed several times since then."

"What do you mean by that?" said the Caterpillar, sternly. "Explain yourself!"

"I can't explain *myself,* I'm afraid, Sir," said Alice, "because I'm not myself, you see."

"I don't see," said the Caterpillar.

"I'm afraid I can't put it more clearly," Alice replied very politely, "for I can't

1. In *The Nursery "Alice,"* Carroll calls attention to the Caterpillar's nose and chin, in Tenniel's drawing, and explains that they are really two of its legs. Ned Sparks took the role of the Caterpillar in Paramount's 1933 movie production of *Alice,* and Richard Haydn supplied the Caterpillar's voice in Walt Disney's 1951 animation of the tale. One of the most striking visual effects in the Disney film was obtained by having the Caterpillar illustrate his words by blowing multicolored smoke rings that assumed the shapes of letters and objects.

understand it myself, to begin with; and being so many different sizes in a day is very confusing."

"It isn't," said the Caterpillar.

"Well, perhaps you haven't found it so yet," said Alice; "but when you have to turn into a chrysalis—you will some day, you know—and then after that into a butterfly, I should think you'll feel it a little queer, won't you?"

"Not a bit," said the Caterpillar.

"Well, perhaps *your* feelings may be different," said Alice: "all I know is, it would feel very queer to *me*."

"You!" said the Caterpillar contemptuously. "Who are *you?*"

Which brought them back again to the beginning of the conversation. Alice felt a little irritated at the Caterpillar's making such *very* short remarks, and she drew herself up and said, very gravely, "I think you ought to tell me who *you* are, first."

"Why?" said the Caterpillar.

Here was another puzzling question; and, as Alice could not think of any good reason, and the Caterpillar seemed to be in a *very* unpleasant state of mind, she turned away.

"Come back!" the Caterpillar called after her. "I've something important to say!"

This sounded promising, certainly. Alice turned and came back again.

"Keep your temper," said the Caterpillar.

"Is that all?" said Alice, swallowing down her anger as well as she could.

"No," said the Caterpillar.

Alice thought she might as well wait, as she had nothing else to do, and perhaps after all it might tell her something worth hearing. For some minutes it puffed away without speaking; but at last it unfolded its arms, took the hookah out of its mouth again, and said, "So you think you're changed, do you?"

"I'm afraid I am, Sir," said Alice. "I can't remember things as I used—and I don't keep the same size for ten minutes together!"

"Can't remember *what* things?" said the Caterpillar.

"Well, I've tried to say '*How doth the little busy bee*,' but it all came different!" Alice replied in a very melancholy voice.

"Repeat '*You are old, Father William,*'" said the Caterpillar.

Alice folded her hands, and began:—**2**

2. "You are old, father William," one of the undisputed masterpieces of nonsense verse, is a clever parody of Robert Southey's (1774–1843) long-forgotten didactic poem, *The Old Man's Comforts and How He Gained Them.*

"*You are old, father William,*" *the young man cried,*
"*The few locks which are left you are grey;*
You are hale, father William, a hearty old man;
Now tell me the reason, I pray."

"*In the days of my youth,*" *father William replied,*
"*I remember'd that youth would fly fast,*
And abus'd not my health and my vigour at first,
That I never might need them at last."

"*You are old, father William,*" *the young man cried,*
"*And pleasures with youth pass away.*
And yet you lament not the days that are gone;
Now tell me the reason, I pray."

"*In the days of my youth,*" *father William replied,*
"*I remember'd that youth could not last;*
I thought of the future, whatever I did,
That I never might grieve for the past."

"*You are old, father William,*" *the young man cried,*
"*And life must be hast'ning away;*
You are cheerful and love to converse upon death;
Now tell me the reason, I pray."

"*I am cheerful, young man,*" *father William replied,*
"*Let the cause thy attention engage;*
In the days of my youth I remember'd my God!
And He hath not forgotten my age."

Although Southey had an enormous literary output of both prose and poetry, he is little read today except for a few short poems such as *The Inchcape Rock* and *The Battle of Blenheim,* and for his version of the immortal folk tale about Goldilocks and the three bears.

3. In the original version of this poem, in *Alice's Adventures Underground,* the price of the ointment is five shillings.

"You are old, father William," the young man said,
    "And your hair has become very white;
And yet you incessantly stand on your head —
    Do you think, at your age, it is right?"

"In my youth," father William replied to his son,
    "I feared it might injure the brain;
But, now that I'm perfectly sure I have none,
    Why, I do it again and again."

'You are old," said the youth, "as I mentioned before,
    And have grown most uncommonly fat;
Yet you turned a back-somersault in at the door —
    Pray what is the reason of that?"

"In my youth," said the sage, as he shook his grey locks,
    "I kept all my limbs very supple
By the use of this ointment—one shilling the box—**3**
    Allow me to sell you a couple?"

"You are old," said the youth, "and your jaws
  are too weak
  For anything tougher than suet;
Yet you finished the goose, with the bones and
  the beak —
  Pray, how did you manage to do it?"

"In my youth," said his father, "I took to the
  law,
  And argued each case with my wife;
And the muscular strength, which it gave to
  my jaw,
  Has lasted the rest of my life."

"You are old," said the youth, "one would
  hardly suppose
  That your eye was as steady as ever;
Yet you balanced an eel on the end of your
  nose —
  What made you so awfully clever?"

"I have answered three questions, and that is
  enough,"
  Said his father. "Don't give yourself airs!
Do you think I can listen all day to such stuff?
  Be off, or I'll kick you down stairs!"

71

"That is not said right," said the Caterpillar.

"Not *quite* right, I'm afraid," said Alice timidly: "some of the words have got altered."

"It is wrong from beginning to end," said the Caterpillar, decidedly; and there was silence for some minutes.

The Caterpillar was the first to speak.

"What size do you want to be?" it asked.

"Oh, I'm not particular as to size," Alice hastily replied; "only one doesn't like changing so often, you know."

"I *don't* know," said the Caterpillar.

Alice said nothing: she had never been so much contradicted in all her life before, and she felt that she was losing her temper.

"Are you content now?" said the Caterpillar.

"Well, I should like to be a *little* larger, Sir, if you wouldn't mind," said Alice: "three inches is such a wretched height to be."

"It is a very good height indeed!" said the Caterpillar angrily, rearing itself upright as it spoke (it was exactly three inches high).

"But I'm not used to it!" pleaded poor Alice in a piteous tone. And she thought to herself, "I wish the creatures wouldn't be so easily offended!"

"You'll get used to it in time," said the

Caterpillar; and it put the hookah into its mouth and began smoking again.

This time Alice waited patiently until it chose to speak again. In a minute or two the Caterpillar took the hookah out of its mouth, and yawned once or twice, and shook itself. Then it got down off the mushroom, and crawled away into the grass, merely remarking, as it went, "One side will make you grow taller, and the other side will make you grow shorter."[4]

"One side of *what?* The other side of *what?*" thought Alice to herself.

"Of the mushroom," said the Caterpillar, just as if she had asked it aloud; and in another moment it was out of sight.

Alice remained looking thoughtfully at the mushroom for a minute, trying to make out which were the two sides of it; and, as it was perfectly round, she found this a very difficult question. However, at last she stretched her arms round it as far as they would go, and broke off a bit of the edge with each hand.

"And now which is which?" she said to herself, and nibbled a little of the right-hand bit to try the effect. The next moment she felt a violent blow underneath her chin: it had struck her foot!

She was a good deal frightened by this very sudden change, but she felt that there was no time to be lost, as she was shrinking rapidly: so she set to work at once to

4. In *Alice's Adventures Underground* the Caterpillar tells Alice that the *top* of the mushroom will make her grow taller and the *stalk* will make her grow shorter.

eat some of the other bit. Her chin was pressed so closely against her foot, that there was hardly room to open her mouth; but she did it at last, and managed to swallow a morsel of the left-hand bit.

*   *   *   *   *
  *   *   *   *   *
  *   *   *   *   *

"Come, my head's free at last!" said Alice in a tone of delight, which changed into alarm in another moment, when she found that her shoulders were nowhere to be found: all she could see, when she looked down, was an immense length of neck, which seemed to rise like a stalk out of a sea of green leaves that lay far below her.

"What *can* all that green stuff be?" said Alice. "And where *have* my shoulders got to? And oh, my poor hands, how is it I can't see you?" She was moving them about, as she spoke, but no result seemed to follow, except a little shaking among the distant green leaves.

As there seemed to be no chance of getting her hands up to her head, she tried to get her head down to *them,* and was delighted to find that her neck would bend about easily in any direction, like a serpent. She had just succeeded in curving it down into a graceful zigzag, and was going to dive in among the leaves, which she found to be nothing but the tops of the trees under which she had been wandering, when a sharp hiss made her draw back in a hurry: a large pigeon had flown into her face, and was beating her violently with its wings.

"Serpent!" screamed the Pigeon.

"I'm *not* a serpent!" said Alice indignantly. "Let me alone!"

"Serpent, I say again!" repeated the Pigeon, but in a more subdued tone, and added, with a kind of sob, "I've tried every way, but nothing seems to suit them!"

"I haven't the least idea what you're talking about," said Alice.

"I've tried the roots of trees, and I've tried banks, and I've tried hedges," the Pigeon went on, without attending to her; "but those serpents! There's no pleasing them!"

Alice was more and more puzzled, but she thought there was no use in saying anything more till the Pigeon had finished.

"As if it wasn't trouble enough hatching the eggs," said the Pigeon; "but I must be on the look-out for serpents night and day! Why, I haven't had a wink of sleep these three weeks!"

"I'm very sorry you've been annoyed," said Alice, who was beginning to see its meaning.

"And just as I'd taken the highest tree in the wood," continued the Pigeon, raising its voice to a shriek, "and just as I was

thinking I should be free of them at last,
they must needs come wriggling down
from the sky! Ugh, Serpent!"

"But I'm *not* a serpent, I tell you!" said
Alice. "I'm a—I'm a—"

"Well! *What* are you?" said the Pigeon.
"I can see you're trying to invent something!"

"I—I'm a little girl," said Alice, rather
doubtfully, as she remembered the number of changes she had gone through, that
day.

"A likely story indeed!" said the Pigeon
in a tone of the deepest contempt. "I've
seen a good many little girls in my time,
but never *one* with such a neck as that!
No, no! You're a serpent; and there's no
use denying it. I suppose you'll be telling
me next that you never tasted an egg!"

"I *have* tasted eggs, certainly," said
Alice, who was a very truthful child; "but
little girls eat eggs quite as much as serpents do, you know."

"I don't believe it," said the Pigeon;
"but if they do, why, then they're a kind
of serpent: that's all I can say."

This was such a new idea to Alice, that
she was quite silent for a minute or two,
which gave the Pigeon the opportunity of
adding, "You're looking for eggs, I know
that well enough; and what does it matter to me whether you're a little girl or a
serpent?"

"It matters a good deal to *me*," said Alice hastily; "but I'm not looking for eggs, as it happens; and, if I was, I shouldn't want *yours:* I don't like them raw."

"Well, be off, then!" said the Pigeon in a sulky tone, as it settled down again into its nest. Alice crouched down among the trees as well as she could, for her neck kept getting entangled among the branches, and every now and then she had to stop and untwist it. After a while she remembered that she still held the pieces of mushroom in her hands, and she set to work very carefully, nibbling first at one and then at the other, and growing sometimes taller and sometimes shorter, until she had succeeded in bringing herself down to her usual height.

It was so long since she had been anything near the right size, that it felt quite strange at first; but she got used to it in a few minutes, and began talking to herself, as usual, "Come, there's half my plan done now! How puzzling all these changes are! I'm never sure what I'm going to be, from one minute to another! However, I've got back to my right size: the next thing is, to get into that beautiful garden —how *is* that to be done, I wonder?" As she said this, she came suddenly upon an open place, with a little house in it about four feet high. "Whoever lives there," thought Alice, "it'll never do to come upon them *this* size: why, I should frighten them out of their wits!" So she began nibbling at the right-hand bit again, and did not venture to go near the house till she had brought herself down to nine inches high.

CHAPTER VI

Pig and Pepper

For a minute or two she stood looking at the house, and wondering what to do next, when suddenly a footman in livery came running out of the wood—(she considered him to be a footman because he was in livery: otherwise, judging by his face only, she would have called him a fish)—and rapped loudly at the door with his knuckles. It was opened by another footman in livery, with a round face and large eyes like a frog; and both footmen, Alice noticed, had powdered hair that curled all over their heads. She felt very curious to know what it was all about, and crept a little way out of the wood to listen.

The Fish-Footman began by producing from under his arm a great letter, nearly as large as himself, and this he handed over to the other, saying, in a solemn tone,

"For the Duchess. An invitation from the
Queen to play croquet." The Frog-Foot-
man repeated, in the same solemn tone,
only changing the order of the words a
little, "From the Queen. An invitation
for the Duchess to play croquet."

Then they both bowed low, and their
curls got entangled together.

Alice laughed so much at this that she
had to run back into the wood for fear of
their hearing her; and, when she next
peeped out, the Fish-Footman was gone,
and the other was sitting on the ground
near the door, staring stupidly up into
the sky.

Alice went timidly up to the door, and
knocked.

"There's no sort of use in knocking,"
said the Footman, "and that for two reasons. First, because I'm on the same side
of the door as you are. Secondly, because
they're making such a noise inside, no
one could possibly hear you." And certainly there *was* a most extraordinary
noise going on within—a constant howling and sneezing, and every now and then
a great crash, as if a dish or kettle had
been broken to pieces.

"Please, then," said Alice, "how am I
to get in?"

"There might be some sense in your
knocking," the Footman went on, without
attending to her, "if we had the door between us. For instance, if you were *in-*

side, you might knock, and I could let you out, you know." He was looking up into the sky all the time he was speaking, and this Alice thought decidedly uncivil. "But perhaps he can't help it," she said to herself; "his eyes are so *very* nearly at at the top of his head. But at any rate he might answer questions.—How am I to get in?" she repeated, aloud.

"I shall sit here," the Footman remarked, "till to-morrow—"

At this moment the door of the house opened, and a large plate came skimming out, straight at the Footman's head: it just grazed his nose, and broke to pieces against one of the trees behind him.

"—or next day, maybe," the Footman continued in the same tone, exactly as if nothing had happened.

"How am I to get in?" asked Alice again, in a louder tone.

"*Are* you to get in at all?" said the Footman. "That's the first question, you know."

It was, no doubt: only Alice did not like to be told so. "It's really dreadful," she muttered to herself, "the way all the creatures argue. It's enough to drive one crazy!"

The Footman seemed to think this a good opportunity for repeating his remark, with variations. "I shall sit here," he said, "on and off, for days and days."

"But what am *I* to do?" said Alice.

1. A glance at the portrait of the *Ugly Duchess,* by the sixteenth-century Flemish painter Quintin Matsys (it is reproduced in Langford Reed's book on Carroll) leaves little doubt that it served as the model for Tenniel's duchess. Matsys's duchess is popularly supposed to be Margaretha Maultasch, a fourteenth-century duchess of Carinthia and Tyrol. "Maultasch," meaning "pocket-mouth," was a name given to her because of the shape of her mouth. The unhappy life of poor Margaret, who had the reputation of being the ugliest woman in history, is told by Lion Feuchtwanger in his novel *The Ugly Duchess.* (See "A Portrait of the Ugliest Princess in History," by W. A. Baillie-Grohman, *Burlington Magazine,* April 1921)

"Anything you like," said the Footman, and began whistling.

"Oh, there's no use in talking to him," said Alice desperately: "he's perfectly idiotic!" And she opened the door and went in.

The door led right into a large kitchen, which was full of smoke from one end to the other: the Duchess[1] was sitting on a three-legged stool in the middle, nursing a baby: the cook was leaning over the fire, stirring a large cauldron which seemed to be full of soup.

"There's certainly too much pepper in that soup!" Alice said to herself, as well as she could for sneezing.

There was certainly too much of it in the *air.* Even the Duchess sneezed occasionally; and as for the baby, it was sneezing and howling alternately without a moment's pause. The only two creatures in the kitchen, that did *not* sneeze, were the cook, and a large cat, which was lying on the hearth and grinning from ear to ear.

"Please would you tell me," said Alice, a little timidly, for she was not quite sure whether it was good manners for her to speak first, "why your cat grins like that?"

"It's a Cheshire cat,"[2] said the Duchess, "and that's why. Pig!"

She said the last word with such sudden violence that Alice quite jumped; but she saw in another moment that it was addressed to the baby, and not to her, so she took courage, and went on again:—

"I didn't know that Cheshire cats always grinned; in fact, I didn't know that cats *could* grin."

"They all can," said the Duchess; "and most of 'em do."

"I don't know of any that do," Alice said very politely, feeling quite pleased to have got into a conversation.

"You don't know much," said the Duchess; "and that's a fact."

Alice did not at all like the tone of this remark, and thought it would be as well to introduce some other subject of conversation. While she was trying to fix on one, the cook took the cauldron of soup off the fire, and at once set to work throw-

2. "Grin like a Cheshire cat" was a common phrase in Carroll's day. Its origin is not known. The two leading theories are: (1) A sign painter in Cheshire (the county, by the way, where Carroll was born) painted grinning lions on the signboards of inns in the area (see *Notes and Queries*, No. 130, April 24, 1852, page 402), (2) Cheshire cheeses were at one time molded in the shape of a grinning cat (see *Notes and Queries*, No. 55, Nov. 16, 1850, page 412.) "This has a peculiar Carrollian appeal," writes Dr. Phyllis Greenacre in her psychoanalytic study of Carroll, "as it provokes the fantasy that the cheesy cat may eat the rat that would eat the cheese." The Cheshire Cat is not in the original manuscript, *Alice's Adventures Underground*.

ing everything within her reach at the
Duchess and the baby—the fire-irons
came first; then followed a shower of
saucepans, plates, and dishes. The Duchess took no notice of them, even when
they hit her; and the baby was howling
so much already, that it was quite impossible to say whether the blows hurt it or
not.

"Oh, *please* mind what you're doing!"
cried Alice, jumping up and down in an
agony of terror. "Oh, there goes his *precious* nose!" as an unusually large saucepan flew close by it, and very nearly
carried it off.

"If everybody minded their own business," the Duchess said, in a hoarse growl,
"the world would go round a deal faster
than it does."

"Which would *not* be an advantage,"
said Alice, who felt very glad to get an
opportunity of showing off a little of her
knowledge. "Just think what work it
would make with the day and night! You
see the earth takes twenty-four hours to
turn round on its axis—"

"Talking of axes," said the Duchess,
"chop off her head!"

Alice glanced rather anxiously at the
cook, to see if she meant to take the hint;
but the cook was busily stirring the soup,
and seemed not to be listening, so she
went on again: "Twenty-four hours, I
think; or is it twelve? I—"

"Oh, don't bother *me*," said the Duchess. "I never could abide figures!" And with that she began nursing her child again, singing a sort of lullaby to it as she did so, and giving it a violent shake at the end of every line:——**3**

> "Speak roughly to your little boy,
>   And beat him when he sneezes:
> He only does it to annoy,
>   Because he knows it teases."

CHORUS

(in which the cook and the baby joined):——

> "Wow! wow! wow!"

While the Duchess sang the second verse of the song, she kept tossing the baby violently up and down, and the poor little thing howled so, that Alice could hardly hear the words:——

> "I speak severely to my boy,
>   And beat him when he sneezes:
> For he can thoroughly enjoy
>   The pepper when he pleases!"

CHORUS

> "Wow! wow! wow!"

"Here! You may nurse it a bit, if you like!" the Duchess said to Alice, flinging the baby at her as she spoke. "I must go and get ready to play croquet with the Queen," and she hurried out of the room. The cook threw a frying-pan after her as she went, but it just missed her.

Alice caught the baby with some dif-

3. The original of this burlesque is *Speak Gently,* a happily unremembered poem attributed by some authorities to one G. W. Langford and by other authorities to David Bates, a Philadelphia rhymster.

John M. Shaw, in *The Parodies of Lewis Carroll and their Originals* (the catalog and notes of an exhibition at the Florida State University Library, December 1960) reports that he was unsuccessful in his search for Langford's version; in fact he failed to find Langford himself. Shaw did find the poem on page 15 of *The Eolian,* a book of verse published by Bates in 1849. Shaw points out that Bates' son, in a preface to his father's *Poetical Works* (1870) states that his father had indeed written this widely-quoted poem.

> *Speak gently! It is better far*
>   *To rule by love than fear;*
> *Speak gently; let no harsh words mar*
>   *The good we might do here!*
>
> *Speak gently! Love doth whisper low*
>   *The vows that true hearts bind;*
> *And gently Friendship's accents flow;*
>   *Affection's voice is kind.*
>
> *Speak gently to the little child!*
>   *Its love be sure to gain;*
> *Teach it in accents soft and mild;*
>   *It may not long remain.*
>
> *Speak gently to the young, for they*
>   *Will have enough to bear;*
> *Pass through this life as best they may,*
>   *'Tis full of anxious care!*
>
> *Speak gently to the aged one,*
>   *Grieve not the care-worn heart;*
> *Whose sands of life are nearly run,*
>   *Let such in peace depart!*
>
> *Speak gently, kindly, to the poor;*
>   *Let no harsh tone be heard;*
> *They have enough they must endure,*
>   *Without an unkind word!*
>
> *Speak gently to the erring; know*
>   *They may have toiled in vain;*
> *Perchance unkindness made them so;*
>   *Oh, win them back again!*

Speak gently! He who gave his life
  To bend man's stubborn will,
When elements were in fierce strife,
  Said to them, "Peace, be still."

Speak gently! 'tis a little thing
  Dropped in the heart's deep well;
The good, the joy, that it may bring,
  Eternity shall tell.

ficulty, as it was a queer-shaped little crea-ture, and held out its arms and legs in all directions, "just like a starfish," thought Alice. The poor little thing was snorting like a steam-engine when she caught it, and kept doubling itself up and straight-ening itself out again, so that altogether, for the first minute or two, it was as much as she could do to hold it.

As soon as she had made out the proper way of nursing it (which was to twist it up into a sort of knot, and then keep tight hold of its right ear and left foot, so as to prevent its undoing itself), she carried it out into the open air. "If I don't take this child away with me," thought Alice, "they're sure to kill it in a day or two. Wouldn't it be murder to leave it be-hind?" She said the last words out loud, and the little thing grunted in reply (it had left off sneezing by this time). "Don't grunt," said Alice; "that's not at all a proper way of expressing yourself."

The baby grunted again, and Alice looked very anxiously into its face to see what was the matter with it. There could be no doubt that it had a *very* turn-up nose, much more like a snout than a real nose: also its eyes were getting extremely small for a baby: altogether Alice did not like the look of the thing at all. "But perhaps it was only sobbing," she thought, and looked into its eyes again, to see if there were any tears.

No, there were no tears. "If you're going to turn into a pig, my dear," said Alice, seriously, "I'll have nothing more to do with you. Mind now!" The poor little thing sobbed again, (or grunted, it was impossible to say which), and they went on for some while in silence.

Alice was just beginning to think to herself, "Now, what am I to do with this creature, when I get it home?" when it grunted again, so violently, that she looked down into its face in some alarm. This time there could be *no* mistake about it: it was neither more nor less than a pig, and she felt that it would be quite absurd for her to carry it any further.[4]

So she set the little creature down, and felt quite relieved to see it trot away quietly into the wood. "If it had grown up," she said to herself, "it would have made a dreadfully ugly child: but it makes rather a handsome pig, I think." And she began thinking over other children she knew, who might do very well as pigs, and was just saying to herself, "if one only knew the right way to change them—" when she was a little startled by seeing the Cheshire Cat sitting on a bough of a tree a few yards off.[5]

The Cat only grinned when it saw Alice. It looked good-natured, she thought: still it had *very* long claws and a great

4. It was surely not without malice that Carroll turned a male baby into a pig, for he had a low opinion of little boys. In *Sylvie and Bruno Concluded* an unpleasant child named Uggug ("a hideous fat boy . . . with the expression of a prize-pig") finally turns into a porcupine. Carroll now and then made an effort to be friendly with a little boy, but usually only when the lad had sisters that Carroll wanted to meet. In one of his concealed-rhyme letters (a letter that seems to be prose but on closer inspection turns out to be verse) he closed a P.S. with these lines:

My best love to yourself,—to your Mother
My kindest regards — to your small,
Fat, impertinent, ignorant brother
My hatred — I think that is all.

(Letter 21, to Maggie Cunnynghame, in *A Selection from the Letters of Lewis Carroll to His Child-friends*, edited by Evelyn M. Hatch.)

Tenniel's picture of Alice holding the pig-baby appears, with the baby redrawn as a human one, on the front of the envelope holding The Wonderland Postage-Stamp Case. This was a cardboard case designed to hold postage stamps, invented by Carroll and sold by a firm in Oxford. When you slip the case out of its envelope, you find on the front of it the same picture except that the baby has become a pig, as in Tenniel's original drawing. The back of the envelope and case provide a similar transformation from Tenniel's picture of the grinning Cheshire Cat to the picture in which the cat has mostly faded away. Slipped into the case was a tiny booklet titled *Eight or Nine Words about Letter Writing*. This delightfully written essay by Carroll opens as follows:

Some American writer has said "the snakes in this district may be divided into one species — the venomous."

many teeth, so she felt that it ought to be treated with respect.

"Cheshire Puss," she began, rather timidly, as she did not at all know whether it would like the name: however, it only grinned a little wider. "Come, it's pleased so far," thought Alice, and she went on. "Would you tell me, please, which way I ought to go from here?"

"That depends a good deal on where you want to get to," said the Cat.

"I don't much care where—" said Alice.

"Then it doesn't matter which way you go," said the Cat.[6]

"—so long as I get *somewhere*," Alice added as an explanation.

"Oh, you're sure to do that," said the Cat, "if you only walk long enough."

Alice felt that this could not be denied, so she tried another question. "What sort of people live about here?"

"In *that* direction," the Cat said, waving its right paw round, "lives a Hatter: and in *that* direction," waving the other paw, "lives a March Hare. Visit either you like: they're both mad."**7**

"But I don't want to go among mad people," Alice remarked.

"Oh, you can't help that," said the Cat: "we're all mad here. I'm mad. You're mad."**8**

"How do you know I'm mad?" said Alice.

"You must be," said the Cat, "or you wouldn't have come here."

Alice didn't think that proved it at all: however, she went on: "And how do you know that you're mad?"

"To begin with," said the Cat, "a dog's not mad. You grant that?"

"I suppose so," said Alice.

"Well, then," the Cat went on, "you see a dog growls when it's angry, and wags its tail when it's pleased. Now *I* growl when I'm pleased, and wag my tail when I'm angry. Therefore I'm mad."

"*I* call it purring, not growling," said Alice.

"Call it what you like," said the Cat. "Do you play croquet with the Queen to-day?"

"I should like it very much," said Alice, "but I haven't been invited yet."

"You'll see me there," said the Cat, and vanished.

The same principle applies here. Postage-Stamp-Cases may be divided into one species, the "Wonderland." Imitations of it will soon appear, no doubt: but they cannot include the two Pictorial Surprises, which are copyright.

You don't see why I call them 'Surprises'? Well, take the Case in your left hand, and regard it attentively. You see Alice nursing the Duchess's Baby? (An entirely new combination, by the way: it doesn't occur in the book.) Now, with your right thumb and forefinger, lay hold of the little book, and suddenly pull it out. *The Baby has turned into a Pig!* If *that* doesn't surprise you, why, I suppose you wouldn't be surprised if your own Mother-in-law suddenly turned into a Gyroscope!

5. In *The Nursery "Alice"* Carroll calls attention to the Fox Glove showing in the background of Tenniel's drawing for this scene (it can be seen also in the previous illustration). Foxes do not wear gloves, Carroll explains to his young readers. "The right word is 'Folk's-Gloves.' Did you ever hear that Fairies used to be called 'the good Folk'?"

6. These remarks are among the most quoted passages in the *Alice* books. A recent echo is heard in Jack Kerouac's forgettable novel, *On the Road:*

". . . we gotta go and never stop going till we get there."
"Where we going, man?"
"I don't know but we gotta go."

John Kemeny places Alice's question, and the Cat's famous answer, at the head of his chapter on science and values in *A Philosopher Looks at Science*, 1959. In fact each chapter of Kemeny's book is preceded by an appropriate quote from *Alice*. The Cat's answer expresses very precisely the eternal cleavage between science and ethics. As Kemeny makes clear, science cannot tell us where to go, but after this decision is made on other grounds, it *can* tell us the best way to get there.

7. The phrases "mad as a hatter" and "mad as a March hare" were common at the time Carroll wrote, and of course that was why he created the two characters. "Mad as a hatter" may have been a corruption of the earlier "mad as an adder" but more likely owes its origin to the fact that until recently hatters actually did go mad. The mercury used in curing felt (there are now laws against its use in most states and in parts of Europe) was a common cause of mercury poisoning. Victims developed a tremor called "hatter's shakes," which affected their eyes and limbs and addled their speech. In advanced stages they developed hallucinations and other psychotic symptoms. "Mad as a March hare" alludes to the frenzied capers of the male hare during March, its rutting season.

8. Compare the Cheshire Cat's remarks with the following entry, of February 9, 1856, in Carroll's diary:

> Query: when we are dreaming and, as often happens, have a dim consciousness of the fact and try to wake, do we not say and do things which in waking life would be insane? May we not then sometimes define insanity as an inability to distinguish which is the waking and which the sleeping life? We often dream without the least suspicion of unreality: 'Sleep hath its own world,' and it is often as lifelike as the other.

In Plato's *Theaetetus*, Socrates and Theaetetus discuss this topic as follows:

> THEAETETUS: "I certainly cannot undertake to argue that madmen or dreamers think truly, when they imagine, some of them that they are gods, and others that they can fly, and are flying in their sleep."
> SOCRATES: "Do you see another question which can be raised about these phenomena, notably about dreaming and waking?"
> THEAETETUS: "What question?"
> SOCRATES: "A question which I think that you must often have heard per-

Alice was not much surprised at this, she was getting so well used to queer things happening. While she was still looking at the place where it had been, it suddenly appeared again.

"By-the-bye, what became of the baby?" said the Cat. "I'd nearly forgotten to ask."

"It turned into pig," Alice answered very quietly, just as if the Cat had come back in a natural way.

"I thought it would," said the Cat, and vanished again.

Alice waited a little, half expecting to see it again, but it did not appear, and after a minute or two she walked on in the direction in which the March Hare was said to live. "I've seen hatters before," she said to herself: "the March Hare will be much the most interesting, and perhaps, as this is May, it won't be raving mad—at least not so mad as it was in March." As she said this, she looked up, and there was the Cat again, sitting on a branch of a tree.

"Did you say 'pig,' or 'fig'?" said the Cat.

"I said 'pig,'" replied Alice; "and I wish you wouldn't keep appearing and vanishing so suddenly: you make one quite giddy!"

"All right," said the Cat; and this time it vanished quite slowly, beginning with the end of the tail, and ending with the grin, which remained some time after the rest of it had gone.

"Well! I've often seen a cat without a grin," thought Alice; "but a grin without a cat! It's the most curious thing I ever saw in all my life!"**9**

She had not gone much farther before she came in sight of the house of the March Hare: she thought it must be the right house, because the chimneys were shaped like ears and the roof was thatched with fur. It was so large a house, that she did not like to go nearer till she had nibbled some more of the left-hand bit of mushroom, and raised herself to about two feet high: even then she walked up towards it rather timidly, saying to herself, "Suppose it should be raving mad after all! I almost wish I'd gone to see the Hatter instead!"

sons ask: how can you determine whether at this moment we are sleeping, and all our thoughts are a dream; or whether we are awake, and talking to one another in the waking state?"

THEAETETUS: "Indeed, Socrates, I do not know how to prove the one any more than the other, for in both cases the facts precisely correspond; and there is no difficulty in supposing that during all this discussion we have been talking to one another in a dream; and when in a dream we seem to be narrating dreams, the resemblance of the two states is quite astonishing."

SOCRATES: "You see, then, that a doubt about the reality of sense is easily raised, since there may even be a doubt whether we are awake or in a dream. And as our time is equally divided between sleeping and waking, in either sphere of existence the soul contends that the thoughts which are present to our minds at the time are true; and during one half of our lives we affirm the truth of the one, and, during the other half, of the other; and are equally confident of both."

THEAETETUS: "Most true."

SOCRATES: "And may not the same be said of madness and the other disorders? The difference is only that the times are not equal."

(Cf. Chapter 12, Note 4, and *Through the Looking-Glass*, Chapter 4, Note 7.)

9. The phrase "grin without a cat" is not a bad description of pure mathematics. Although mathematical theorems often can be usefully applied to the structure of the external world, the theorems themselves are abstractions that belong in another realm "remote from human passions," as Bertrand Russell once put it in a memorable passage, "remote even from the pitiful facts of Nature . . . an ordered cosmos, where pure thought can dwell as in its natural home, and where one, at least, of our nobler impulses can escape from the dreary exile of the actual world."

CHAPTER VII

A Mad Tea-Party

There was a table set out under a tree in front of the house, and the March Hare and the Hatter[1] were having tea at it: a Dormouse[2] was sitting between them, fast asleep, and the other two were using it as a cushion, resting their elbows on it, and talking over its head. "Very uncomfortable for the Dormouse," thought Alice; "only, as it's asleep, I suppose it doesn't mind."

The table was a large one, but the three were all crowded together at one corner of it. "No room! No room!" they cried out when they saw Alice coming. "There's *plenty* of room!" said Alice indignantly, and she sat down in a large arm-chair at one end of the table.

"Have some wine," the March Hare said in an encouraging tone.

Alice looked all round the table, but

1. There is good reason to believe that Tenniel adopted a suggestion of Carroll's that he draw the Hatter to resemble one Theophilus Carter, a furniture dealer near Oxford (and no grounds whatever for the widespread belief at the time that the Hatter was a burlesque of Prime Minister Gladstone). Carter was known in the area as the Mad Hatter, partly because he always wore a top hat and partly because of his eccentric ideas. His invention of an "alarm clock bed" that woke the sleeper by tossing him out on the floor (it was exhibited at the Crystal Palace in 1851) may help explain why Carroll's Hatter is so concerned with time as well as with arousing a sleepy dormouse. One notes also that items of furniture—table, armchair, writing desk — are prominent in this episode.

The Hatter, Hare, and Dormouse do not appear in *Alice's Adventures Underground;* the entire chapter was a later addition to the tale. The Hare and Hatter reappear as the King's messengers, Haigha and Hatta, in Chapter 6 of *Through the Looking-Glass.* In

Paramount's 1933 motion picture of *Alice*, Edward Everett Horton was the Hatter, Charles Ruggles the March Hare. Ed Wynn supplied the Hatter's voice in Walt Disney's 1951 animation, and Jerry Colonna spoke the part of the Hare.

"It is impossible to describe Bertrand Russell," writes Norbert Wiener in Chapter 14 of his autobiography *Ex-Prodigy*, "except by saying that he looks like the Mad Hatter . . . the caricature of Tenniel almost argues an anticipation on the part of the artist." Wiener goes on to point out the likenesses of philosophers J. M. E. McTaggart and E. E. Moore, two of Russell's fellow dons at Cambridge, to the Dormouse and March Hare respectively. The three men were known in the community as the Mad Tea Party of Trinity.

2. The British dormouse is a tree-living rodent that resembles a small squirrel much more than it does a mouse. The name is from the Latin *dormire,* to sleep, and has reference to the animal's habit

there was nothing on it but tea. "I don't see any wine," she remarked.

"There isn't any," said the March Hare.

"Then it wasn't very civil of you to offer it," said Alice angrily.

"It wasn't very civil of you to sit down without being invited," said the March Hare.

"I didn't know it was *your* table," said Alice: "it's laid for a great many more than three."

"Your hair wants cutting," said the Hatter. He had been looking at Alice for some time with great curiosity, and this was his first speech.

"You should learn not to make personal remarks," Alice said with some severity: "It's very rude."

The Hatter opened his eyes very wide

on hearing this; but all he *said* was, "Why is a raven like a writing-desk?"**3**

"Come, we shall have some fun now!" thought Alice. "I'm glad they've begun asking riddles—I believe I can guess that," she added aloud.

"Do you mean that you think you can find out the answer to it?" said the March Hare.

"Exactly so," said Alice.

"Then you should say what you mean," the March Hare went on.

"I do," Alice hastily replied; "at least —at least I mean what I say—that's the same thing, you know."

"Not the same thing a bit!" said the Hatter. "Why, you might just as well say that 'I see what I eat' is the same thing as 'I eat what I see'!"

"You might just as well say," added the March Hare, "that 'I like what I get' is the same thing as 'I get what I like'!"

"You might just as well say," added the Dormouse, which seemed to be talking in its sleep, "that 'I breathe when I sleep' is the same thing as 'I sleep when I breathe'!"

"It *is* the same thing with you," said the Hatter, and here the conversation dropped, and the party sat silent for a minute, while Alice thought over all she could remember about ravens and writing-desks, which wasn't much.

The Hatter was the first to break the

of winter hibernation. Unlike the squirrel, the dormouse is nocturnal, so that even in May (the month of Alice's adventure) it remains in a torpid state throughout the day. In *Some Reminiscences of William Michael Rossetti,* 1906, we are told that the dormouse may have been modeled after Dante Gabriel Rossetti's pet wombat, which had a habit of sleeping on the table. Carroll knew all the Rossettis and occasionally visited them.

3. The Mad Hatter's famous unanswered riddle was the object of much parlor speculation in Carroll's time. His own answer (given in a new preface that he wrote for the 1896 edition) is as follows:

> Enquiries have been so often addressed to me, as to whether any answer to the Hatter's Riddle can be imagined, that I may as well put on record here what seems to me to be a fairly appropriate answer, viz: "Because it can produce a few notes, tho they are *very* flat; and it is never put with the wrong end in front!" This, however, is merely an afterthought; the Riddle, as originally invented, had no answer at all.

Other answers have been proposed, notably by Sam Loyd the American puzzle genius, in his posthumous *Cyclopedia of Puzzles,* 1914, page 114. In keeping with Carroll's alliterative style Loyd offers as his best solution: because the notes for which they are noted are not noted for being musical notes. Other Loyd suggestions: because Poe wrote on both; bills and tales are among their characteristics; because they both stand on their legs, conceal their steels (steals), and ought to be made to shut up.

4. Alice's remark that the day is the fourth, coupled with the previous chapter's revelation that the month is May, establishes the date of Alice's underground adventure as May 4. May 4, 1852, was Alice Liddell's birthday. She was ten in 1862, the year Carroll first told and recorded the story, but her age in the story is almost certainly seven (see Note 1, Chapter 1, of *Through the Looking-Glass*). On the last page of the hand-lettered manuscript, *Alice's Adventures Underground*, which Carroll gave to Alice, he pasted a photograph of her that he had taken in 1859, when she was seven.

In his book *The White Knight*, A. L. Taylor reports that on May 4, 1862, there was exactly two days' difference between the lunar and calendar months. This, Taylor argues, suggests that the Mad Hatter's watch ran on lunar time and accounts for his remark that his watch is "two days wrong." If Wonderland is near the earth's center, Taylor points out, the position of the sun would be useless for time-telling, whereas phases of the moon remain unambiguous. The conjecture is also supported by the close connection of "lunar" with "lunacy," but it is hard to believe that Carroll had all this in mind.

5. An even funnier watch is the Outlandish Watch owned by the German professor in Chapter 23 of *Sylvie and Bruno*. Setting its hands back in time has the result of setting events themselves back to the time indicated by the hands; an interesting anticipation of H. G. Wells's *The Time Machine*. But that is not all. Pressing a "reversal peg" on the Outlandish Watch starts events moving *backward;* a kind of looking-glass reversal of time's linear dimension.

One is reminded also of an earlier piece by Carroll in which he proves that a stopped clock is more

silence. "What day of the month is it?" he said, turning to Alice: he had taken his watch out of his pocket, and was looking at it uneasily, shaking it every now and then, and holding it to his ear.

Alice considered a little, and then said, "The fourth."**4**

"Two days wrong!" sighed the Hatter. "I told you butter wouldn't suit the works!" he added, looking angrily at the March Hare.

"It was the *best* butter," the March Hare meekly replied.

"Yes, but some crumbs must have got in as well," the Hatter grumbled: "you shouldn't have put it in with the bread-knife."

The March Hare took the watch and looked at it gloomily: then he dipped it into his cup of tea, and looked at it again: but he could think of nothing better to say than his first remark, It was the *best* butter, you know."

Alice had been looking over his shoulder with some curiosity. "What a funny watch!"**5** she remarked. "It tells the day of the month, and doesn't tell what o'clock it is!"

"Why should it?" muttered the Hatter. "Does *your* watch tell you what year it is?"

"Of course not," Alice replied very readily: "but that's because it stays the same year for such a long time together."

"Which is just the case with *mine*," said the Hatter.

Alice felt dreadfully puzzled. The Hatter's remark seemed to her to have no sort of meaning in it, and yet it was certainly English. "I don't quite understand you," she said, as politely as she could.

"The Dormouse is asleep again," said the Hatter, and he poured a little hot tea upon its nose.

The Dormouse shook its head impatiently, and said, without opening its eyes, "Of course, of course: just what I was going to remark myself."

"Have you guessed the riddle yet?" the Hatter said, turning to Alice again.

"No, I give it up," Alice replied. "What's the answer?"

"I haven't the slightest idea," said the Hatter.

"Nor I," said the March Hare.

Alice sighed wearily. "I think you might do something better with the time," she said, "than wasting it in asking riddles that have no answers."

"If you knew Time as well as I do," said the Hatter, "you wouldn't talk about wasting *it*. It's *him*."

"I don't know what you mean," said Alice.

"Of course you don't!" the Hatter said, tossing his head contemptuously. "I dare say you never even spoke to Time!"

"Perhaps not," Alice cautiously re-

accurate than one that loses a minute a day. The first clock is exactly right twice every twenty-four hours, whereas the other clock is exactly right only once in two years. "You *might* go on to ask," Carroll adds, "'How am I to know when eight o'clock *does* come? My clock will not tell me.' Be patient: you know that when eight o'clock comes your clock is right; very good; then your rule is this: keep your eyes fixed on the clock and the *very moment it is right* it will be eight o'clock."

6. The Hatter's song parodies the first verse of Jane Taylor's well-known poem, *The Star*.

Twinkle, twinkle, little star,
How I wonder what you are!
Up above the world so high,
Like a diamond in the sky.

When the blazing sun is gone,
When he nothing shines upon,
Then you show your little light,
Twinkle, twinkle, all the night.

Then the traveller in the dark
Thanks you for your tiny spark:
He could not see which way to go,
If you did not twinkle so.

In the dark blue sky you keep,
And often through my curtains peep,
For you never shut your eye
Till the sun is in the sky.

As your bright and tiny spark
Lights the traveller in the dark,
Though I know not what you are,
Twinkle, twinkle, little star.

Carroll's burlesque may contain what professional comics call an "inside joke." Bartholomew Price, a distinguished professor of mathematics at Oxford and a good friend of Carroll's, was known among his students by the nickname "The Bat." His lectures no doubt had a way of soaring high above the heads of his listeners.

plied; "but I know I have to beat time when I learn music."

"Ah! That accounts for it," said the Hatter. "He won't stand beating. Now, if you only kept on good terms with him, he'd do almost anything you liked with the clock. For instance, suppose it were nine o'clock in the morning, just time to begin lessons: you'd only have to whisper a hint to Time, and round goes the clock in a twinkling! Half-past one, time for dinner!"

("I only wish it was," the March Hare said to itself in a whisper.)

"That would be grand, certainly," said Alice thoughtfully; "but then — I shouldn't be hungry for it, you know."

"Not at first, perhaps," said the Hatter: "but you could keep it to half-past one as long as you liked."

"Is that the way *you* manage?" Alice asked.

The Hatter shook his head mournfully. "Not I!" he replied. "We quarreled last March—just before *he* went mad, you know—" (pointing with his teaspoon at the March Hare), "—it was at the great concert given by the Queen of Hearts, and I had to sing.[6]

'Twinkle, twinkle, little bat!
How I wonder what you're at!'

You know the song, perhaps?"

"I've heard something like it," said Alice.

"It goes on, you know," the Hatter continued, "in this way:—

'Up above the world you fly,
Like a tea-tray in the sky.
Twinkle, twinkle—' "

Here the Dormouse shook itself, and began singing in its sleep *"Twinkle, twinkle, twinkle, twinkle—"* and went on so long that they had to pinch it to make it stop.

"Well, I'd hardly finished the first verse," said the Hatter, "when the Queen bawled out 'He's murdering the time![7] Off with his head!' "

"How dreadfully savage!" exclaimed Alice.

"And ever since that," the Hatter went on in a mournful tone, "he won't do a thing I ask! It's always six o'clock now."

A bright idea came into Alice's head. "Is that the reason so many tea-things are put out here?" she asked.

"Yes, that's it," said the Hatter with a sigh: "it's always tea-time,[8] and we've no time to wash the things between whiles."

"Then you keep moving round, I suppose?" said Alice.

"Exactly so," said the Hatter: "as the things get used up."

"But what happens when you come to the beginning again?" Alice ventured to ask.

7. The equivalent contemporary expression is "killing time"; that is, spending time in an unprofitable way. Here the phrase also alludes to the Hatter's mangling of the song's meter.

8. This was written before five-o'clock tea had become the general custom in England. It was intended to refer to the fact that the Liddells sometimes served tea at six o'clock, the children's supper-time. Arthur Stanley Eddington, as well as less distinguished writers on relativity theory, have compared the Mad Tea Party, where it is always six o'clock, with that portion of De Sitter's model of the cosmos in which time stands eternally still. (See Chapter 10 of Eddington's *Space Time and Gravitation.*)

9. The three little sisters are the three Liddell sisters. Elsie is L.C. (Lorina Charlotte), Tillie refers to Edith's family nickname Matilda, and Lacie is an anagram of Alice.

This is the second time that Carroll has punned on the word "Liddell." His first play with the sound similarity of "Liddell" and "little" is in the first stanza of his prefatory poem where "little" is used three times to refer to the "cruel Three" of the next stanza. We know how "Liddell" was pronounced because in Carroll's day the students at Oxford composed the following couplet:

I am the Dean and this is Mrs. Liddell.
She plays the first, and I the second fiddle.

The rhyme is given by Roger Green in *The Diaries of Lewis Carroll*, Vol. 1, page 169.

10. Molasses.

"Suppose we change the subject," the March Hare interrupted, yawning. "I'm getting tired of this. I vote the young lady tells us a story."

"I'm afraid I don't know one," said Alice, rather alarmed at the proposal.

"Then the Dormouse shall!" they both cried. "Wake up, Dormouse!" And they pinched it on both sides at once.

The Dormouse slowly opened his eyes. "I wasn't asleep," it said in a hoarse, feeble voice, "I heard every word you fellows were saying."

"Tell us a story!" said the March Hare.

"Yes, please do!" pleaded Alice.

"And be quick about it," added the Hatter, "or you'll be asleep again before it's done."

"Once upon a time there were three little sisters," the Dormouse began in a great hurry; "and their names were Elsie, Lacie, and Tillie;[9] and they lived at the bottom of a well—"

"What did they live on?" said Alice, who always took a great interest in questions of eating and drinking.

"They lived on treacle,"[10] said the Dormouse, after thinking a minute or two.

"They couldn't have done that, you know," Alice gently remarked. "They'd have been ill."

"So they were," said the Dormouse; "*very* ill."

Alice tried a little to fancy to herself what such an extraordinary way of living would be like, but it puzzled her too much: so she went on: "But why did they live at the bottom of a well?"

"Take some more tea," the March Hare said to Alice, very earnestly.

"I've had nothing yet," Alice replied in an offended tone: "so I can't take more."

"You mean you can't take *less*," said the Hatter: "it's very easy to take *more* than nothing."

"Nobody asked *your* opinion," said Alice.

"Who's making personal remarks now?" the Hatter asked triumphantly.

Alice did not quite know what to say to this: so she helped herself to some tea and bread-and-butter, and then turned to the Dormouse, and repeated her question. "Why did they live at the bottom of a well?"

The Dormouse again took a minute or two to think about it, and then said, "It was a treacle-well."

"There's no such thing!" Alice was beginning very angrily, but the Hatter and the March Hare went "Sh! Sh!" and the Dormouse sulkily remarked, "If you can't be civil, you'd better finish the story for yourself."

"No, please go on!" Alice said very

humbly. "I won't interrupt you again. I dare say there may be *one*."

"One, indeed!" said the Dormouse indignantly. However, he consented to go on. "And so these three little sisters—they were learning to draw, you know—"

"What did they draw?" said Alice, quite forgetting her promise.

"Treacle," said the Dormouse, without considering at all this time.

"I want a clean cup," interrupted the Hatter: "let's all move one place on."

He moved on as he spoke, and the Dormouse followed him: the March Hare moved into the Dormouse's place, and Alice rather unwillingly took the place of the March Hare. The Hatter was the only one who got any advantage from the change; and Alice was a good deal worse off than before, as the March Hare had just upset the milk-jug into his plate.

Alice did not wish to offend the Dormouse again, so she began very cautiously: "But I don't understand. Where did they draw the treacle from?"

"You can draw water out of a water-well," said the Hatter; "so I should think you could draw treacle out of a treacle-well—eh, stupid?"

"But they were *in* the well," Alice said to the Dormouse, not choosing to notice this last remark.

"Of course they were," said the Dormouse: "well in."

This answer so confused poor Alice, that she let the Dormouse go on for some time without interrupting it.

"They were learning to draw," the Dormouse went on, yawning and rubbing its eyes, for it was getting very sleepy; "and they drew all manner of things—everything that begins with an M—"

"Why with an M?" said Alice.

"Why not?" said the March Hare.

Alice was silent.

The Dormouse had closed its eyes by this time, and was going off into a doze; but, on being pinched by the Hatter, it woke up again with a little shriek, and went on: "—that begins with an M, such as mouse-traps, and the moon, and memory, and muchness—you know you say things are 'much of a muchness'—11 did you ever see such a thing as a drawing of a muchness!"

"Really, now you ask me," said Alice, very much confused, "I don't think—"

"Then you shouldn't talk," said the Hatter.

This piece of rudeness was more than Alice could bear: she got up in great disgust, and walked off: the Dormouse fell asleep instantly, and neither of the others took the least notice of her going, though she looked back once or twice, half hoping that they would call after her: the last time she saw them, they were trying to put the Dormouse into the teapot.

11. "Much of a muchness" is still a colloquial British phrase meaning that two things are pretty much the same. In both England and the U.S. an equivalent phrase is "six of one and half a dozen of the other."

"At any rate I'll never go *there* again!" said Alice, as she picked her way through the wood. "It's the stupidest tea-party I ever was at in all my life!"

Just as she said this, she noticed that one of the trees had a door leading right into it. "That's very curious!" she thought. "But everything's curious to-day. I think I may as well go in at once." And in she went.

Once more she found herself in the long hall, and close to the little glass table. "Now, I'll manage better this time," she said to herself, and began by taking the little golden key, and unlocking the door that led into the garden. Then she set to work nibbling at the mushroom (she had kept a piece of it in her pocket) till she was about a foot high: then she walked down the little passage: and *then*—she found herself at last in the beautiful garden, among the bright flower-beds and the cool fountains.

CHAPTER VIII

The Queen's Croquet-Ground

A large rose-tree stood near the entrance of the garden: the roses growing on it were white, but there were three gardeners at it, busily painting them red. Alice thought this a very curious thing, and she went nearer to watch them, and, just as she came up to them, she heard one of them say, "Look out now, Five! Don't go splashing paint over me like that!"

"I couldn't help it," said Five, in a sulky tone. "Seven jogged my elbow."

On which Seven looked up and said, "That's right, Five! Always lay the blame on others!"

"*You'd* better not talk!" said Five. "I heard the Queen say only yesterday you deserved to be beheaded."

"What for?" said the one who had spoken first.

"That's none of *your* business, Two!" said Seven.

"Yes, it *is* his business!" said Five. "And I'll tell him—it was for bringing the cook tulip-roots instead of onions."

Seven flung down his brush, and had just begun, "Well, of all the unjust things—" when his eye chanced to fall upon Alice, as she stood watching them, and he checked himself suddenly: the others looked round also, and all of them bowed low.

"Would you tell me, please," said Alice, a little timidly, "why you are painting those roses?"

Five and Seven said nothing, but looked at Two. Two began, in a low voice, "Why, the fact is, you see, Miss, this here ought to have been a *red* rose-tree, and we put a white one in by mistake; and, if the Queen was to find it out, we should all have our heads cut off, you know. So you see, Miss, we're doing our best, afore she comes, to—" At this moment, Five, who been anxiously looking across the garden, called out "The Queen! The Queen!" and the three gardeners instantly threw themselves flat upon their faces. There was a sound of many footsteps, and Alice looked round, eager to see the Queen.

First came ten soldiers carrying clubs: these were all shaped like the three gardeners. oblong and flat, with their hands

106

and feet at the corners: next the ten courtiers: these were ornamented all over with diamonds, and walked two and two, as the soldiers did. After these came the royal children: there were ten of them, and the little dears came jumping merrily along, hand in hand, in couples: they were all ornamented with hearts.[1] Next came the guests, mostly Kings and Queens, and among them Alice recognized the White Rabbit: it was talking in a hurried nervous manner, smiling at everything that was said, and went by without noticing her. Then followed the Knave of Hearts, carrying the King's crown on a crimson velvet cushion; and, last of all this grand procession, came THE KING AND THE QUEEN OF HEARTS.

Alice was rather doubtful whether she ought not to lie down on her face like the three gardeners, but she could not remember ever having heard of such a rule at processions; "and besides, what would be the use of a procession," thought she, "if people had all to lie down on their faces, so that they couldn't see it?" So she stood where she was, and waited.

When the procession came opposite to Alice, they all stopped and looked at her, and the Queen said, severely, "Who is this?" She said it to the Knave of Hearts, who only bowed and smiled in reply.

"Idiot!" said the Queen, tossing her head impatiently; and, turning to Alice,

1. Among the spot cards the spades are the gardeners, the clubs are soldiers, diamonds are courtiers, and the hearts are the ten royal children. The court cards are of course members of the court. Note how cleverly throughout this chapter Carroll has linked the behavior of his animated cards with the behavior of actual playing cards. They lie flat on their faces, they cannot be identified from their backs, they are easily turned over, and they bend themselves into croquet arches.

she went on: "What's your name, child?"

"My name is Alice, so please your Majesty," said Alice very politely; but she added, to herself, "Why, they're only a pack of cards, after all. I needn't be afraid of them!"

"And who are *these?*" said the Queen, pointing to the three gardeners who were lying round the rose-tree; for, you see, as they were lying on their faces, and the pattern on their backs was the same as the rest of the pack, she could not tell whether they were gardeners, or soldiers, or courtiers, or three of her own children.

"How should *I* know?" said Alice, surprised at her own courage. "It's no business of *mine.*"

The Queen turned crimson with fury, and, after glaring at her for a moment like a wild beast, began screaming, "Off with her head!**2** Off with—"

"Nonsense!" said Alice, very loudly and decidedly, and the Queen was silent.

The King laid his hand upon her arm, and timidly said, "Consider, my dear: she is only a child!"

The Queen turned angrily away from him, and said to the Knave, "Turn them over!"

The Knave did so, very carefully, with one foot.

"Get up!" said the Queen in a shrill, loud voice, and the three gardeners instantly jumped up, and began bowing to the King, the Queen, the royal children, and everybody else.

"Leave off that!" screamed the Queen. "You make me giddy." And then, turning to the rose-tree, she went on, "What *have* you been doing here?"

"May it please your Majesty," said Two, in a very humble tone, going down on one knee as he spoke, "we were trying—"

"*I* see!" said the Queen, who had meanwhile been examining the roses. "Off with

2. "I pictured to myself the Queen of Hearts," Carroll wrote in his article "Alice on the Stage" (cited in previous notes), "as a sort of embodiment of ungovernable passion —a blind and aimless Fury." Her constant orders for beheadings are shocking to those modern critics of children's literature who feel that juvenile fiction should be free of all violence and especially violence with Freudian undertones. Even the Oz books of L. Frank Baum, so singularly free of the horrors to be found in Grimm and Andersen, contain many scenes of decapitation. As far as I know, there have been no empirical studies of how children react to such scenes and what harm if any is done to their psyche. My guess is that the normal child finds it all very amusing and is not damaged in the least, but that books like *Alice's Adventures in Wonderland* and *The Wizard of Oz* should not be allowed to circulate indiscriminately among adults who are undergoing analysis.

their heads!" and the procession moved on, three of the soldiers remaining behind to execute the unfortunate gardeners, who ran to Alice for protection.

"You shan't be beheaded!" said Alice, and she put them into a large flower-pot that stood near. The three soldiers wandered about for a minute or two, looking for them, and then quietly marched off after the others.

"Are their heads off?" shouted the Queen.

"Their heads are gone, if it please your Majesty!" the soldiers shouted in reply.

"That's right!" shouted the Queen. "Can you play croquet?"

The soldiers were silent, and looked at Alice, as the question was evidently meant for her.

"Yes!" shouted Alice.

"Come on, then!" roared the Queen, and Alice joined the procession, wondering very much what would happen next.

"It's—it's a very fine day!" said a timid voice at her side. She was walking by the White Rabbit, who was peeping anxiously into her face.

"Very," said Alice. "Where's the Duchess?"

"Hush! Hush!" said the Rabbit in a low, hurried tone. He looked anxiously over his shoulder as he spoke, and then raised himself upon tiptoe, put his mouth close to her ear, and whispered, "She's under sentence of execution."

"What for?" said Alice.

"Did you say 'What a pity!'?" the Rabbit asked.

"No, I didn't," said Alice. "I don't think it's at all a pity. I said 'What for?' "

"She boxed the Queen's ears—" the Rabbit began. Alice gave a little scream of laughter. "Oh, hush!" the Rabbit whispered in a frightened tone. "The Queen will hear you! You see she came rather late, and the Queen said—"

"Get to your places!" shouted the Queen in a voice of thunder, and people began running about in all directions, tumbling up against each other: however, they got settled down in a minute or two, and the game began.

Alice thought she had never seen such a curious croquet-ground in her life: it was all ridges and furrows: the croquet balls were live hedgehogs, and the mallets live flamingoes,[3] and the soldiers had to double themselves up and stand on their hands and feet, to make the arches.

The chief difficulty Alice found at first was in managing her flamingo: she succeeded in getting its body tucked away, comfortably enough, under her arm, with its legs hanging down, but generally, just as she had got its neck nicely straightened out, and was going to give the hedgehog

3. In Carroll's original manuscript of *Alice* as well as in the sketches he made for it, the mallets are ostriches instead of flamingoes. Carroll spent a great deal of time inventing new and unusual ways of playing familiar games. His rules for Castle Croquet, a complicated game that he often played with the Liddell sisters, were published in 1863 and will be found reprinted in *The Lewis Carroll Picture Book*. The same volume contains a reprint of his rules for Lanrick, a game played with checkers on a checkerboard. His pamphlet on "Circular Billiards" has not been reprinted. Of some two hundred pamphlets that Carroll had printed about twenty deal with original games.

a blow with its head, it *would* twist itself round and look up in her face, with such a puzzled expression that she could not help bursting out laughing; and, when she had got its head down, and was going to begin again, it was very provoking to find that the hedgehog had unrolled itself, and was in the act of crawling away: besides all this, there was generally a ridge or a furrow in the way wherever she wanted to send the hedgehog to, and, as the doubled-up soldiers were always getting up and walking off to other parts of the ground, Alice soon came to the conclusion that it was a very difficult game indeed.

The players all played at once, without waiting for turns, quarrelling all the while, and fighting for the hedgehogs; and in a very short time the Queen was in a furious passion, and went stamping about, and shouting, "Off with his head!" or "Off with her head!" about once in a minute.

Alice began to feel very uneasy: to be sure, she had not as yet had any dispute with the Queen, but she knew that it might happen any minute, "and then," thought she, "what would become of me? They're dreadfully fond of beheading people here: the great wonder is, that there's any one left alive!"

She was looking about for some way of escape, and wondering whether she could get away without being seen, when she noticed a curious appearance in the air: it puzzled her very much at first, but after watching it a minute or two she made it out to be a grin, and she said to herself, "It's the Cheshire Cat: now I shall have somebody to talk to."

"How are you getting on?" said the Cat, as soon as there was mouth enough for it to speak with.

Alice waited till the eyes appeared, and then nodded. "It's no use speaking to it," she thought, "till its ears have come, or at least one of them." In another minute the whole head appeared, and then Alice put down her flamingo, and began an account of the game, feeling very glad she had some one to listen to her. The Cat seemed to think that there was enough of it now in sight, and no more of it appeared.

"I don't think they play at all fairly," Alice began, in rather a complaining tone, "and they all quarrel so dreadfully one can't hear oneself speak—and they don't seem to have any rules in particular: at least, if there are, nobody attends to them —and you've no idea how confusing it is all the things being alive: for instance, there's the arch I've got to go through next walking about at the other end of the ground—and I should have croqueted the Queen's hedgehog just now, only it ran away when it saw mine coming!"

4. "A cat may look at a king" is a familiar English proverb meaning that there are things an inferior may do in the presence of a superior.

"How do you like the Queen?" said the Cat in a low voice.

"Not at all," said Alice: "she's so extremely—" Just then she noticed that the Queen was close behind her, listening: so she went on "—likely to win, that it's hardly worth while finishing the game."

The Queen smiled and passed on.

"Who *are* you talking to?" said the King, coming up to Alice, and looking at the Cat's head with great curiosity.

"It's a friend of mine—a Cheshire Cat," said Alice: "allow me to introduce it."

"I don't like the look of it at all," said the King: "however, it may kiss my hand, if it likes."

"I'd rather not," the Cat remarked.

"Don't be impertinent," said the King, "and don't look at me like that!" He got behind Alice as he spoke.

"A cat may look at a king," said Alice. "I've read that in some book, but I don't remember where."4

"Well, it must be removed," said the King very decidedly; and he called to the Queen, who was passing at the moment, "My dear! I wish you would have this cat removed!"

The Queen had only one way of settling all difficulties, great or small. "Off with his head!" she said without even looking round.

"I'll fetch the executioner myself,"

said the King eagerly, and he hurried off.

Alice thought she might as well go back and see how the game was going on, as she heard the Queen's voice in the distance, screaming with passion. She had already heard her sentence three of the players to be executed for having missed their turns, and she did not like the look of things at all, as the game was in such confusion that she never knew whether it was her turn or not. So she went off in search of her hedgehog.

The hedgehog was engaged in a fight with another hedgehog, which seemed to Alice an excellent opportunity for croqueting one of them with the other: the only difficulty was, that her flamingo was gone across to the other side of the garden, where Alice could see it trying in a helpless sort of way to fly up into a tree.

By the time she had caught the flamingo and brought it back, the fight was over, and both the hedgehogs were out of sight: "but it doesn't matter much," thought Alice, "as all the arches are gone from this side of the ground." So she tucked it away under her arm, that it might not escape again, and went back to have a little more conversation with her friend.

When she got back to the Cheshire Cat, she was surprised to find quite a large crowd collected round it: there was a dispute going on between the executioner,

the King, and the Queen, who were all talking at once, while all the rest were quite silent, and looked very uncomfortable.

The moment Alice appeared, she was appealed to by all three to settle the question, and they repeated their arguments to her, though, as they all spoke at once, she found it very hard to make out exactly what they said.

The executioner's argument was, that you couldn't cut off a head unless there was a body to cut it off from: that he had

116

never had to do such a thing before, and he wasn't going to begin at *his* time of life.

The King's argument was, that anything that had a head could be beheaded, and that you weren't to talk nonsense.

The Queen's argument was that, if something wasn't done about it in less than no time, she'd have everybody executed, all round. (It was this last remark that had made the whole party look so grave and anxious.)

Alice could think of nothing else to say but "It belongs to the Duchess: you'd better ask *her* about it."

"She's in prison," the Queen said to the executioner: "fetch her here." And the executioner went off like an arrow.

The Cat's head began fading away the moment he was gone, and, by the time he had come back with the Duchess, it had entirely disappeared: so the King and the executioner ran wildly up and down looking for it, while the rest of the party went back to the game.

CHAPTER IX

The Mock Turtle's Story

"You can't think how glad I am to see you again, you dear old thing!" said the Duchess, as she tucked her arm affectionately into Alice's, and they walked off together.

Alice was very glad to find her in such a pleasant temper, and thought to herself that perhaps it was only the pepper that had made her so savage when they met in the kitchen.

"When *I'm* a Duchess," she said to herself (not in a very hopeful tone, though), "I won't have any pepper in my kitchen *at all*. Soup does very well without — Maybe it's always pepper that makes people hot-tempered," she went on, very much pleased at having found out a new kind of rule, "and vinegar that makes them sour—and camomile[1] that makes them bitter—and—and barley-sugar[2] and

1. Camomile was an extremely bitter medicine, widely used in Victorian England. It was extracted from the plant of the same name.

2. Barley-sugar is a transparent, brittle candy that used to be made by boiling cane sugar with a concoction of barley.

119

such things that make children sweet-tempered. I only wish people knew *that:* then they wouldn't be so stingy about it, you know—"

She had quite forgotten the Duchess by this time, and was a little startled when she heard her voice close to her ear. "You're thinking about something, my dear, and that makes you forget to talk. I can't tell you just now what the moral of that is, but I shall remember it in a bit."

"Perhaps it hasn't one," Alice ventured to remark.

"Tut, tut, child!" said the Duchess. "Everything's got a moral, if only you can find it." And she squeezed herself up closer to Alice's side as she spoke.

Alice did not much like her keeping so close to her: first, because the Duchess was *very* ugly: and secondly, because she was exactly the right height to rest her chin on Alice's shoulder, and it was an uncomfortably sharp chin. However, she did not like to be rude: so she bore it as well as she could.

"The game's going on rather better now," she said, by way of keeping up the conversation a little.

" 'Tis so," said the Duchess: "and the moral of that is—'Oh, 'tis love, 'tis love, that makes the world go round!' "

"Somebody said," Alice whispered,

"that it's done by everybody minding their own business!" **3**

"Ah, well! It means much the same thing," said the Duchess, digging her sharp little chin into Alice's shoulder as she added, "and the moral of *that* is—'Take care of the sense, and the sounds will take care of themselves.' "**4**

"How fond she is of finding morals in things!" Alice thought to herself.

"I dare say you're wondering why I don't put my arm round your waist," the Duchess said, after a pause: "the reason is, that I'm doubtful about the temper of your flamingo. Shall I try the experiment?"

"He might bite," Alice cautiously replied, not feeling at all anxious to have the experiment tried.

"Very true," said the Duchess: "flamingoes and mustard both bite. And the moral of that is—'Birds of a feather flock together.' "

"Only mustard isn't a bird," Alice remarked.

"Right, as usual," said the Duchess: "what a clear way you have of putting things!"

"It's a mineral, I *think*," said Alice.

"Of course it is," said the Duchess, who seemed ready to agree to everything that Alice said: "there's a large mustard-mine near here. And the moral of that is —

3. The "somebody" was the Duchess herself, in Chapter 6.

4. Surely few American readers have recognized this for what it is, an extremely ingenious switch on the British proverb, "Take care of the pence and the pounds will take care of themselves." The Duchess's remark is sometimes quoted as a good rule to follow in writing prose or even poetry. Unsound, of course.

'The more there is of mine, the less there is of yours.' "

"Oh, I know!" exclaimed Alice, who had not attended to this last remark, "it's a vegetable. It doesn't look like one, but it is."

"I quite agree with you," said the Duchess; "and the moral of that is—'Be what you would seem to be'—or, if you'd like it put more simply—'Never imagine yourself not to be otherwise than what it might appear to others that what you were or might have been was not otherwise than what you had been would have appeared to them to be otherwise.' "

"I think I should understand that better," Alice said very politely, "if I had it written down: but I can't quite follow it as you say it."

"That's nothing to what I could say if I chose," the Duchess replied, in a pleased tone.

"Pray don't trouble yourself to say it any longer than that," said Alice.

"Oh, don't talk about trouble!" said the Duchess. "I make you a present of everything I've said as yet."

"A cheap sort of present!" thought Alice. "I'm glad people don't give birthday presents like that!" But she did not venture to say it out loud.

"Thinking again?" the Duchess asked, with another dig of her sharp little chin.

"I've a right to think," said Alice

sharply, for she was beginning to feel a little worried.

"Just about as much right," said the Duchess, "as pigs have to fly: and the m—"

But here, to Alice's great surprise, the Duchess's voice died away, even in the middle of her favourite word 'moral,' and the arm that was linked into hers began to tremble. Alice looked up, and there stood the Queen in front of them, with her arms folded, frowning like a thunderstorm.

"A fine day, your Majesty!" the Duchess began in a low, weak voice.

"Now, I give you fair warning," shouted the Queen, stamping on the ground as she spoke; "either you or your head must be off, and that in about half no time! Take your choice!"

The Duchess took her choice, and was gone in a moment.

"Let's go on with the game," the Queen said to Alice; and Alice was too much frightened to say a word, but slowly followed her back to the croquet-ground.

The other guests had taken advantage of the Queen's absence, and were resting in the shade: however, the moment they saw her, they hurried back to the game, the Queen merely remarking that a moment's delay would cost them their lives.

All the time they were playing the Queen never left off quarrelling with the other players, and shouting "Off with his head!" or "Off with her head!" Those

5. Mock turtle soup is an imitation of green turtle soup, usually made from veal. This explains why Tenniel drew his Mock Turtle with the head, hind hoofs, and tail of a calf.

6. The gryphon, or griffin, is a fabulous monster with the head and wings of an eagle and the lower body of a lion. In the *Purgatorio*, Canto 29, of Dante's *Divine Comedy* (that lesser-known tour of Wonderland by way of a hole in the ground), the chariot of the Church is pulled by a gryphon. The beast was a common medieval symbol for the union of God and man in Christ. Here both the Gryphon and Mock Turtle are obvious satires on the sentimental college alumnus, of which Oxford has always had an unusually large share.

whom she sentenced were taken into custody by the soldiers, who of course had to leave off being arches to do this, so that, by the end of half an hour or so, there were no arches left, and all the players, except the King, the Queen, and Alice, were in custody, and under sentence of execution.

Then the Queen left off, quite out of breath, and said to Alice, "Have you seen the Mock Turtle yet?"

"No," said Alice. "I don't even know what a Mock Turtle is."

"It's the thing Mock Turtle Soup[5] is made from," said the Queen.

"I never saw one, or heard of one," said Alice.

"Come on, then," said the Queen, "and he shall tell you his history."

As they walked off together, Alice heard the King say in a low voice, to the company generally, "You are all pardoned." "Come, *that's* a good thing!" she said to herself, for she had felt quite unhappy at the number of executions the Queen had ordered.

They very soon came upon a Gryphon,[6] lying fast asleep in the sun. (If you don't know what a Gryphon is, look at the picture.) "Up, lazy thing!" said the Queen, "and take this young lady to see the Mock Turtle, and to hear his history. I must go back and see after some executions I have ordered;" and she walked off, leaving Alice alone with the Gryphon.

Alice did not quite like the look of the creature, but on the whole she thought it would be quite as safe to stay with it as to go after that savage Queen: so she waited.

The Gryphon sat up and rubbed its eyes: then it watched the Queen till she was out of sight: then it chuckled. "What fun!" said the Gryphon, half to itself, half to Alice.

"What *is* the fun?" said Alice.

"Why, *she*," said the Gryphon. "It's all her fancy, that: they never executes nobody, you know. Come on!"

"Everybody says 'come on!' here," thought Alice, as she went slowly after it: "I never was so ordered about before, in all my life, never!"

They had not gone far before they saw the Mock Turtle in the distance, sitting sad and lonely on a little ledge of rock, and, as they came nearer, Alice could hear

125

him sighing as if his heart would break. She pitied him deeply. "What is his sorrow?" she asked the Gryphon. And the Gryphon answered, very nearly in the same words as before, "It's all his fancy, that: he hasn't got no sorrow, you know. Come on!"

So they went up to the Mock Turtle, who looked at them with large eyes full of tears, but said nothing.

"This here young lady," said the Gryphon, "she wants for to know your history, she do."

"I'll tell it her," said the Mock Turtle in a deep, hollow tone. "Sit down, both of you, and don't speak a word till I've finished."

So they sat down, and nobody spoke for some minutes. Alice thought to herself, "I don't see how he can *ever* finish, if he doesn't begin." But she waited patiently.

"Once," said the Mock Turtle at last, with a deep sigh, "I was a real Turtle."

These words were followed by a very long silence, broken only by an occasional exclamation of "Hjckrrh!" from the Gryphon, and the constant heavy sobbing of the Mock Turtle. Alice was very nearly getting up and saying, "Thank you, Sir, for your interesting story," but she could not help thinking there *must* be more to come, so she sat still and said nothing.

"When we were little," the Mock Tur-

tle went on at last, more calmly, though still sobbing a little now and then, "we went to school in the sea. The master was an old Turtle—we used to call him Tortoise—"

"Why did you call him Tortoise, if he wasn't one?" Alice asked.

"We called him Tortoise because he taught us,"**7** said the Mock Turtle angrily. "Really you are very dull!"

"You ought to be ashamed of yourself

7. Carroll used this pun again in his article "What the Tortoise said to Achilles," in *Mind*, April 1895. After explaining a disconcerting logical paradox to Achilles, the tortoise remarks: "And *would* you mind, as a personal favor — considering what a lot of instruction this colloquy of ours will provide for the Logicians of the Nineteenth Century — *would* you mind adopting a pun that my cousin the Mock-Turtle will then make, and allowing yourself to be re-named Taught-Us?"

Achilles buries his face in his hands, then in low tones of despair he counters with another pun: "As you please! Provided that *you*, for *your* part, will adopt a pun the Mock-Turtle never made, and allow yourself to be renamed A Kill-Ease!"

8. The phrase "French, music and washing — extra" often appeared on boarding-school bills. It meant, of course, that there was an extra charge for French and music, and for having one's laundry done by the school.

for asking such a simple question," added the Gryphon; and then they both sat silent and looked at poor Alice, who felt ready to sink into the earth. At last the Gryphon said to the Mock Turtle, "Drive on, old fellow! Don't be all day about it!" and he went on in these words:—

"Yes, we went to school in the sea, though you mayn't believe it—"

"I never said I didn't!" interrupted Alice.

"You did," said the Mock Turtle.

"Hold your tongue!" added the Gryphon, before Alice could speak again. The Mock Turtle went on.

"We had the best of educations—in fact, we went to school every day—"

"*I've* been to a day-school, too," said Alice. "You needn't be so proud as all that."

"With extras?" asked the Mock Turtle, a little anxiously.

"Yes," said Alice: "we learned French and music."

"And washing?" said the Mock Turtle.

"Certainly not!" said Alice indignantly.

"Ah! Then yours wasn't a really good school," said the Mock Turtle in a tone of great relief. "Now, at *ours,* they had, at the end of the bill, 'French, music, *and washing*—extra.' " **8**

"You couldn't have wanted it much," said Alice; "living at the bottom of the sea."

128

"I couldn't afford to learn it," said the Mock Turtle with a sigh. "I only took the regular course."

"What was that?" enquired Alice.

"Reeling and Writing,[9] of course, to begin with," the Mock Turtle replied; "and then the different branches of Arithmetic—Ambition, Distraction, Uglification and Derision."

"I never heard of 'Uglification,' " Alice ventured to say. "What is it?"

The Gryphon lifted up both its paws in surprise. "Never heard of uglifying!" it exclaimed. "You know what to beautify is, I suppose?"

"Yes," said Alice doubtfully: "it means —to—make—anything—prettier."

"Well, then," the Gryphon went on, "if you don't know what to uglify is, you *are* a simpleton."

Alice did not feel encouraged to ask any more questions about it: so she turned to the Mock Turtle, and said, "What else had you to learn?"

"Well, there was Mystery," the Mock Turtle replied, counting off the subjects on his flappers,—"Mystery, ancient and modern, with Seaography: then Drawling —the Drawling-master was an old conger-eel, that used to come once a week: *he* taught us Drawling, Stretching, and Fainting in Coils."

"What was *that* like?" said Alice.

9. Needless to say, all the Mock Turtle's subjects are puns (reading, writing, addition, subtraction, multiplication, division, history, geography, drawing, sketching, painting in oils, Latin, Greek). In fact, this chapter and the one to follow fairly swarm with puns. Children find puns very funny, but most contemporary authorities on what children are supposed to like believe that puns lower the literary quality of juvenile books.

"Well, I can't show it you, myself," the Mock Turtle said: "I'm too stiff. And the Gryphon never learnt it."

"Hadn't time," said the Gryphon: "I went to the Classical master, though. He was an old crab, *he* was."

"I never went to him," the Mock Turtle said with a sigh. "He taught Laughing and Grief, they used to say."

"So he did, so he did," said the Gryphon, sighing in his turn; and both creatures hid their faces in their paws.

"And how many hours a day did you do lessons?" said Alice, in a hurry to change the subject.

"Ten hours the first day," said the Mock Turtle: "nine the next, and so on."

"What a curious plan!" exclaimed Alice.

"That's the reason they're called lessons," the Gryphon remarked: "because they lessen from day to day."

This was quite a new idea to Alice, and she thought it over a little before she made her next remark. "Then the eleventh day must have been a holiday?"

"Of course it was," said the Mock Turtle.

"And how did you manage on the twelfth?" Alice went on eagerly.

"That's enough about lessons," the Gryphon interrupted in a very decided tone. "Tell her something about the games now."

CHAPTER X

The Lobster Quadrille

The Mock Turtle sighed deeply, and drew the back of one flapper across his eyes. He looked at Alice and tried to speak, but, for a minute or two, sobs choked his voice. "Same as if he had a bone in his throat," said the Gryphon; and it set to work shaking him and punching him in the back. At last the Mock Turtle recovered his voice, and, with tears running down his cheeks, he went on again:—

"You may not have lived much under the sea—" ("I haven't," said Alice) —"and perhaps you were never even introduced to a lobster—" (Alice began to say "I once tasted—" but checked herself hastily, and said, "No, never") "—so you can have no idea what a delightful thing a Lobster-Quadrille is!"[1]

1. The quadrille, a kind of square dance in five figures, was one of the most difficult of the ballroom dances fashionable at the time Carroll wrote his tale. The Liddell children had been taught the dance by a private tutor.

In one of his letters to a little girl, Carroll described his own dancing technique as follows:

As to dancing, my dear, I *never* dance, unless I am allowed to do it *in my own peculiar way*. There is no use trying to describe it: it has to be seen to be believed. The last house I tried it in, the floor broke through. But then it was a poor sort of floor — the beams were only six inches thick, hardly worth calling beams at all: stone arches are much more sensible, when any dancing, *of my peculiar kind*, is to be done. Did you ever see the Rhinoceros, and the Hippopotamus, at the Zoological Gardens, trying to dance a minuet together? It is a touching sight.

131

"No, indeed," said Alice. "What sort of a dance is it?"

"Why," said the Gryphon, "you first form into a line along the seashore—"

"Two lines!" cried the Mock Turtle. "Seals, turtles, salmon, and so on: then, when you've cleared all the jelly-fish out of the way—"

"*That* generally takes some time," interrupted the Gryphon.

"—you advance twice—"

"Each with a lobster as a partner!" cried the Gryphon.

"Of course," the Mock Turtle said: "advance twice, set to partners—"

"—change lobsters, and retire in same order," continued the Gryphon.

"Then, you know," the Mock Turtle went on, "you throw the—"

"The lobsters!" shouted the Gryphon, with a bound into the air.

"—as far out to sea as you can—"

"Swim after them!" screamed the Gryphon.

"Turn a somersault in the sea!" cried the Mock Turtle, capering wildly about.

"Change lobsters again!" yelled the Gryphon at the top of its voice.

"Back to land again, and—that's all the first figure," said the Mock Turtle, suddenly dropping his voice; and the two creatures, who had been jumping about like mad things all this time, sat down again very sadly and quietly, and looked at Alice.

"It must be a very pretty dance," said Alice timidly.

"Would you like to see a little of it?" said the Mock Turtle.

"Very much indeed," said Alice.

"Come, let's try the first figure!" said the Mock Turtle to the Gryphon. "We can do it without lobsters, you know. Which shall sing?"

"Oh, *you* sing," said the Gryphon. "I've forgotten the words."

So they began solemnly dancing round and round Alice, every now and then treading on her toes when they passed too close, and waving their fore-paws to mark the time, while the Mock Turtle sang this, very slowly and sadly:—**2**

2. The Mock Turtle's song parodies the first line and adopts the meter of Mary Howitt's poem (in turn based on an older song) *The Spider and the Fly*. The first stanza of Mrs. Howitt's version reads:

"Will you walk into my parlour?"
  said the spider to the fly.
" 'Tis the prettiest little parlour that
  ever you did spy.
The way into my parlour is up a
  winding stair,
And I've got many curious things to
  show when you are there."
"Oh, no, no," said the little fly, "to
  ask me is in vain,
For who goes up your winding stair
  can ne'er come down again."

In Carroll's original manuscript the Mock Turtle sings a different song:

Beneath the waters of the sea
Are lobsters thick as thick can be —
They love to dance with you and me.
My own, my gentle Salmon!

CHORUS
Salmon, come up! Salmon, go down!
Salmon, come twist your tail around!
Of all the fishes of the sea
There's none so good as Salmon!

Here Carroll is parodying a Negro minstrel song, the chorus of which begins:

Sally come up! Sally go down!
Sally come twist your heel around!

An entry in Carroll's diary on July 3, 1862 (the day before the famous expedition up the river Thames), mentions hearing the Liddell sisters (at a rainy-day get-together in the Deanery) sing this minstrel song "with great spirit."

3. A whiting is a food fish in the cod family.

4. "Shingle" is a British word for that portion of the seaside where the beach is covered with large rounded stones and pebbles.

"Will you walk a little faster?" said a whiting[3] to a snail,
"There's a porpoise close behind us, and he's treading on my tail.
See how eagerly the lobsters and the turtles all advance!
They are waiting on the shingle[4]—will you come and join the dance?
    Will you, won't you, will you, won't you, will you join the dance?
    Will you, won't you, will you, won't you, won't you join the dance?

"You can really have no notion how delightful it will be
When they take us up and throw us, with the lobsters, out to sea!"
But the snail replied "Too far, too far!" and gave a look askance—
Said he thanked the whiting kindly, but he would not join the dance.
    Would not, could not, would not, could not, would not join the dance.
    Would not, could not, would not, could not, could not join the dance.

"What matters it how far we go?" his scaly friend replied.
"There is another shore, you know, upon the other side.
The further off from England the nearer is to France—
Then turn not pale, beloved snail, but come and join the dance.
    Will you, won't you, will you, won't you, will you join the dance?
    Will you, won't you, will you, won't you, won't you join the dance?"

"Thank you, it's a very interesting dance to watch," said Alice, feeling very glad that it was over at last: "and I do so like that curious song about the whiting!"

"Oh, as to the whiting," said the Mock Turtle, "they—you've seen them, of course?"

"Yes," said Alice, "I've often seen them at dinn—" she checked herself hastily.

"I don't know where Dinn may be," said the Mock Turtle; "but, if you've seen them so often, of course you know what they're like?"

"I believe so," Alice replied thought-

135

5. "When I wrote that," Carroll is quoted as saying (in Stuart Collingwood's *The Life and Letters of Lewis Carroll*, page 402), "I believed that whiting really did have their tails in their mouths, but I have since been told that fishmongers put the tail through the eye, not in the mouth at all."

fully. "They have their tails in their mouths[5]—and they're all over crumbs."

"You're wrong about the crumbs," said the Mock Turtle: "crumbs would all wash off in the sea. But they *have* their tails in their mouths; and the reason is—" here the Mock Turtle yawned and shut his eyes. "Tell her about the reason and all that," he said to the Gryphon.

"The reason is," said the Gryphon, "that they *would* go with the lobsters to the dance. So they got thrown out to sea. So they had to fall a long way. So they got their tails fast in their mouths. So they couldn't get them out again. That's all."

"Thank you," said Alice, "it's very interesting. I never knew so much about a whiting before."

"I can tell you more than that, if you like," said the Gryphon. "Do you know why it's called a whiting?"

"I never thought about it," said Alice. "Why?"

"It does the boots and shoes," the Gryphon replied very solemnly.

Alice was thoroughly puzzled. "Does the boots and shoes!" she repeated in a wondering tone.

"Why, what are *your* shoes done with?" said the Gryphon. "I mean, what makes them so shiny?"

Alice looked down at them, and considered a little before she gave her an-

swer. "They're done with blacking, I believe."

"Boots and shoes under the sea," the
Gryphon went on in a deep voice, "are
done with whiting. Now you know."

"And what are they made of?" Alice
asked in a tone of great curiosity.

"Soles and eels, of course," the Gryphon replied, rather impatiently: "any
shrimp could have told you that."

"If I'd been the whiting," said Alice,
whose thoughts were still running on the
song, "I'd have said to the porpoise,
'Keep back, please! We don't want *you*
with us!' "

"They were obliged to have him with
them," the Mock Turtle said. "No wise
fish would go anywhere without a porpoise."

"Wouldn't it, really?" said Alice, in a
tone of great surprise.

"Of course not," said the Mock Turtle.
"Why, if a fish came to *me,* and told me
he was going a journey, I should say 'With
what porpoise?' "

"Don't you mean 'purpose'?" said
Alice.

"I mean what I say," the Mock Turtle
replied in an offended tone. And the
Gryphon added "Come, let's hear some
of *your* adventures."

"I could tell you my adventures—beginning from this morning," said Alice a

little timidly; "but it's no use going back to yesterday, because I was a different person then."

"Explain all that," said the Mock Turtle.

"No, no! The adventures first," said the Gryphon in an impatient tone: "explanations take such a dreadful time."

So Alice began telling them her adventures from the time when she first saw the White Rabbit. She was a little nervous about it, just at first, the two creatures got so close to her, one on each side, and opened their eyes and mouths so *very* wide; but she gained courage as she went on. Her listeners were perfectly quiet till she got to the part about her repeating *"You are old, Father William,"* to the Caterpillar, and the words all coming different, and then the Mock Turtle drew a long breath, and said, "That's very curious!"

"It's all about as curious as it can be," said the Gryphon.

"It all came different!" the Mock Turtle repeated thoughtfully. "I should like to hear her try and repeat something now. Tell her to begin." He looked at the Gryphon as if he thought it had some kind of authority over Alice.

"Stand up and repeat *' 'Tis the voice of the sluggard,' "* said the Gryphon.

"How the creatures order one about, and make one repeat lessons!" thought

Alice. "I might just as well be at school at once." However, she got up, and began to repeat it, but her head was so full of the Lobster-Quadrille, that she hardly knew what she was saying; and the words came very queer indeed:—**6**

" 'Tis the voice of the Lobster: I heard him declare
'You have baked me too brown, I must sugar my hair.'
As a duck with its eyelids, so he with his nose
Trims his belt and his buttons, and turns out his toes.
When the sands are all dry, he is gay as a lark,
And will talk in contemptuous tones of the Shark:
But, when the tide rises and sharks are around,
His voice has a timid and tremulous sound."

"That's different from what *I* used to say when I was a child," said the Gryphon.

"Well, *I* never heard it before," said the Mock Turtle; "but it sounds uncommon nonsense."

Alice said nothing: she had sat down with her face in her hands, wondering if anything would *ever* happen in a natural way again.

"I should like to have it explained," said the Mock Turtle.

"She can't explain it," said the Gryphon hastily. "Go on with the next verse."

"But about his toes?" the Mock Turtle

6. The first line of this poem calls to mind the Biblical phrase "the voice of the turtle" (*Song of Songs* 2:12); actually it is a parody of the opening lines of *The Sluggard*, a dismal poem by Isaac Watts (see Note 4 of Chapter 2), which was well known to Carroll's readers.

'Tis the voice of the sluggard; I heard him complain,
"You have wak'd me too soon, I must slumber again."
As the door on its hinges, so he on his bed,
Turns his sides and his shoulders and his heavy head.

"A little more sleep, and a little more slumber;"
Thus he wastes half his days, and his hours without number,
And when he gets up, he sits folding his hands,
Or walks about sauntering, or trifling he stands.

I pass'd by his garden, and saw the wild brier,

*The thorn and the thistle grow
    broader and higher;
The clothes that hang on him are
    turning to rags;
And his money still wastes till he
    starves or he begs.*

*I made him a visit, still hoping to
    find
That he took better care for
    improving his mind:
He told me his dreams, talked of
    eating and drinking;
But he scarce reads his Bible, and
    never loves thinking.*

*Said I then to my heart, "Here's a
    lesson for me,"
This man's but a picture of what I
    might be:
But thanks to my friends for their
    care in my breeding,
Who taught me betimes to love
    working and reading.*

Carroll's burlesque of Watts's doggerel underwent a good many changes. Before 1886 all editions of *Alice* had a first verse of four lines and a second verse that was interrupted after the second line. Carroll supplied the missing two lines for William Boyd's *Songs from Alice in Wonderland*, a book published in 1870. The full stanza then read:

*I passed by his garden, and marked,
    with one eye,
How the owl and the oyster were
    sharing a pie,
While the duck and the Dodo, the
    lizard and cat
Were swimming in milk round the
    brim of a hat.*

In 1886 Carroll revised and enlarged the poem to sixteen lines for the stage musical of *Alice*. This is the final version, which appears in editions of Alice after 1886. It is hard to believe, but an Essex vicar actually wrote a letter to *The St. James' Gazette* accusing Carroll of irreverence because of the Biblical allusion in the first line of his parody.

persisted. "How *could* he turn them out with his nose, you know?"

"It's the first position in dancing," Alice said; but she was dreadfully puzzled by the whole thing, and longed to change the subject.

"Go on with the next verse," the Gryphon repeated: "it begins '*I passed by his garden.*'" Alice did not dare to disobey, though she felt sure it would all come wrong, and she went on in a trembling voice:—

"I passed by his garden, and marked, with one eye,
How the Owl and the Panther were sharing a pie:
The Panther took pie-crust, and gravy, and meat,
While the Owl had the dish as its share of the treat.
When the pie was all finished, the Owl, as a boon,
Was kindly permitted to pocket the spoon:
While the Panther received knife and fork with a growl,
And concluded the banquet by—" **7**

"What *is* the use of repeating all that stuff," the Mock Turtle interrupted, "if you don't explain it as you go on? It's by far the most confusing thing *I* ever heard!"

"Yes, I think you'd better leave off," said the Gryphon, and Alice was only too glad to do so.

"Shall we try another figure of the Lob-

140

ster-Quadrille?" the Gryphon went on.
"Or would you like the Mock Turtle to
sing you another song?"

"Oh, a song, please, if the Mock Turtle
would be so kind," Alice replied, so
eagerly that the Gryphon said, in a
rather offended tone, "Hm! No account-
ing for tastes! Sing her '*Turtle Soup,*' will
you, old fellow?"

The Mock Turtle sighed deeply, and
began, in a voice choked with sobs, to
sing this:—8

> "Beautiful Soup, so rich and green,
>   Waiting in a hot tureen!
> Who for such dainties would not
>   stoop?
> Soup of the evening, beautiful Soup!
> Soup of the evening, beautiful Soup!
>
>   Beau—ootiful Soo—oop!
>   Beau—ootiful Soo—oop!
> Soo—oop of the e—e—evening,
>   Beautiful, beautiful Soup!
>
> "Beautiful Soup! Who cares for fish,
>   Game, or any other dish?
> Who would not give all else for two p
>   ennyworth only of Beautiful Soup?
> Pennyworth only of beautiful Soup?
>
>   Beau—ootiful Soo—oop!
>   Beau—ootiful Soo—oop!
> Soo—oop of the e—e—evening,
>   Beautiful, beauti—FUL SOUP!"

"Chorus again!" cried the Gryphon,
and the Mock Turtle had just begun to

7. The grim final words, "eating
the owl," appear in the 1886
printed edition of Savile Clarke's
operetta. Another and probably
earlier version of the last couplet,
given in Stuart Collingwood's biography, runs:

> But the panther obtained both
>   the fork and the knife,
> So, when *he* lost his temper, the
>   owl lost its life.

8. On August 1, 1862, Carroll records in his diary that the Liddell
sisters sang for him the popular
song "Star of the Evening." The
words and music were by James M.
Sayles.

> *Beautiful star in heav'n so bright,*
> *Softly falls thy silv'ry light,*
> *As thou movest from earth afar,*
> *Star of the evening, beautiful star.*
>
> CHORUS:
>
> *Beautiful star,*
> *Beautiful star,*
> *Star of the evening, beautiful star.*
>
> *In Fancy's eye thou seem'st to say,*
> *Follow me, come from earth away.*
> *Upward thy spirit's pinions try,*
> *To realms of love beyond the sky.*
>
> *Shine on, oh star of love divine,*
> *And may our soul's affection twine*
> *Around thee as thou movest afar,*
> *Star of the twilight, beautiful star.*

Carroll's second stanza, with its
e. e. cummings-like partition of
"pennyworth," does not appear in
the original manuscript. The divi-
sions of "beautiful," "soup," and
"evening" suggest the manner in
which the original song was sung.
Cary Grant sobbed through the
song in his role of the Mock Turtle
in Paramount's undistinguished
1933 movie version of *Alice.*

repeat it, when a cry of "The trial's beginning!" was heard in the distance.

"Come on!" cried the Gryphon, and, taking Alice by the hand, it hurried off, without waiting for the end of the song.

"What trial is it?" Alice panted as she ran; but the Gryphon only answered "Come on!" and ran the faster, while more and more faintly came, carried on the breeze that followed them, the melancholy words:—

"Soo—oop of the e—e—evening,
Beautiful, beautiful Soup!"

CHAPTER XI

Who Stole the Tarts?

The King and Queen of Hearts were seated on their throne when they arrived, with a great crowd assembled about them —all sorts of little birds and beasts, as well as the whole pack of cards: the Knave was standing before them, in chains, with a soldier on each side to guard him; and near the King was the White Rabbit, with a trumpet in one hand, and a scroll of parchment in the other. In the very middle of the court was a table, with a large dish of tarts upon it: they looked so good, that it made Alice quite hungry to look at them—"I wish they'd get the trial done," she thought, "and hand round the refreshments!" But there seemed to be no chance of this; so she began looking at everything about her to pass away the time.

Alice had never been in a court of justice before, but she had read about them in books, and she was quite pleased to find that she knew the name of nearly everything there. "That's the judge," she said to herself, "because of his great wig."

The judge, by the way, was the King; and, as he wore his crown over the wig (look at the frontispiece if you want to see how he did it), he did not look at all comfortable, and it was certainly not becoming.

"And that's the jury-box," thought Alice; "and those twelve creatures," (she was obliged to say "creatures," you see, because some of them were animals, and some were birds), "I suppose they are the jurors." She said this last word two or three times over to herself, being rather proud of it: for she thought, and rightly too, that very few little girls of her age knew the meaning of it at all. However, "jurymen" would have done just as well.

The twelve jurors were all writing very busily on slates. "What are they doing?" Alice whispered to the Gryphon. "They can't have anything to put down yet, before the trial's begun."

"They're putting down their names," the Gryphon whispered in reply, "for fear they should forget them before the end of the trial."

"Stupid things!" Alice began in a loud indignant voice; but she stopped herself hastily, for the White Rabbit cried out, "Silence in the court!" and the King put on his spectacles and looked anxiously round, to make out who was talking.

Alice could see, as well as if she were looking over their shoulders, that all the jurors were writing down "Stupid things!" on their slates, and she could even make out that one of them didn't know how to spell "stupid," and that he had to ask his neighbour to tell him. "A nice muddle their slates'll be in, before the trial's over!" thought Alice.

One of the jurors had a pencil that squeaked. This, of course, Alice could *not* stand, and she went round the court and got behind him, and very soon found an opportunity of taking it away. She did it so quickly that the poor little juror (it was Bill, the Lizard) could not make out at all what had become of it; so, after hunting all about for it, he was obliged to write with one finger for the rest of the day; and this was of very little use, as it left no mark on the slate.

"Herald, read the accusation!" said the King.

On this the White Rabbit blew three blasts on the trumpet, and then unrolled the parchment-scroll, and read as follows:—**1**

1. This familiar nursery rhyme fits so neatly into Carroll's fantasy of living playing cards that he reprints it without alteration. In *Alice's Adventures Underground* the trial of the Knave of Hearts, which here takes up two chapters, is covered in just a few paragraphs.

145

"The Queen of Hearts, she made some tarts,
    All on a summer day:
The Knave of Hearts, he stole those tarts
    And took them quite away!"

"Consider your verdict," the King said to the jury.

"Not yet, not yet!" the Rabbit hastily interrupted. "There's a great deal to come before that!"

"Call the first witness," said the King; and the White Rabbit blew three blasts on the trumpet, and called out "First witness!"

The first witness was the Hatter. He came in with a teacup in one hand and a piece of bread-and-butter in the other. "I beg pardon, your Majesty," he began, "for bringing these in; but I hadn't quite finished my tea when I was sent for."

"You ought to have finished," said the King. "When did you begin?"

The Hatter looked at the March Hare, who had followed him into the court, arm-in-arm with the Dormouse. "Fourteenth of March, I *think* it was," he said.

"Fifteenth," said the March Hare.

"Sixteenth," said the Dormouse.

"Write that down," the King said to the jury; and the jury eagerly wrote down all three dates on their slates, and then added them up, and reduced the answer to shillings and pence.

"Take off your hat," the King said to the Hatter.

"It isn't mine," said the Hatter.

"Stolen!" the King exclaimed, turning to the jury, who instantly made a memorandum of the fact.

"I keep them to sell," the Hatter added as an explanation: "I've none of my own. I'm a hatter."

Here the Queen put on her spectacles, and began staring hard at the Hatter, who turned pale and fidgeted.

"Give your evidence," said the King; "and don't be nervous, or I'll have you executed on the spot."

This did not seem to encourage the witness at all: he kept shifting from one foot to the other, looking uneasily at the Queen, and in his confusion he bit a large piece out of his teacup instead of the bread-and-butter.

Just at this moment Alice felt a very curious sensation, which puzzled her a good deal until she made out what it was: she was beginning to grow larger again, and she thought at first she would get up and leave the court; but on second thoughts she decided to remain where she was as long as there was room for her.

"I wish you wouldn't squeeze so," said the Dormouse, who was sitting next to her. "I can hardly breathe."

"I can't help it," said Alice very meekly: "I'm growing."

147

2. The Queen is recalling the occasion, described in Chapter 7, on which the Hatter murdered the time by singing " 'Twinkle, twinkle, little bat!' "

"You've no right to grow *here*," said the Dormouse.

"Don't talk nonsense," said Alice more boldly: "you know you're growing too."

"Yes, but *I* grow at a reasonable pace," said the Dormouse: "not in that ridiculous fashion." And he got up very sulkily and crossed over to the other side of the court.

All this time the Queen had never left off staring at the Hatter, and, just as the Dormouse crossed the court, she said, to one of the officers of the court, "Bring me the list of the singers in the last concert!" on which the wretched Hatter trembled so, that he shook off both his shoes.**2**

"Give your evidence," the King repeated angrily, "or I'll have you executed, whether you are nervous or not."

"I'm a poor man, your Majesty," the Hatter began, in a trembling voice, "and I hadn't begun my tea—not above a week or so—and what with the bread-and-butter getting so thin—and the twinkling of the tea—"

"The twinkling of *what?*" said the King.

"It *began* with the tea," the Hatter replied.

"Of course twinkling *begins* with a T!" said the King sharply. "Do you take me for a dunce? Go on!"

"I'm a poor man," the Hatter went on,

148

"and most things twinkled after that—
only the March Hare said—"

"I didn't!" the March Hare interrupted
in a great hurry.

"You did!" said the Hatter.

"I deny it!" said the March Hare.

"He denies it," said the King: "leave
out that part."

"Well, at any rate, the Dormouse said
—" the Hatter went on, looking anxiously
round to see if he would deny it too; but
the Dormouse denied nothing, being fast
asleep.

"After that," continued the Hatter, "I
cut some more bread-and-butter—"

"But what did the Dormouse say?" one
of the jury asked.

"That I can't remember," said the Hatter.

"You *must* remember," remarked the
King, "or I'll have you executed."

The miserable Hatter dropped his teacup and bread-and-butter, and went down
on one knee. "I'm a poor man, your Majesty," he began.

"You're a *very* poor *speaker*," said the
King.

Here one of the guinea-pigs cheered,
and was immediately suppressed by the
officers of the court. (As that is rather a
hard word, I will just explain to you how
it was done. They had a large canvas bag,
which tied up at the mouth with strings:

149

into this they slipped the guinea-pig, head first, and then sat upon it.)

"I'm glad I've seen that done," thought Alice. "I've so often read in the newspapers, at the end of trials, 'There was some attempt at applause, which was immediately suppressed by the officers of the court,' and I never understood what it meant till now."

"If that's all you know about it, you may stand down," continued the King.

"I can't go no lower," said the Hatter: "I'm on the floor, as it is."

"Then you may *sit* down," the King replied.

Here the other guinea-pig cheered, and was suppressed.

"Come, that finishes the guinea-pigs!" thought Alice. "Now we shall get on better."

"I'd rather finish my tea," said the Hatter, with an anxious look at the Queen, who was reading the list of singers.

"You may go," said the King, and the Hatter hurriedly left the court, without even waiting to put his shoes on.

"—and just take his head off outside," the Queen added to one of the officers; but the Hatter was out of sight before the officer could get to the door.

"Call the next witness!" said the King.

The next witness was the Duchess's cook. She carried the pepper-box in her

hand, and Alice guessed who it was, even before she got into the court, by the way the people near the door began sneezing all at once.

"Give your evidence," said the King.

"Shan't," said the cook.

The King looked anxiously at the White Rabbit, who said, in a low voice, "Your Majesty must cross-examine *this* witness."

"Well, if I must, I must," the King said with a melancholy air, and, after folding his arms and frowning at the cook till his eyes were nearly out of sight, he said, in a deep voice, "What are tarts made of?"

"Pepper, mostly," said the cook.

"Treacle," said a sleepy voice behind her.

"Collar that Dormouse!" the Queen shrieked out. "Behead that Dormouse! Turn that Dormouse out of court! Suppress him! Pinch him! Off with his whiskers!"

For some minutes the whole court was in confusion, getting the Dormouse turned out, and, by the time they had settled down again, the cook had disappeared.

"Never mind!" said the King, with an air of great relief. "Call the next witness." And, he added, in an under-tone to the Queen, "Really, my dear, *you* must cross-examine the next witness. It quite makes my forehead ache!"

Alice watched the White Rabbit as he fumbled over the list, feeling very curious to see what the next witness would be like, "—for they haven't got much evidence *yet*," she said to herself. Imagine her surprise, when the White Rabbit read out, at the top of his shrill little voice, the name "Alice!"

CHAPTER XII

Alice's Evidence

"Here!" cried Alice, quite forgetting in the flurry of the moment how large she had grown in the last few minutes, and she jumped up in such a hurry that she tipped over the jury-box with the edge of her skirt, upsetting all the jurymen on to the heads of the crowd below, and there they lay sprawling about, reminding her very much of a globe of gold-fish she had accidentally upset the week before.[1]

"Oh, I *beg* your pardon!" she exclaimed in a tone of great dismay, and began picking them up again as quickly as she could, for the accident of the gold-fish kept running in her head, and she had a vague sort of idea that they must be collected at once and put back into the jury-box, or they would die.

"The trial cannot proceed," said the King, in a very grave voice, "until all the

[1] In *The Nursery "Alice"* Carroll points out that all twelve jury members are visible in Tenniel's drawing of this scene, and he lists them as a frog, dormouse, rat, ferret, hedgehog, lizard, bantam cock, mole, duck, squirrel, storkling, mousling. Of the last two Carroll writes: "Mr. Tenniel says the screaming bird is a *Storkling* (of course you know what *that* is?) and the little white head is a *Mousling*. Isn't it a little *Darling*?"

jurymen are back in their proper places —*all*," he repeated with great emphasis, looking hard at Alice as he said so.

Alice looked at the jury-box, and saw that, in her haste, she had put the Lizard in head downwards, and the poor little thing was waving its tail about in a melancholy way, being quite unable to move. She soon got it out again, and put it right; "not that it signifies much," she said to herself; "I should think it would be *quite*

as much use in the trial one way up as the other."

As soon as the jury had a little recovered from the shock of being upset, and their slates and pencils had been found and handed back to them, they set to work very diligently to write out a history of the accident, all except the Lizard, who seemed too much overcome to do anything but sit with its mouth open, gazing up into the roof of the court.

"What do you know about this business?" the King said to Alice.

"Nothing," said Alice.

"Nothing *whatever?*" persisted the King.

"Nothing whatever," said Alice.

"That's very important," the King said, turning to the jury. They were just beginning to write this down on their slates, when the White Rabbit interrupted: "*Un*important, your Majesty means of course," he said, in a very respectful tone, but frowning and making faces at him as he spoke.

"*Un*important, of course, I meant," the King hastily said, and went on to himself in an undertone, "important— unimportant — unimportant — important—" as if he were trying which word sounded best.

Some of the jury wrote it down "important," and some "unimportant." Alice could see this, as she was near enough to look over their slates; "but it doesn't matter a bit," she thought to herself.

At this moment the King, who had been for some time busily writing in his note-book, called out "Silence!" and read out from his book, "Rule Forty-two. *All persons more than a mile high to leave the court.*"

Everybody looked at Alice.

"*I'm* not a mile high," said Alice.

"You are," said the King.

"Nearly two miles high," added the Queen.

"Well, I shan't go, at any rate," said Alice; "besides, that's not a regular rule: you invented it just now."

"It's the oldest rule in the book," said the King.

"Then it ought to be Number One," said Alice.

The King turned pale, and shut his notebook hastily. "Consider your verdict," he said to the jury, in a low trembling voice.

"There's more evidence to come yet, please your Majesty," said the White Rabbit, jumping up in a great hurry: "this paper has just been picked up."

"What's in it?" said the Queen.

"I haven't opened it yet," said the White Rabbit; "but it seems to be a letter, written by the prisoner to—to somebody."

"It must have been that," said the King, "unless it was written to nobody, which isn't usual, you know."

"Who is it directed to?" said one of the jurymen.

"It isn't directed at all," said the White Rabbit: "in fact, there's nothing written on the *outside*." He unfolded the paper as he spoke, and added, "It isn't a letter, after all: it's a set of verses."

"Are they in the prisoner's handwriting?" asked another of the jurymen.

"No, they're not," said the White Rabbit, "and that's the queerest thing about it." (The jury all looked puzzled.)

"He must have imitated somebody else's hand," said the King. (The jury all brightened up again.)

"Please, your Majesty," said the Knave, "I didn't write it, and they can't prove that I did: there's no name signed at the end."

"If you didn't sign it," said the King, "that only makes the matter worse. You *must* have meant some mischief, or else you'd have signed your name like an honest man."

There was a general clapping of hands at this: it was the first really clever thing the King had said that day.

"That *proves* his guilt, of course," said the Queen: "so, off with—."

"It doesn't prove anything of the sort!"

2. The White Rabbit's evidence consists of six verses with confused pronouns and very little sense. They are taken in considerably revised form from Carroll's eight-verse nonsense poem, *She's All My Fancy Painted Him*, which first appeared in *The Comic Times* of London in 1855. The first line of the original copies the first line of "Alice Gray," a sentimental song by William Mee that was popular at the time. The rest of the poem has no resemblance to the song except in meter.

Carroll's earlier version, with his introductory note, follows:

This affecting fragment was found in MS. among the papers of the well-known author of "Was it You or I?" a tragedy, and the two popular novels, "Sister and Son," and "The Niece's Legacy, or the Grateful Grandfather."

She's all my fancy painted him
(I make no idle boast);
If he or you had lost a limb,
Which would have suffered most?

He said that you had been to her,
And seen me here before;
But, in another character,
She was the same of yore.

There was not one that spoke to us,
Of all that thronged the street:
So he sadly got into a 'bus,
And pattered with his feet.

They sent him word I had not gone
(We know it to be true):
If she should push the matter on,
What would become of you?

They gave her one, they gave me two,
They gave us three or more;
They all returned from him to you,
Though they were mine before.

If I or she should chance to be
Involved in this affair,
He trusts to you to set them free,
Exactly as we were.

It seemed to me that you had been
(Before she had this fit)
An obstacle, that came between
Him, and ourselves, and it.

said Alice. "Why, you don't even know what they're about!"

"Read them," said the King.

The White Rabbit put on his spectacles. "Where shall I begin, please your Majesty?" he asked.

"Begin at the beginning," the King said, very gravely, "and go on till you come to the end: then stop."

There was dead silence in the court, whilst the White Rabbit read out these verses:—**2**

"They told me you had been to her,
    And mentioned me to him:
She gave me a good character,
    But said I could not swim.

He sent them word I had not gone
    (We know it to be true):
If she should push the matter on,
    What would become of you?

I gave her one, they gave him two,
    You gave us three or more;
They all returned from him to you,
    Though they were mine before.

If I or she should chance to be
    Involved in this affair,
He trusts to you to set them free,
    Exactly as we were.

My notion was that you had been
    (Before she had this fit)
An obstacle that came between
    Him, and ourselves, and it.

Don't let him know she liked them best,
    For this must ever be
A secret, kept from all the rest,
    Between yourself and me."

"That's the most important piece of evidence we've heard yet," said the King, rubbing his hands; "so now let the jury—"

"If any one of them can explain it," said Alice, (she had grown so large in the last few minutes that she wasn't a bit afraid of interrupting him), "I'll give him sixpence. *I* don't believe there's an atom of meaning in it."

The jury all wrote down on their slates, "*She* doesn't believe there's an atom of meaning in it," but none of them attempted to explain the paper.

"If there's no meaning in it," said the King, "that saves a world of trouble, you know, as we needn't try to find any. And yet I don't know," he went on, spreading out the verses on his knee, and looking at them with one eye; "I seem to see some meaning in them, after all. '—*said I could not swim*—' you can't swim, can you?" he added, turning to the Knave.

The Knave shook his head sadly. "Do I look like it?" he said. (Which he certainly did *not,* being made entirely of cardboard.)

"All right, so far," said the King; and he went on muttering over the verses to himself: "'*We know it to be true*—' that's the jury, of course—'*If she should push the matter on*'—that must be the Queen—'*What would become of you?*'— What, indeed!—'*I gave her one, they*

*Don't let him know she liked them
     best,
 For this must ever be
A secret, kept from all the rest,
 Between yourself and me.*

Did Carroll introduce this poem into his story because the song behind it tells of the unrequited love of a man for a girl named Alice? I quote from John M. Shaw's booklet (cited in Note 3 of Chapter 6) the song's opening stanzas:

*She's all my fancy painted her,
 She's lovely, she's divine,
But her heart it is another's,
 She never can be mine.*

*Yet loved I as man never loved,
 A love without decay,
O, my heart, my heart is breaking
 For the love of Alice Gray.*

159

3. A similar reaction to a pun is one of the five characteristic traits of a snark, as we learn in the second "fit" of Carroll's *The Hunting of the Snark:*

> *The third is its slowness in taking a jest;*
> *Should you happen to venture on one,*
> *It will sigh like a thing that is deeply distressed:*
> *And it always looks grave at a pun.*

gave him two—' why, that must be what he did with the tarts, you know—"

"But it goes on *'they all returned from him to you,'* " said Alice.

"Why, there they are!" said the King triumphantly, pointing to the tarts on the table. "Nothing can be clearer than *that.* Then again—*'before she had this fit—'* you never had fits, my dear, I think?" he said to the Queen.

"Never!" said the Queen, furiously, throwing an inkstand at the Lizard as she spoke. (The unfortunate little Bill had left off writing on his slate with one finger, as he found it made no mark; but he now hastily began again, using the ink, that was trickling down his face, as long as it lasted.)

"Then the words don't *fit* you," said the King, looking round the court with a smile. There was a dead silence.**3**

"It's a pun!" the King added in an angry tone, and everybody laughed. "Let the jury consider their verdict,"

the King said, for about the twentieth
time that day.

"No, no!" said the Queen. "Sentence
first—verdict afterwards."

"Stuff and nonsense!" said Alice loudly.
"The idea of having the sentence first!"

"Hold your tongue!" said the Queen,
turning purple.

"I won't!" said Alice.

"Off with her head!" the Queen
shouted at the top of her voice. Nobody
moved.

"Who cares for *you?*" said Alice (she
had grown to her full size by this time).
"You're nothing but a pack of cards!"

At this the whole pack rose up into
the air, and came flying down upon her;

she gave a little scream, half of fright and half of anger, and tried to beat them off, and found herself lying on the bank, with her head in the lap of her sister, who was gently brushing away some dead leaves that had fluttered down from the trees upon her face.

"Wake up, Alice dear!" said her sister. "Why, what a long sleep you've had!"

"Oh, I've had such a curious dream!" said Alice. And she told her sister, as well as she could remember them, all these strange Adventures of hers that you have just been reading about; and, when she had finished, her sister kissed her, and said, "It *was* a curious dream, dear, certainly; but now run in to your tea: it's getting late." So Alice got up and ran off, thinking while she ran, as well she might, what a wonderful dream it had been.

But her sister sat still just as she left her, leaning her head on her hand, watching the setting sun, and thinking of little Alice and all her wonderful Adventures, till she too began dreaming after a fashion, and this was her dream:—

First, she dreamed about little Alice herself: once again the tiny hands were clasped upon her knee, and the bright eager eyes were looking up into hers— she could hear the very tones of her voice, and see that queer little toss of her head to keep back the wandering hair that *would* always get into her eyes—and still as she listened, or seemed to listen, the whole place around her became alive with the strange creatures of her little sister's dream.[4]

The long grass rustled at her feet as the White Rabbit hurried by—the frightened Mouse splashed his way through the neighbouring pool—she could hear the rattle of the teacups as the March Hare and his friends shared their never-ending meal, and the shrill voice of the Queen ordering off her unfortunate guests to execution—once more the pig-baby was sneezing on the Duchess's knee, while plates and dishes crashed around it—once more the shriek of the Gryphon, the squeaking of the Lizard's slate-pencil, and the choking of the suppressed guinea-pigs, filled the air, mixed up with the distant sob of the miserable Mock Turtle.

So she sat on, with closed eyes, and half believed herself in Wonderland, though she knew she had but to open them again, and all would change to dull reality—the grass would be only rustling in the wind, and the pool rippling to the waving of the reeds—the rattling tea-cups would change to tinkling sheep-bells, and the Queen's shrill cries to the voice of the shepherd boy—and the sneeze of the baby, the shriek of the Gryphon, and all the other queer noises, would change (she knew) to the confused clamour of the busy farm-yard—while the lowing of the

4. This dream-within-a-dream motif (Alice's sister dreaming of Alice's dream) reoccurs in a more complicated form in the sequel. See *Through the Looking-Glass,* Chapter 4, Note 7.

cattle in the distance would take the place of the Mock Turtle's heavy sobs.

Lastly, she pictured to herself how this same little sister of hers would, in the after-time, be herself a grown woman; and how she would keep, through all her riper years, the simple and loving heart of her childhood; and how she would gather about her other little children, and make *their* eyes bright and eager with many a strange tale, perhaps even with the dream of Wonderland of long ago; and how she would feel with all their simple sorrows, and find a pleasure in all their simple joys, remembering her own child-life, and the happy summer days.

THROUGH
THE LOOKING-GLASS
AND WHAT
Alice
FOUND THERE

1. Carroll's description of the chess problem, which underlies the book's action, is accurate. One is at loss to account for the statement on page 48 of *A Handbook of the Literature of the Rev. C. L. Dodgson,* by Sidney Williams and Falconer Madan, that "no attempt" is made to execute a normal checkmate. The final mate is completely orthodox. It is true, however, as Carroll himself points out, that red and white do not alternate moves properly, and some of the "moves" listed by Carroll are not represented by actual movements of the pieces on the board (for example, Alice's first, third, ninth and tenth "moves," and the "castling" of the queens).

The most serious violation of chess rules occurs near the end of the problem, when the White King is placed in check by the Red Queen without either side taking account of the fact. "Hardly a move has a sane purpose, from the point of view of chess," writes Mr. Madan. It is true that both sides play an exceedingly careless game, but what else could one expect from the mad creatures behind the mirror? At one point the White Queen passes up a chance to checkmate and on another occasion she flees from the Red Knight when she could have captured him. Both oversights, however, are in keeping with her absent-mindedness.

Considering the staggering difficulties involved in dovetailing a chess game wih an amusing nonsense fantasy, Carroll does a remarkable job. At no time, for example, does Alice exchange words with a piece that is not then on a square alongside her own. Queens bustle about doing things while their husbands remain relatively fixed and impotent, just as in actual chess games. The White Knight's eccentricities fit admirably the eccentric way in which Knights move; even the tendency of the Knights to fall off their horses, on one side or the other, suggests the knight's move, which is two squares in one direction followed by one square to the right or left. In order to assist the reader in integrating the chess moves with the story, each move will be noted in the text at the precise point where it occurs.

The rows of the giant chessboard are separated from each other by brooks. The columns are divided by hedges. Throughout the problem Alice remains on the queen's file except for her final move when (as queen) she captures the Red Queen to checkmate the dozing Red King. It is amusing to note that it is the Red Queen who persuades Alice to advance along her file to the eighth square. The Queen is protecting herself with this advice, for white has at the outset an easy, though inelegant, checkmate in three moves. The White Knight first checks at KKt.3. If the Red King moves to either Q6 or Q5, white can mate with the Queen at QB3. The only alternative is for the Red King to move to K4. The White Queen then checks on QB5, forcing the Red King to K3. The Queen then mates on Q6. This calls, of course, for an alertness of mind not possessed by either the Knight or Queen.

Attempts have been made to work out a better sequence of chess moves that would both fit the narrative and at the same time conform to all the rules of the game. The most ambitious attempt of this sort that I have come across is to be found in the *British Chess Magazine* of May 1910 (Vol. 30, page 181). Donald M. Liddell presents an entire chess game, starting with the Bird Opening and ending with a mate by Alice when she enters the eighth square on her sixty-sixth move! The choice of opening is appropriate, for no chess expert

(Continued on Page 172)

Author's Preface

As the chess-problem, given on the next page, has puzzled some of my readers, it may be well to explain that it is correctly worked out, so far as the *moves* are concerned. The *alternation* of Red and White is perhaps not so strictly observed as it might be, and the "castling" of the three Queens is merely a way of saying that they entered the palace: but the "check" of the White King at move 6, the capture of the Red Knight at move 7, and the final "checkmate" of the Red King, will be found, by any one who will take the trouble to set the pieces and play the moves as directed, to be strictly in accordance with the laws of the game.[1]

The new words, in the poem "Jabberwocky," have given rise to some differences of opinion as to their pronunciation: so it may be well to give instructions on *that* point also. Pronounce "slithy" as if it were the two words "sly, the": make the 'g' *hard* in "gyre" and "gimble": and pronounce "rath" to rhyme with "bath."

Christmas, 1896.

171

RED

WHITE

White Pawn (Alice) to play, and win in eleven moves.

ever had a more hilarious and eccentric style of play than the Englishman H. E. Bird. Whether Donald Liddell is related to *the* Liddells I have not been able to determine.

In the Middle Ages and Renaissance chess games were sometimes played with human pieces on enormous fields (see Rabelais's *Gargantua and Pantagruel*, Book 5, Chapters 24 and 25), but I know of no earlier attempt than Carroll's to base a fictional narrative on animated chess pieces. It has been done many times since, mostly by science-fiction writers. A recent example is Poul Anderson's fine short story *The Immortal Game (Fantasy and Science Fiction,* February 1954).

For many reasons chess pieces are singularly appropriate to the second *Alice* book. They complement the playing cards of the first book, permitting the return of kings and queens; the loss of knaves is more than offset by the acquisition of knights. Alice's bewildering changes of size in the first book are replaced by equally bewildering changes of place, occasioned of course by the movements of chess pieces over the board. By a happy accident chess also ties in beautifully with the mirror-reflection motif. Not only do rooks, bishops, and knights come in pairs, but the asymmetric arrangement of one player's pieces at the start of a game (asymmetric because of the positions of king and queen) is an exact mirror reflection of his opponent's pieces. Finally, the mad quality of the chess game conforms to the mad logic of the looking-glass world.

1. ALICE MEETS R. Q.	1. R. Q. TO K. R'S 4TH
2. ALICE THROUGH Q'S 3D *(by railway)* TO Q'S 4TH *(Tweedledum and Tweedledee)*	2. W. Q. TO Q. B'S 4TH *(after shawl)*
3. ALICE MEETS W. Q. *(with shawl)*	3. W. Q. TO Q. B'S 5TH *(becomes sheep)*
4. ALICE TO Q'S 5TH *(shop, river, shop)*	4. W. Q. TO K. B'S 8TH *(leaves egg on shelf)*
5. ALICE TO Q'S 6TH *(Humpty Dumpty)*	5. W. Q. TO Q. B'S 8TH *(flying from R. Kt.)*
6. ALICE TO Q'S 7TH *(forest)*	6. R. KT. TO K'S 2ND (CH.)
7. W. KT. TAKES R. KT.	7. W. KT. TO K. B'S 5TH
8. ALICE TO Q'S 8TH *(coronation)*	8. R. Q. TO K'S SQ. *(examination)*
9. ALICE BECOMES QUEEN	9. QUEENS CASTLE
10. ALICE CASTLES *(feast)*	10. W. Q. TO Q. R'S 6TH *(soup)*
11. ALICE TAKES R. Q. AND WINS	

Child of the pure unclouded brow
  And dreaming eyes of wonder!
Though time be fleet, and I and thou
  Are half a life asunder,
Thy loving smile will surely hail
The love-gift of a fairy-tale.

I have not seen thy sunny face,
  Nor heard thy silver laughter:
No thought of me shall find a place
  In thy young life's hereafter—**2**
Enough that now thou wilt not fail
To listen to my fairy-tale.

A tale begun in other days,
  When summer suns were glowing—
A simple chime, that served to time
  The rhythm of our rowing—
Whose echoes live in memory yet,
Though envious years would say 'forget.'

Come, harken then, ere voice of dread,
  With bitter tidings laden,
Shall summon to unwelcome bed
  A melancholy maiden!
We are but older children, dear,
Who fret to find our bedtime near.

2. Although the majority of Carroll's child-friends broke off contact with him (or he with them) after their adolescence, the sad presentiment of these lines proved groundless. Among the finest tributes ever paid to Carroll are the recollections of him expressed by Alice in her later years.

Without, the frost, the blinding snow,
    The storm-wind's moody madness—
Within, the firelight's ruddy glow,
    And childhood's nest of gladness.
The magic words shall hold thee fast:
Thou shalt not heed the raving blast.

And, though the shadow of a sigh
    May tremble through the story,
For 'happy summer days'[3] gone by,
    And vanish'd summer glory—
It shall not touch, with breath of bale,
The pleasance[4] of our fairy-tale.

CHAPTER I

Looking-Glass House

One thing was certain, that the *white* kitten had had nothing to do with it—it was the black kitten's fault entirely. For the white kitten had been having its face washed by the old cat for the last quarter of an hour (and bearing it pretty well, considering): so you see that it *couldn't* have had any hand in the mischief.

The way Dinah washed her children's faces was this: first she held the poor thing down by its ear with one paw, and then with the other paw she rubbed its face all over, the wrong way, beginning at the nose: and just now, as I said, she was hard at work on the white kitten, which was lying quite still and trying to purr—no doubt feeling that it was all meant for its good.

But the black kitten had been finished with earlier in the afternoon, and so, while Alice was sitting curled up in a corner of the great armchair, half talking to herself and half asleep, the kitten had been having a grand game of romps with the ball of worsted Alice had been trying to wind up, and had been rolling it up and down till it had all come undone again; and there it was, spread over the hearth-rug, all knots and tangles, with the kitten running after its own tail in the middle.

"Oh, you wicked wicked little thing!" cried Alice, catching up the kitten, and giving it a little kiss to make it understand that it was in disgrace. "Really, Dinah ought to have taught you better manners! You *ought*, Dinah, you know you ought!" she added, looking reproachfully at the old cat, and speaking in as cross a voice as she could manage—and then she scrambled back into the arm-chair, taking the kitten and the worsted with her, and began winding up the ball again. But she didn't get on very fast, as she was talking all the time, sometimes to the kitten, and sometimes to herself. Kitty sat very demurely on her knee, pretending to watch the progress of the winding, and now and then putting out one paw and gently touching the ball, as if it would be glad to help if it might.

"Do you know what to-morrow is, Kitty?" Alice began. "You'd have guessed if you'd been up in the window with me

—only Dinah was making you tidy, so you couldn't. I was watching the boys getting in sticks for the bonfire—and it wants plenty of sticks, Kitty! Only it got so cold, and it snowed so, they had to leave off. Never mind, Kitty, we'll go and see the bonfire[1] to-morrow." Here Alice wound two or three turns of the worsted round the kitten's neck, just to see how it would look: this led to a scramble, in which the ball rolled down upon the floor, and yards and yards of it got unwound again.

"Do you know, I was so angry, Kitty," Alice went on, as soon as they were comfortably settled again, "when I saw all the

1. It was characteristic of Carroll, with his love of sharp contrast, to open his sequel on an indoor, midwinter scene. (The previous book opens out of doors on a warm May afternoon.) The wintry weather also harmonizes with the wintry symbols of age and approaching death that enter into his prefatory and terminal poems. The preparation for a bonfire and Alice's remark "Do you know what tomorrow is, Kitty?" suggest that the date was November 4, the day before Guy Fawkes Day. (The holiday was annually celebrated at Christ Church with a huge bonfire in Peckwater Quadrangle.) This is supported by Alice's statement to the White Queen (Chapter 5) that she is *exactly* seven and one half years old, for Alice Liddell's birthday was May 4, and the previous

trip to Wonderland occurred on May 4, when Alice presumably was exactly seven (see Note 4, Chapter 7 of the previous book).

This leaves open the question of whether the year is 1859 (when Alice actually was seven), 1860, 1861, or 1862 when Carroll told and wrote down the story of Alice's first adventure. November 4, 1859, was a Friday. In 1860 it was Sunday, in 1861 Monday, and in 1862 Tuesday. The last date seems the most plausible in view of Alice's remark to the kitten (in the next paragraph but one) that she is saving up her punishments until a week from Wednesday.

2. Snowdrop was the name of a kitten belonging to one of Carroll's early child-friends, Mary Macdonald. Mary was the daughter of Carroll's good friend George Macdonald, the Scottish poet and novelist, and author of such well-known children's fantasies as *The Princess and the Goblin* and *At the Back of the North Wind*. The Macdonald children were in part responsible for Carroll's decision to publish *Alice's Adventures in Wonderland*. To test the story's general appeal, he asked Mrs. Macdonald to read the manuscript to her children. The reception was enthusiastic. Greville, age six (who later recalled the occasion in his book *George Macdonald and His Wife*), declared that there ought to be sixty thousand copies of it.

mischief you had been doing, I was very nearly opening the window, and putting you out into the snow! And you'd have deserved it, you little mischievous darling! What have you got to say for yourself? Now don't interrupt me!" she went on, holding up one finger. "I'm going to tell you all your faults. Number one: you squeaked twice while Dinah was washing your face this morning. Now you can't deny it, Kitty: I heard you! What's that you say?" (pretending that the kitten was speaking). "Her paw went into your eye? Well, that's *your* fault, for keeping your eyes open—if you'd shut them tight up, it wouldn't have happened. Now don't make any more excuses, but listen! Number two: you pulled Snowdrop**2** away by the tail just as I had put down the saucer of milk before her! What, you were thirsty, were you? How do you know she wasn't thirsty too? Now for number three: you unwound every bit of the worsted while I wasn't looking!

"That's three faults, Kitty, and you've not been punished for any of them yet. You know I'm saving up all your punishments for Wednesday week — Suppose they had saved up all *my* punishments?" she went on, talking more to herself than the kitten. "What *would* they do at the end of a year? I should be sent to prison, I suppose, when the day came. Or—let me see—suppose each punishment was to be going without a dinner: then, when the miserable day came, I should have to go without fifty dinners at once! Well, I shouldn't mind *that* much! I'd far rather go without them than eat them!

"Do you hear the snow against the windowpanes, Kitty? How nice and soft it sounds! Just as if some one was kissing the window all over outside. I wonder if the snow *loves* the trees and fields, that it kisses them so gently? And then it covers them up snug, you know, with a white quilt; and perhaps it says 'go to sleep, darlings, till the summer comes again.' And when they wake up in the summer, Kitty, they dress themselves all in green, and dance about—whenever the wind blows—oh, that's very pretty!" cried Alice, dropping the ball of worsted to clap her hands. "And I do so *wish* it was true! I'm sure the woods look sleepy in the autumn, when the leaves are getting brown.

"Kitty, can you play chess? Now, don't smile, my dear, I'm asking it seriously. Because, when we were playing just now, you watched just as if you understood it: and when I said 'Check!' you purred! Well, it *was* a nice check, Kitty, and really I might have won, if it hadn't been for that nasty Knight, that came wriggling[3] down among my pieces. Kitty, dear, let's pretend—" And here I wish I could tell you half the things Alice used to say, beginning with her favourite phrase "Let's

3. "Wriggling" is a good description of how the knight moves across a chessboard.

179

4. The looking-glass theme seems to have been a late addition to the story. We have the word of Alice Liddell that a good part of the book was based on chess tales that Carroll told the Liddell girls at a time when they were learning excitedly how to play the game. It was not until 1868 that another Alice, Carroll's distant cousin Alice Raikes, played a role in suggesting the mirror motif. This is how she told the story in the London *Times,* January 22, 1932:

As children, we lived in Onslow Square and used to play in the garden behind the houses. Charles Dodgson used to stay with an old uncle there, and walk up and down, his hands behind him, on the strip of lawn. One day, hearing my name, he called me to him saying, "So you are another Alice. I'm very fond of Alices. Would you like to come and see something which is rather puzzling?" We followed him into his house which opened, as ours did, upon the garden, into a room full of furniture with a tall mirror standing across one corner.
"Now," he said, giving me an orange, "first tell me which hand you have got that in." "The right," I said. "Now," he said, "go and stand before that glass, and tell me which hand the little girl you see there has got it in." After some perplexed contemplation, I said, "The left hand." "Exactly," he said, "and how do you explain that?" I couldn't explain it, but seeing that some solution was expected, I ventured, "If I was on the *other* side of the glass, wouldn't the orange still be in my right hand?" I can remember his laugh. "Well done, little Alice," he said. "The best answer I've had yet."
I heard no more then, but in after years was told that he said that had given him his first idea for *Through the Looking-Glass,* a copy of which, together with each of his other books, he regularly sent me.

In a mirror all asymmetrical objects (objects not superposable on their mirror images) "go the other way." There are many references

pretend." She had had quite a long argument with her sister only the day before—all because Alice had begun with "Let's pretend we're kings and queens;" and her sister, who liked being very exact, had argued that they couldn't, because there were only two of them, and Alice had been reduced at last to say "Well, *you* can be one of them, then, and *I'll* be all the rest." And once she had really frightened her old nurse by shouting suddenly in her ear, "Nurse! Do let's pretend that I'm a hungry hyæna, and you're a bone!"

But this is taking us away from Alice's speech to the kitten. "Let's pretend that you're the Red Queen, Kitty! Do you know, I think if you sat up and folded your arms, you'd look exactly like her. Now do try, there's a dear!" And Alice got the Red Queen off the table, and set it up before the kitten as a model for it to imitate: however, the thing didn't succeed, principally, Alice said, because the kitten wouldn't fold its arms properly. So, to punish it, she held it up to the Looking-glass, that it might see how sulky it was, "—and if you're not good directly," she added, "I'll put you through into Looking-glass House. How would you like *that?*"

"Now, if you'll only attend, Kitty, and not talk so much, I'll tell you all my ideas about Looking-glass House. First, there's the room you can see through the glass—

that's just the same as our drawing-room, only the things go the other way.[4] I can see all of it when I get upon a chair—all but the bit just behind the fireplace. Oh! I do so wish I could see *that* bit! I want so much to know whether they've a fire in the winter: you never *can* tell, you know, unless our fire smokes, and then smoke comes up in that room too—but that may be only pretence, just to make it look as if they had a fire. Well then, the books are something like our books, only the words go the wrong way: I know *that*, because I've held up one of our books to the glass, and then they hold up one in the other room.

"How would you like to live in Looking-glass House, Kitty? I wonder if they'd give you milk in there? Perhaps Looking-glass milk isn't good to drink[5]—but oh, Kitty! now we come to the passage. You can just see a little *peep* of the passage in Looking-glass House, if you leave the door of our drawing-room wide open: and it's very like our passage as far as you can see, only you know it may be quite different on beyond. Oh, Kitty, how nice it would be if we could only get through into Looking-glass House! I'm sure it's got, oh! such beautiful things in it! Let's pretend there's a way of getting through into it, somehow, Kitty. Let's pretend the glass has got all soft like gauze, so that we can

(Continued on Page 184)

in the book to such left-right reversals. Tweedledee and Tweedledum are, as we shall see, mirror-image twins; the White Knight sings of squeezing a right foot into a left shoe; and it may not be accidental that there are several references to corkscrews, for the helix is an asymmetric structure with distinct right and left forms. If we extend the mirror-reflection theme to include the reversal of any asymmetric relation, we hit upon a note that dominates the entire story. It would take too much space to list here all the instances, but the following examples make the point. To approach the Red Queen, Alice walks backward; in the railway carriage the Guard tells her she is traveling the wrong way; the King has two messengers, "one to come, and one to go." The White Queen explains the advantages of living backward in time; the looking-glass cake is handed around first, then sliced. Odd and even numbers, the combinatorial equivalent of left and right, are worked into the story at several points (e.g., the White Queen requests jam every other day). In a sense, nonsense itself is a sanity-insanity inversion. The ordinary world is turned upside down and backward; it becomes a world in which things go every way except the way they are supposed to.

Inversion themes occur, of course, throughout all of Carroll's nonsense writing. In the first *Alice* book Alice wonders if cats eat bats or bats eat cats, and she is told that to say what she means is not the same as meaning what she says. When she eats the left side of the mushroom, she grows large; the right side has the reverse effect. These changes in size, which take place so often in the first book, are in themselves reversals (e.g., instead of a large girl and small puppy we have a large puppy and small girl). In *Sylvie and Bruno* we learn about "imponderal," an anti-gravity wool that can be stuffed into parcel-post packages to make them weigh less than nothing; a watch that reverses time; black light; Fortunatus's purse, a projective plane with outside inside and inside outside. We learn that E-V-I-L is simply L-I-V-E backward.

In real life also Carroll milked the notion of inversion as much as he could to amuse his child-friends. One of his letters speaks of a doll whose right hand becomes "left" when the left hand drops off; another letter tells how he sometimes goes to bed so soon after getting up that he finds himself back in bed *before* he gets up. He wrote letters in mirror writing that had to be held to a mirror to be read. He wrote letters that had to be read by starting at the last word and reading to the first. He had a collection of music boxes and one of his favorite stunts was to play them backward. He drew funny pictures that changed to different pictures when you turned them upside down.

Even in serious moments Carroll's mind, like that of the White Knight, seemed to function best when he was seeing things upside down. He invented a new method of multiplication in which the multiplier is written backward and *above* the multiplicand. *The Hunting of the Snark,* he tells us, was actually composed backward. The final line, "For the Snark *was* a Boojum, you see," came into his head as a sudden inspiration, then he fashioned a stanza to fit the line and finally a poem to fit the stanza.

Closely related to Carroll's inversion humor is his humor of logical contradiction. The Red Queen knows of a hill so large that, compared to it, this hill is a valley; dry biscuits are eaten to quench thirst; a messenger whispers by shouting; Alice runs as fast as she can to stay

in the same place. It is not surprising to learn that Carroll was fond of the Irish bull, of which logical contradiction is the essence. He once wrote to his sister: "Please analyze logically the following piece of reasoning: *Little Girl:* 'I'm *so* glad I don't like asparagus.' *Friend:* 'Why, my dear?' *Little Girl:* 'Because if I *did* like it, I should have to eat it — and I can't bear it!'" One of Carroll's acquaintances recalled hearing him speak about a friend he knew whose feet were so big that he had to put his trousers on over his head.

Treating a "null class" (a set with no members) as though it were an existing thing is another rich source of Carrollian logical nonsense. The March Hare offers Alice some nonexistent wine; Alice wonders where the flame of a candle is when the candle is not burning; the map in *The Hunting of the Snark* is "a perfect and absolute blank"; the King of Hearts thinks it unusual to write letters to nobody, and the White King compliments Alice on having keen enough eyesight to see nobody at a great distance down the road.

Why was Carroll's humor so interwoven with logical twists of these sorts? We shall not enter here into the question of whether Carroll's interest in logic and mathematics is a sufficient explanation, or whether there were unconscious compulsions that made it necessary for him to be forever warping and stretching, compressing and inverting, reversing and distorting the familiar world. Surely the thesis advanced by Florence Becker Lennon in her otherwise admirable biography *Victoria Through the Looking Glass* is hardly adequate. She argues that Carroll was born left-handed but forced to use his right hand, and that "he took his revenge by doing a little reversing himself." Unfortunately there is only the flimsiest, most unconvincing evidence that Carroll was born left-handed. Even if true, it seems a woefully inadequate explanation for the origin of Carrollian nonsense.

5. Alice's speculation about looking-glass milk has a significance greater than Carroll suspected. It was not until several years after the publication of *Through the Looking-Glass* that stereochemistry found positive evidence that organic substances had an asymmetric arrangement of atoms. Isomers are substances that have molecules composed of exactly the same atoms, but with these atoms linked together in structures that are topologically quite different. Stereoisomers are isomers that are identical even in topological structure, but, owing to the asymmetric nature of this structure, they come in mirror-image pairs, like right and left shoes. All organic substances are stereoisometric. Sugar is a common example; in right-handed form it is called dextrose, in left-handed form, levulose. Because the intake of food involves complicated chemical reactions between asymmetric food and asymmetric substances in the body, there often are marked differences in the taste, smell, and digestibility of left- and right-handed forms of the same organic substance. No laboratory or cow has yet produced reversed milk, but if the asymmetric structure of ordinary milk were to be reflected, it is a safe bet that this looking-glass milk would *not* be good to drink.

In this judgment on looking-glass milk only a reversal of the structure by which the milk's atoms are linked to each other is considered. Of course a true mirror reflection of milk would also reverse the structure of the elementary particles themselves. In 1957 two Chinese-American physicists, Tsung Dao Lee and Chen Ning Yang, received the Nobel prize for theoretical work that led to the "gay and wonderful discovery" (in Robert Oppenheimer's happy phrase) that some elementary particles are asymmetric. It now appears likely that particles and their antiparticles (that is, identical particles with opposite charges) are, like stereoisomers, nothing more than mirror-image forms of the same structure. If this is true, then looking-glass milk would be composed of "anti-matter," which would not even be drinkable by Alice; both milk and Alice would explode as soon as they came in contact. Of course an anti-Alice, on the other side of the looking-glass, would find anti-milk as tasty and nourishing as usual.

Readers who would like to learn more about the philosophical and scientific implications of left- and right-handedness are referred to Hermann Weyl's delightful little book on *Symmetry*, 1952; Philip Morrison's article, "The Overthrow of Parity," in *Scientific American*, April 1957; and my paper "Is Nature Ambidextrous?" in *Philosophy and Phenomenological Research*, December 1952. On the lighter side there is my discussion of left-right topics in the last chapter of *The Scientific American Book of Mathematical Puzzles and Diversions*, 1959, and my story "Left or Right?" in *Esquire*, February 1951. The classic science-fiction tale involving left-right reversal is "The Plattner Story" by H. G. Wells. And one must not overlook *The New Yorker's* Department of Amplification, December 15, 1956, page 164, in which Dr. Edward Teller comments with Carrollian wit on a previously published *New Yorker* poem (November 10, 1956, page 52) that describes the explosion that occurred when Dr. Teller shook hands with Dr. Edward Anti-Teller.

At the time this is written, there is considerable speculation among atomic scientists about the possibility of creating anti-matter in the laboratory, keeping it suspended in space by magnetic forces, then combining it with matter to achieve a total conversion of nuclear mass into energy (in contrast to both fusion and fission in which only a small portion of mass is so converted). The road to ultimate nuclear power may, therefore, lie on the other side of the looking glass.

6. The mantel.

get through. Why, it's turning into a sort of mist now, I declare! It'll be easy enough to get through—" She was up on the chimney-piece[6] while she said this, though she hardly knew how she had got there. And certainly the glass *was* beginning to melt way, just like a bright silvery mist.

In another moment Alice was through the glass, and had jumped lightly down into the Looking-glass room. The very first thing she did was to look whether

there was a fire in the fireplace, and she was quite pleased to find that there was a real one, blazing away as brightly as the one she had left behind. "So I shall be as warm here as I was in the old room," thought Alice: "warmer, in fact, because there'll be no one here to scold me away from the fire. Oh, what fun it'll be, when they see me through the glass in here, and can't get at me!"

Then she began looking about, and noticed that what could be seen from the

7. Note that, in addition to the grinning face on the back of the clock, Tenniel has added a face to the back of the vase. It was a Victorian custom to put artificial flowers as well as clocks under glass bell jars.

old room was quite common and uninteresting, but that all the rest was as different as possible. For instance, the pictures on the wall next the fire seemed to be all alive, and the very clock on the chimney-piece (you know you can only see the back of it in the Looking-glass⁷) had got the face of a little old man, and grinned at her.

"They don't keep this room so tidy as the other," Alice thought to herself, as she noticed several of the chessmen down in the hearth among the cinders; but in another moment, with a little "Oh!" of surprise, she was down on her hands and knees watching them. The chessmen were walking about, two and two!

"Here are the Red King and the Red Queen," Alice said (in a whisper, for fear

of frightening them), "and there are the White King and the White Queen sitting on the edge of the shovel—and here are two Castles walking arm in arm[8]—I don't think they can hear me," she went on, as she put her head closer down, "and I'm nearly sure they can't see me. I feel somehow as if I was getting invisible—"

Here something began squeaking on the table behind Alice, and made her turn her head just in time to see one of the White Pawns roll over and begin kicking: she watched it with great curiosity to see what would happen next.

"It is the voice of my child!" the White Queen cried out, as she rushed past the King, so violently that she knocked him over among the cinders. "My precious Lily! My imperial kitten!" and she began scrambling wildly up the side of the fender.

"Imperial fiddlestick!" said the King, rubbing his nose, which had been hurt by the fall. He had a right to be a *little* annoyed with the Queen, for he was covered with ashes from head to foot.

Alice was very anxious to be of use, and, as the poor little Lily was nearly screaming herself into a fit, she hastily picked up the Queen and set her on the table by the side of her noisy little daughter.

The Queen gasped, and sat down: the rapid journey through the air had quite taken away her breath, and for a minute

8. Notice how Tenniel has suggested mirror reflections in his pairing of chess pieces in the illustration for this scene. Carroll makes no mention of bishops in his story (to avoid offending the clergy?), but several are clearly visible in the drawing, dressed in ecclesiastical robes.

or two she could do nothing but hug the little Lily in silence. As soon as she had recovered her breath a little, she called out to the White King, who was sitting sulkily among the ashes, "Mind the volcano!"

"What volcano?" said the King, looking up anxiously into the fire, as if he thought that was the most likely place to find one.

"Blew—me—up," panted the Queen, who was still a little out of breath. "Mind you come up—the regular way—don't get blown up!"

Alice watched the White King as he slowly struggled up from bar to bar, till at last she said "Why, you'll be hours and hours getting to the table, at that rate. I'd far better help you, hadn't I?" but the King took no notice of the question: it was quite clear that he could neither hear her nor see her.

So Alice picked him up very gently, and lifted him across more slowly than she had lifted the Queen, that she mightn't take his breath away; but, before she put him on the table, she thought she might as well dust him a little, he was so covered with ashes.

She said afterwards that she had never seen in all her life such a face as the King made, when he found himself held in the air by an invisible hand, and being dusted: he was far too much astonished

to cry out, but his eyes and his mouth
went on getting larger and larger, and
rounder and rounder, till her hand shook
so with laughing that she nearly let him
drop upon the floor.

"Oh! *please* don't make such faces, my
dear!" she cried out, quite forgetting that
the King couldn't hear her. "You make
me laugh so that I can hardly hold you!
And don't keep your mouth so wide open!
All the ashes will get into it—there, now
I think you're tidy enough!" she added,
as she smoothed his hair, and set him upon
the table near the Queen.

The King immediately fell flat on his
back, and lay perfectly still; and Alice
was a little alarmed at what she had done,
and went round the room to see if she
could find any water to throw over him.
However, she could find nothing but a
bottle of ink, and when she got back with
it she found he had recovered, and he
and the Queen were talking together in a
frightened whisper—so low, that Alice
could hardly hear what they said.

The King was saying "I assure you, my
dear, I turned cold to the very ends of
my whiskers!"

To which the Queen replied "You
haven't got any whiskers."

"The horror of that moment," the
King went on, "I shall never, *never* forget!"

"You will, though," the Queen said,

189

"if you don't make a memorandum of it."

Alice looked on with great interest as the King took an enormous memorandum-book out of his pocket, and began writing. A sudden thought struck her, and she took hold of the end of the pencil, which came some way over his shoulder, and began writing for him.

The poor King looked puzzled and unhappy, and struggled with the pencil for some time without saying anything; but Alice was too strong for him, and at last he panted out "My dear! I really *must* get a thinner pencil. I can't manage this one a bit: it writes all manner of things that I don't intend—"

"What manner of things?" said the Queen, looking over the book (in which Alice had put *'The White Knight is sliding down the poker. He balances very badly'*)[9] "That's not a memorandum of *your* feelings!"

There was a book lying near Alice on the table, and while she sat watching the White King (for she was still a little anxious about him, and had the ink all ready to throw over him, in case he fainted again), she turned over the leaves, to find some part that she could read, "—for it's all in some language I don't know," she said to herself.

It was like this.[10]

JABBERWOCKY

*'Twas brillig, and the slithy toves
Did gyre and gimble in the wabe:
All mimsy were the borogoves,
And the mome raths outgrabe.*

She puzzled over this for some time, but at last a bright thought struck her. "Why, it's a Looking-glass book, of course! And, if I hold it up to a glass, the words will all go the right way again."

This was the poem that Alice read.[11]

JABBERWOCKY

'Twas brillig, and the slithy[12] toves[13]
  Did gyre[14] and gimble[15] in the wabe:
All mimsy[16] were the borogoves,[17]
  And the mome[18] raths[19] outgrabe.[20]

"Beware the Jabberwock,[21] my son!
  The jaws that bite, the claws that catch!
Beware the Jubjub[22] bird, and shun
  The frumious[23] Bandersnatch!"[24]

He took his vorpal[25] sword in hand:
  Long time the manxome[26] foe he sought—
So rested he by the Tumtum[27] tree,
  And stood awhile in thought.

And, as in uffish[28] thought he stood,
  The Jabberwock, with eyes of flame,
Came whiffling[29] through the tulgey wood,
  And burbled[30] as it came!

One, two! One, two! And through and through
  The vorpal blade went snicker-snack!
He left it dead, and with its head
  He went galumphing[31] back.

(Continued on Page 197)

11. The opening stanza of *Jabberwocky* first appeared in *Mischmasch*, the last of a series of private little "periodicals" that young Carroll wrote, illustrated and hand-lettered for the amusement of his brothers and sisters. In an issue dated 1855 (Carroll was then twenty-three), under the heading "Stanza of Anglo-Saxon Poetry," the following "curious fragment" appears:

Carroll then proceeds to interpret the words as follows:

BRYLLYG (derived from the verb to BRYL or BROIL), 'the time of broiling dinner, i.e. the close of the afternoon.'

SLYTHY (compounded of SLIMY and LITHE). 'Smooth and active.'

TOVE. A species of Badger. They had smooth white hair, long hind legs, and short horns like a stag; lived chiefly on cheese.

GYRE, verb (derived from GYAOUR or GIAOUR, 'a dog'). To scratch like a dog.

GYMBLE (whence GIMBLET). 'To screw out holes in anything.'

WABE (derived from the verb to SWAB or SOAK). 'The side of a hill' (from its being *soaked* by the rain).

MIMSY (whence MIMSERABLE and MISERABLE). 'Unhappy.'

BOROGOVE. An extinct kind of Parrot. They had no wings, beaks turned up, and made their nests under sundials: lived on veal.

MOME (hence SOLEMOME, SOLEMONE, and SOLEMN). 'Grave.'

RATH. A species of land turtle. Head erect: mouth like a shark: forelegs curved out so that the animal walked on its knees: smooth green body: lived on swallows and oysters.

OUTGRABE, past tense of the verb to OUTGRIBE. (It is connected with old verb to GRIKE, or SHRIKE, from which are derived 'shriek' and 'creak'). 'Squeaked.'

Hence the literal English of the passage is: 'It was evening, and the

smooth active badgers were scratching and boring holes in the hill-side; all unhappy were the parrots; and the grave turtles squeaked out.'
There were probably sundials on the top of the hill, and the 'borogoves' were afraid that their nests would be undermined. The hill was probably full of the nests of 'raths', which ran out, squeaking with fear, on hearing the 'toves' scratching outside. This is an obscure, but yet deeply-affecting, relic of ancient Poetry.

It is interesting to compare these explanations with those given by Humpty Dumpty in Chapter 6.

Few would dispute the fact that *Jabberwocky* is the greatest of all nonsense poems in English. It was so well known to English schoolboys in the late nineteenth century that five of its nonsense words appear casually in the conversation of students in Rudyard Kipling's *Stalky & Co.* Alice herself, in the paragraph following the poem, puts her finger on the secret of the poem's charm: ". . . it seems to fill my head with ideas — only I don't know exactly what they are." Although the strange words have no precise meaning, they chime with subtle overtones.

There is an obvious similarity between nonsense verse of this sort and an abstract painting. The realistic artist is forced to copy nature, imposing on the copy as much as he can in the way of pleasing forms and colors; but the abstract artist is free to romp with the paint as much as he pleases. In similar fashion the nonsense poet does not have to search for ingenious ways of combining pattern and sense; he simply adopts a policy that is the opposite of the advice given by the Duchess in the previous book (see Chapter 9, Note 4)— he takes care of the sounds and allows the sense to take care of itself. The words he uses may suggest vague meanings, like an eye here and a foot there in a Picasso abstraction, or they may have no meaning at all — just a

play of pleasant sounds like the play of non-objective colors on a canvas.

Carroll was not, of course, the first to use this technique of double-talk in humorous verse. He was preceded by Edward Lear, and it is a curious fact that nowhere in the writings or letters of these two undisputed leaders of English nonsense did either of them refer to the other, nor is there evidence that they ever met. Since the time of Lear and Carroll there have been attempts to produce a more serious poetry of this sort — poems by the Dadaists, the Italian futurists, and Gertrude Stein, for example — but somehow when the technique is taken too seriously the results seem tiresome. I have yet to meet someone who could recite one of Miss Stein's poetic efforts, but I have known a good many Carrollians who found that they knew the *Jabberwocky* by heart without ever having made a conscious effort to memorize it. Ogden Nash produced a fine piece of nonsense in his poem *Geddondillo* ("The Sharrot scudders nights in the quastran now,/ The dorlim slinks undeceded in the grost . . ."), but even here there seems to be a bit too much straining for effect, whereas *Jabberwocky* has a careless lilt and perfection that makes it the unique thing it is.

Jabberwocky was a favorite of the British astronomer Arthur Stanley Eddington and is alluded to several times in his writings. In *New Pathways in Science* he likens the abstract syntactical structure of the poem to that modern branch of mathematics known as group theory. In *The Nature of the Physical World* he points out that the physicist's description of an elementary particle is really a kind of Jabberwocky; words applied to "something unknown" that is "doing we don't know what." Because the description contains numbers, science is able to impose a certain amount of order on the phenomena and to make successful predictions about them.

"By contemplating eight circulating electrons in one atom and seven circulating electrons in another," Eddington writes, "we begin to realize the difference between oxygen and nitrogen. Eight slithy toves gyre and gimble in the oxygen wabe; seven in nitrogen. By admitting a few numbers even "Jabberwocky" may become scientific. We can now venture on a prediction; if one of its toves escapes, oxygen will be masquerading in a garb properly belonging to nitrogen. In the stars and nebulae we do find such wolves in sheep's clothing which might otherwise have startled us. It would not be a bad reminder of the essential unknownness of the fundamental entities of physics to translate it into "Jabberwocky"; provided all numbers—all metrical attributes—are unchanged, it does not suffer in the least."

Jabberwocky has been translated skillfully into several languages. There are two Latin versions. One by Augustus A. Vansittart, fellow of Trinity College, Cambridge, was issued as a pamphlet by the Oxford University Press in 1881 and will be found on page 144 of Stuart Collingwood's biography of Carroll. The other version, by Carroll's uncle, Hassard H. Dodgson, is in *The Lewis Carroll Picture Book* on page 364. (The Gaberbocchus Press, a whimsical London publishing house, derives its name from Uncle Hassard's Latin word for Jabberwock.)

The following French translation by Frank L. Warrin first appeared in *The New Yorker*, January 10, 1931. (I quote from Mrs. Lennon's book, where it is reprinted.)

LE JASEROQUE

Il brilgue: les tôves lubricilleux
Se gyrent en vrillant dans le guave,
Enmîmés sont les gougebosqueux,
Et le mômerade horsgrave.

Garde-toi du Jaseroque, mon fils!
La gueule qui mord; la griffe qui prend!
Garde-toi de l'oiseau Jube, évite
Le frumieux Band-à-prend.

Son glaive vorpal en main il va-
T-à la recherche du fauve manscant;
Puis arrivé à l'arbre Té-Té,
Il y reste, réfléchissant.

Pendant qu'il pense, tout uffusé
Le Jaseroque, à l'œil flambant,
Vient siblant par le bois tullegeais,
Et burbule en venant.

Un deux, un deux, par le milieu,
Le glaive vorpal fait pat-à-pan!
La bête défaite, avec sa tête,
Il rentre gallomphant.

As-tu tué le Jaseroque?
Viens à mon cœur, fils rayonnais!
O jour frabbejeais! Calleau! Callai!
Il cortule dans sa joie.

Il brilgue: les tôves lubricilleux
Se gyrent en vrillant dans le guave,
Enmîmés sont les gougebosqueux,
Et le mômerade horsgrave.

A magnificent German translation was made by Robert Scott, an eminent Greek scholar who had collaborated with Dean Liddell (Alice's father) on a Greek lexicon. It first appeared in an article, "The Jabberwock Traced to Its True Source," *Macmillan's Magazine*, February 1872. Using the pseudonym of Thomas Chatterton, Scott tells of attending a séance at which the spirit of one Hermann von Schwindel insists that Carroll's poem is simply an English translation of the following old German ballad:

DER JAMMERWOCH

Es brillig war. Die schlichte Toven
Wirrten und wimmelten in Waben;
Und aller-mümsige Burggoven
Die mohmen Räth' ausgraben.

Bewahre doch vor Jammerwoch!
Die Zähne knirschen, Krallen kratzen!

Bewahr' vor Jubjub—Vogel, vor
Frumiösen Banderschnätzchen!

Er griff sein vorpals Schwertchen zu,
Er suchte lang das manchsam'
Ding;

Dann, stehend unten Tumtum Baum,
Er an-zu-denken-fing.

Als stand er tief in Andacht auf,
Des Jammerwochen's Augen-feuer
Durch tulgen Wald mit wiffek kam
Ein burbelnd ungeheuer!

Eins, Zwei! Eins, Zwei!
Und durch und durch
Sein vorpals Schwert
zerschnifer-schnück,

Da blieb es todt! Er, Kopf in Hand,
Geläumfig zog zurück.

Und schlugst Du ja den Jammerwoch?
Umarme mich, mien Böhm' sches
Kind!

O Freuden-Tag! O Halloo-Schlag!
Er chortelt froh-gesinnt.

Es brillig war, &c.

Endless parodies of *Jabberwocky* have been attempted. Three of the best will be found on pages 36 and 37 of Carolyn Wells's anthology, *Such Nonsense*, 1918: *Somewhere-in-Europe Wocky*, *Footballwocky*, and *The Jabberwocky of the Publishers* (" 'Twas Harpers and the Little Browns/ Did Houghton Mifflin the book . . ."). But I incline toward Chesterton's dim view (expressed in his article on Carroll mentioned in the introduction) of all such efforts to do humorous imitations of something humorous. In "Mimsy Were the Borogoves," one of the best-known science fiction tales by Lewis Padgett (pen name for the collaborated work of the late Henry Kuttner and his wife, Catherine L. More), the words of *Jabberwocky* are revealed as symbols from a future language. Rightly understood, they explain a technique for entering a four-dimensional continuum. A similar notion is found in Fredric Brown's magnificently funny mystery novel, *Night of the Jabberwock*. Brown's narrator is an enthusiastic Carrollian. He learns from Yehudi Smith, apparently a member of a society of Carroll admirers called The Vorpal Blades, that Carroll's fantasies are not fiction at all, but realistic reporting about another plane of existence. The clues to the fantasies are cleverly concealed in Carroll's mathematical treatises, especially *Curiosa Mathematica*, and in his non-acrostic poems, which are really acrostics of a subtler kind. No Carrollian can afford to miss *Night of the Jabberwock*. It is the outstanding work of fiction that has close ties to the *Alice* books.

12. The Oxford English Dictionary lists "slithy" as a variant of "sleathy," an obsolete word meaning slovenly, but in Chapter 6 Humpty Dumpty gives "slithy" a different interpretation.

This first line of the poem furnishes an unusual clue in a Carrollian mystery story, "The Jabberwocky Thrust," by Bruce Elliott (using the pseudonym of Maxwell Grant), in *Shadow Mystery* magazine, October–November 1947. The murdered man is found beside a copy of *Alice* that is opened to *Jabberwocky*. His finger covers the word "toves." The first word of the line plus the initial letters of the next four words spell " 'Twas Bats," the first name of the killer.

13. "Toves" should be pronounced to rhyme with "groves," Carroll tells us in his preface to *The Hunting of the Snark*.

14. The Oxford English Dictionary traces "gyre" back to 1420 as a word meaning to turn or whirl around. This agrees with Humpty Dumpty's interpretation.

15. According to the Oxford English Dictionary, "gimble" is a variant spelling of "gimbal." Gimbals are pivoted rings used for various purposes, such as suspending a ship's compass so that it remains horizontal while the ship rolls. Humpty Dumpty makes clear, however, that the verb "gimble" is here used in a different sense.

16. "Mimsy" is the first of eight nonsense words in *Jabberwocky* that are used again in *The Hunting of the Snark*. It appears in Fit 7, verse 9: "And chanted in mimsiest tones." In Carroll's time, according to the Oxford English Dictionary, "mimsey" (with an "e") meant "prim, prudish, contemptible." Perhaps Carroll had this in mind.

17. In his preface to the *Snark,* Carroll writes: "The first 'o' in 'borogoves' is pronounced like the 'o' in 'worry.' Such is Human Perversity." The word is commonly mispronounced as "borogroves" by Carrollian novitiates, and this misspelling even appears in some American editions of the book.

18. "Mome" has a number of obsolete meanings such as mother, a blockhead, a carping critic, a buffoon, none of which, judging from Humpty Dumpty's interpretation, Carroll had in mind.

19. According to Humpty Dumpty, a "rath" is a green pig, but in Carroll's day it was a well-known old Irish word for an enclosure, usually a circular earthen wall, serving as a fort and place of residence for the head of a tribe.

20. "But it fairly lost heart, and outgrabe in despair," *Snark,* Fit 5, verse 10.

21. The Jabberwock is not mentioned in the *Snark,* but in a letter to Mrs. Chataway (the mother of one of his child-friends) Carroll explains that the scene of the *Snark* is "an island frequented by the Jubjub and the Bandersnatch—no doubt the very island where the Jabberwock was slain."

When a class in the Girls' Latin School, Boston, asked Carroll's permission to name their school magazine *The Jabberwock,* he replied:

Mr. Lewis Carroll has much pleasure in giving to the editors of the proposed magazine permission to use the title they wish for. He finds that the Anglo-Saxon word "wocer" or "wocor" signifies "offspring" or "fruit." Taking "jabber" in its ordinary acceptation of ."excited and voluble discussion," this would give the meaning of "the result of much excited discussion." Whether this phrase will have any application to the projected periodical. it will be for the future historian of American literature to determine. Mr. Carroll wishes all success to the forthcoming magazine.

22. The Jubjub is mentioned five times in the *Snark:* Fit 4, verse 18, and Fit 5, verses 8, 9, 21, and 29.

23. ". . . those frumious jaws," *Snark,* Fit 7, verse 5. In the *Snark's* preface Carroll writes:

For instance, take the two words "fuming" and "furious." Make up your mind that you will say both words, but leave it unsettled which you will say first. Now open your mouth and speak. If your thoughts incline ever so little towards "fuming," you will say "fuming-furious"; if they turn, by even a hair's breadth, towards "furious," you will say "furious-fuming"; but if you have that rarest of gifts, a perfectly balanced mind, you will say "frumious." Supposing that, when Pistol uttered the well-known words:

Under which king, Bezonian?
Speak or die!

Justice Shallow had felt certain that it was either William or Richard, but had not been able to settle which, so that he could not possibly say either name before the other, can it be doubted that, rather than die, he would have gasped out "Rilchiam!"?

24. The Bandersnatch is mentioned again in Chapter 7, and in the *Snark,* Fit 7, verses 3, 4, and 6.

25. Alexander L. Taylor, in his book on Carroll, *The White Knight,* shows how to get "vorpal" by taking letters alternately from "verbal" and "gospel," but there is no evidence that Carroll resorted to such involved techniques in coining his words. In fact Carroll wrote to a child-friend: "I am afraid I can't explain 'vorpal blade' for you — nor yet 'tulgey wood.'"

26. "Manx" was the Celtic name for the Isle of Man, hence the word came to be used in England for anything pertaining to the island. Its language was called Manx, its inhabitants Manxmen, and so on. Whether Carroll had this in mind when he coined "manxome" is not known.

27.. "Tum-tum" was a common colloquialism in Carroll's day, referring to the sound of a stringed instrument, especially when monotonously strummed.

28. "The Bellman looked uffish, and wrinkled his brow," *Snark*, Fit 4, verse 1. In a letter to child-friend Maud Standen, 1877, Carroll wrote that "uffish" suggested to him "a state of mind when the voice is gruffish, the manner roughish, and the temper huffish."

29. "Whiffling" is not a Carrollian word. It had a variety of meanings in Carroll's time, but usually had reference to blowing unsteadily in short puffs, hence it came to be a slang term for being variable and evasive. In an earlier century "whiffling" meant smoking and drinking.

30. "If you take the three verbs 'bleat,' 'murmur,' and 'warble,'" Carroll wrote in the letter cited above, "and select the bits I have underlined, it certainly *makes* 'burble': though I am afraid I can't distinctly remember having made it in that way." The word (apparently a combination of "burst" and "bubble") had long been used in England as a variant of "bubble" (e.g., the burbling brook), as well as a word meaning "to perplex, confuse, or muddle" ("His life fal-

len into a horribly burbled state," the Oxford English Dictionary quotes from an 1883 letter of Mrs. Carlyle's). In modern aeronautics "burbling" refers to the turbulence that develops when air is not flowing smoothly around an object.

31. "The Beaver went simply galumphing about," *Snark*, Fit 4, verse 17. This Carrollian word has entered the Oxford English Dictionary, where it is attributed to Carroll and defined as a combination of "gallop" and "triumphant," meaning "to march on exultantly with irregular bounding movements."

32. Tenniel's striking illustration for this stanza was originally intended as the book's frontispiece, but it was so horrendous that Carroll feared it might be best to open the book on a milder scene. In 1871 he conducted a private poll of about thirty mothers by sending them the following printed letter:

I am sending you, with this, a print of the proposed frontispiece for *Through the Looking-glass*. It has been suggested to me that it is too terrible a monster, and likely to alarm nervous and imaginative children; and that at any rate we had better begin the book with a pleasanter subject.

So I am submitting the question to a number of friends, for which purpose I have had copies of the frontispiece printed off.

We have three courses open to us:

(1) To retain it as the frontispiece.

(2) To transfer it to its proper place in the book (where the ballad occurs which it is intended to illustrate) and substitute a new frontispiece.

(3) To omit it altogether.

The last named course would be a great sacrifice of the time and trouble which the picture cost, and it would be a pity to adopt it unless it is really necessary.

I should be grateful to have your opinion, (tested by exhibiting the

"And hast thou slain the Jabberwock?[32]
  Come to my arms, my beamish boy![33]
O frabjous day! Callooh![34] Callay!"
  He chortled[35] in his joy.

'Twas brillig, and the slithy toves
  Did gyre and gimble in the wabe:
All mimsy were the borogoves,
  And the mome raths outgrabe.

"It seems very pretty," she said when she had finished it, "but it's *rather* hard to understand!" (You see she didn't like to confess, even to herself, that she couldn't make it out at all.) "Somehow it seems to fill my head with ideas—only I don't exactly know what they are! However, *somebody* killed *something:* that's clear, at any rate—"[36]

"But oh!" thought Alice, suddenly jumping up, "if I don't make haste, I shall have to go back through the Looking-glass, before I've seen what the rest of the house is like! Let's have a look at the garden first!" She was out of the room in a moment, and ran down stairs—or, at least, it wasn't exactly running, but a new invention for getting down stairs quickly and easily, as Alice said to herself. She just kept the tips of her fingers on the hand-rail, and floated gently down without even touching the stairs with her feet: then she floated on through the hall, and would have gone straight out at the door

picture to any children you think fit) as to which of these courses is best. Evidently most of the mothers favored the second course, for the picture of the White Knight on horseback became the frontispiece.

33. "But oh, beamish nephew, beware of the day," *Snark,* Fit 3, verse 10. This is not a word invented by Carroll. The Oxford English Dictionary traces it back to 1530 as a variant of "beaming," meaning "shining brightly, radiant."

34. A species of arctic duck that winters in northern Scotland is called the calloo after its evening call, "Calloo! Calloo!"

35. "Chortled," a word coined by Carroll, also has worked its way into the Oxford English Dictionary, where it is defined as a blend of "chuckle" and "snort."

36. Still far from clear is whether *Jabberwocky* is in some sense a parody. Roger Green, in the *London Times Literary Supplement,* March 1, 1957, and more recently in *The Lewis Carroll Handbook,* 1962, suggests that Carroll may have had in mind "The Shepherd of the Giant Mountains," a long German ballad about how a young shepherd slays a monstrous Griffin. The ballad had been translated by Carroll's cousin, Menella Bute Smedley, and published in *Sharpe's London Magazine,* March 7 and 21, 1846. "The similarity cannot be pinned down precisely," writes Green. "Much is in the feeling and the atmosphere; the parody is of general style and outlook."

in the same way, if she hadn't caught hold
of the door-post. She was getting a little
giddy with so much floating in the air,
and was rather glad to find herself walking again in the natural way.

CHAPTER II

The Garden of Live Flowers

"I should see the garden far better," said Alice to herself, "if I could get to the top of that hill: and here's a path that leads straight to it—at least, no, it doesn't do *that*—" (after going a few yards along the path, and turning several sharp corners), "but I suppose it will at last. But how curiously it twists! It's more like a corkscrew than a path! Well, *this* turn goes to the hill, I suppose—no, it doesn't! This goes straight back to the house! Well then, I'll try it the other way."

And so she did: wandering up and down, and trying turn after turn, but always coming back to the house, do what she would. Indeed, once, when she turned a corner rather more quickly than usual, she ran against it before she could stop herself.

"It's no use talking about it," Alice

1. Carroll originally planned to use the passion flower here but changed it to tiger-lily when he learned that the name had reference not to human passions but to the Passion of Christ on the Cross. The entire episode is a parody on the talking flowers in section 22 of Tennyson's poem *Maud*.

said, looking up at the house and pretending it was arguing with her. "I'm *not* going in again yet. I know I should have to get through the Looking-glass again—back into the old room—and there'd be an end of all my adventures!"

So, resolutely turning her back upon the house, she set out once more down the path, determined to keep straight on till she got to the hill. For a few minutes all went on well, and she was just saying "I really *shall* do it this time—" when the path gave a sudden twist and shook itself (as she described.it afterwards), and the next moment she found herself actually walking in at the door.

"Oh, it's too bad!" she cried. "I never saw such a house for getting in the way! Never!"

However, there was the hill full in sight, so there was nothing to be done but start again. This time she came upon a large flower-bed, with a border of daisies, and a willow-tree growing in the middle.

"O Tiger-lily!"**1** said Alice, addressing herself to one that was waving gracefully about in the wind, "I *wish* you could talk!"

"We *can* talk," said the Tiger-lily, "when there's anybody worth talking to."

Alice was so astonished that she couldn't speak for a minute: it quite seemed to take her breath away. At

length, as the Tiger-lily only went on waving about, she spoke again, in a timid voice—almost in a whisper. "And can *all* the flowers talk?"

"As well as *you* can," said the Tiger-lily. "And a great deal louder."

"It isn't manners for us to begin, you know," said the Rose, "and I really was wondering when you'd speak! Said I to myself, 'Her face has got *some* sense in it, though it's not a clever one!' Still, you're the right colour, and that goes a long way."

"I don't care about the colour," the Tiger-lily remarked. "If only her petals

201

curled up a little more, she'd be all right."

Alice didn't like being criticized, so she began asking questions. "Aren't you sometimes frightened at being planted out here, with nobody to take care of you?"

"There's the tree in the middle," said the Rose. "What else is it good for?"

"But what could it do, if any danger came?" Alice asked.

"It could bark," said the Rose.

"It says 'Bough-wough!' " cried a Daisy. "That's why its branches are called boughs!"

"Didn't you know *that?*" cried another Daisy. And here they all began shouting together, till the air seemed quite full of little shrill voices. "Silence, every one of you!" cried the Tiger-lily, waving itself passionately from side to side, and trembling with excitement. "They know I can't get at them!" it panted, bending its quivering head towards Alice, "or they wouldn't dare to do it!"

"Never mind!" Alice said in a soothing tone, and, stooping down to the daisies, who were just beginning again, she whispered "If you don't hold your tongues, I'll pick you!"

There was silence in a moment, and several of the pink daisies turned white.

"That's right!" said the Tiger-lily. "The daisies are worst of all. When one speaks, they all begin together, and it's enough to make one wither to hear the way they go on!"

"How is it you can all talk so nicely?" Alice said, hoping to get it into a better temper by a compliment. "I've been in many gardens before, but none of the flowers could talk."

"Put your hand down, and feel the ground," said the Tiger-lily. "Then you'll know why."

Alice did so. "It's very hard," she said; "but I don't see what that has to do with it."

"In most gardens," the Tiger-lily said, "they make the beds too soft—so that the flowers are always asleep."

This sounded a very good reason, and Alice was quite pleased to know it. "I never thought of that before!" she said.

"It's *my* opinion that you never think *at all*," the Rose said, in a rather severe tone.

"I never saw anybody that looked stupider," a Violet[2] said, so suddenly, that Alice quite jumped; for it hadn't spoken before.

"Hold *your* tongue!" cried the Tiger-lily. "As if *you* ever saw anybody! You keep your head under the leaves, and snore away there, till you know no more what's going on in the world, than if you were a bud!"

"Are there any more people in the garden besides me?" Alice said, not choosing

2. In addition to the three Liddell girls, of whom Carroll was so fond, there were two younger Liddell sisters, Rhoda and Violet. They appear in this chapter as the Rose and Violet — the only reference to them in the *Alice* books.

to notice the Rose's last remark.

"There's one other flower in the garden that can move about like you," said the Rose. "I wonder how you do it—" ("You're always wondering," said the Tiger-lily), "but she's more bushy than you are."

"Is she like me?" Alice asked eagerly, for the thought crossed her mind, "There's another little girl in the garden, somewhere!"

"Well, she has the same awkward shape as you," the Rose said: "but she's redder —and her petals are shorter, I think."

"They're done up close, like a dahlia," said the Tiger-lily: "not tumbled about, like yours."

"But that's not *your* fault," the Rose added kindly. "You're beginning to fade, you know—and then one can't help one's petals getting a little untidy."

Alice didn't like this idea at all: so, to change the subject, she asked "Does she ever come out here?"

"I daresay you'll see her soon," said the Rose. "She's one of the kind that has nine spikes, you know."

"Where does she wear them?" Alice asked with some curiosity.

"Why, all round her head, of course," the Rose replied. "I was wondering *you* hadn't got some too. I thought it was the regular rule."

"She's coming!" cried the Larkspur. "I

hear her footstep, thump, thump, along the gravel-walk."**3**

Alice looked round eagerly and found that it was the Red Queen. "She's grown a good deal!" was her first remark. She had indeed: when Alice first found her in the ashes, she had been only three inches high—and here she was, half a head taller than Alice herself!

"It's the fresh air that does it," said the Rose: "wonderfully fine air it is, out here."

"I think I'll go and meet her," said Alice, for, though the flowers were interesting enough, she felt that it would be far grander to have a talk with a real Queen.

"You can't possibly do that," said the Rose: "*I* should advise you to walk the other way."

This sounded nonsense to Alice, so she said nothing, but set off at once towards the Red Queen. To her surprise she lost sight of her in a moment, and found herself walking in at the front-door again.

A little provoked, she drew back, and, after looking everywhere for the Queen (whom she spied out at last, a long way off), she thought she would try the plan, this time, of walking in the opposite direction.

It succeeded beautifully.**4** She had not been walking a minute before she found herself face to face with the Red Queen,

3. Compare with the following stanza from Tennyson's *Maud:*

> There has fallen a splendid tear
> From the passion-flower at the gate.
> She is coming, my dove, my dear;
> She is coming, my life, my fate;
> The red rose cries, "She is near, she
> is near;"
> And the white rose weeps, "She is
> late;"
> The larkspur listens, "I hear, I hear;"
> And the lily whispers, "I wait."

4. An obvious allusion to the fact that forward and back are reversed by a mirror. Walk toward a mirror, the image moves in the opposite direction.

5. In his article "Alice on the Stage," cited earlier, Carroll wrote:

"The Red Queen I pictured as a Fury, but of another type; *her* passion must be cold and calm; she must be formal and strict, yet not unkindly; pedantic to the tenth degree, the concentrated essence of all governesses!"

It has been conjectured that the Red Queen was modeled after Miss Prickett, governess for the Liddell children (who called her by the nickname of "Pricks"). Oxford gossip once linked Carroll and Miss Prickett romantically, because of his frequent visits to the Liddell home, but it soon became evident that Carroll was interested in the children, not the governess. In Paramount's motion picture of *Alice* the role of Red Queen was taken by Edna May Oliver.

and full in sight of the hill she had been so long aiming at.

"Where do you come from?" said the Red Queen. "And where are you going? Look up, speak nicely, and don't twiddle your fingers all the time."**5**

Alice attended to all these directions, and explained, as well as she could, that she had lost her way.

"I don't know what you mean by *your* way," said the Queen: "all the ways about here belong to *me*—but why did you come out here at all?" she added in a kinder tone. "Curtsey while you're thinking what to say. It saves time."

Alice wondered a little at this, but she was too much in awe of the Queen to disbelieve it. "I'll try it when I go home," she thought to herself, "the next time I'm a little late for dinner."

"It's time for you to answer now," the Queen said, looking at her watch: "open your mouth a *little* wider when you speak, and always say 'your Majesty.' "

"I only wanted to see what the garden was like, your Majesty—"

"That's right," said the Queen, patting her on the head, which Alice didn't like at all: "though, when you say 'garden'— *I've* seen gardens, compared with which this would be a wilderness."

Alice didn't dare to argue the point, but went on: "—and I thought I'd try and find my way to the top of that hill—"

"When you say 'hill,'" the Queen interrupted, *"I* could show you hills, in comparison with which you'd call that a valley."

"No, I shouldn't," said Alice, surprised into contradicting her at last: "a hill *can't* be a valley, you know. That would be nonsense—"

The Red Queen shook her head. "You may call it 'nonsense' if you like," she said, "but *I've* heard nonsense, compared with which that would be as sensible as a dictionary!"**6**

Alice curtseyed again, as she was afraid from the Queen's tone that she was a *little* offended: and they walked on in silence till they got to the top of the little hill.

For some minutes Alice stood without speaking, looking out in all directions over the country—and a most curious country it was. There were a number of tiny little brooks running straight across it from side to side, and the ground between was divided up into squares by a number of little green hedges, that reached from brook to brook.

"I declare it's marked out just like a large chess-board!" Alice said at last. "There ought to be some men moving about somewhere—and so there are!" she added in a tone of delight, and her heart began to beat quick with excitement as she went on. "It's a great huge game of

6. Eddington, in the concluding chapter of *The Nature of the Physical World*, quotes this remark of the Red Queen in connection with a subtle discussion of what he calls the physicist's "problem of nonsense." In brief, Eddington argues that, although it may be nonsense for the physicist to affirm a reality of some sort beyond the laws of physics, it is as sensible as a dictionary beside the nonsense of supposing that there is no such reality.

7. So many memorable passages have been written in which life itself is compared to an enormous game of chess that a sizable anthology could be assembled out of them. Sometimes the players are men themselves, seeking to manipulate their fellow-men as one manipulates chess pieces. The following passage is from George Eliot's *Felix Holt:*

"Fancy what a game of chess would be if all the chessmen had passions and intellects, more or less small and cunning; if you were not only uncertain about your adversary's men, but a little uncertain also about your own; if your Knight could shuffle himself on to a new square on the sly; if your Bishop, in disgust at your Castling, could wheedle your Pawns out of their places; and if your Pawns, hating you because they are Pawns, could make away from their appointed posts that you might get checkmate on a sudden. You might be the longest-headed of deductive reasoners, and yet you might be beaten by your own Pawns. You would be especially likely to be beaten, if you depended arrogantly on your mathematical imagination, and regarded your passionate pieces with contempt.

chess that's being played—all over the world[7]—if this *is* the world at all, you know. Oh, what fun it is! How I *wish* I was one of them! I wouldn't mind being a Pawn, if only I might join—though of course I should *like* to be a Queen, best."

She glanced rather shyly at the real Queen as she said this, but her companion only smiled pleasantly, and said "That's easily managed. You can be the White Queen's Pawn, if you like, as Lily's[8] too young to play; and you're in the Second Square to begin with: when you get to the Eighth Square you'll be a Queen—" Just at this moment, somehow or other, they began to run.

Alice never could quite make out, in thinking it over afterwards, how it was that they began: all she remembers is, that they were running hand in hand, and the Queen went so fast that it was all she could do to keep up with her: and still the

Queen kept crying "Faster! Faster!" but Alice felt she *could not* go faster, though she had no breath left to say so.

The most curious part of the thing was, that the trees and the other things round them never changed their places at all: however fast they went, they never seemed to pass anything. "I wonder if all the things move along with us?" thought poor puzzled Alice. And the Queen seemed to guess her thoughts, for she cried "Faster! Don't try to talk!"

Not that Alice had any idea of doing *that*. She felt as if she would never be able to talk again, she was getting so much out of breath: and still the Queen cried "Faster! Faster!" and dragged her along. "Are we nearly there?" Alice managed to pant out at last.

"Nearly there!" the Queen repeated. "Why, we passed it ten minutes ago! Faster!" And they ran on for a time in silence, with the wind whistling in Alice's ears, and almost blowing her hair off her head, she fancied.

"Now! Now!" cried the Queen. "Faster! Faster!" And they went so fast that at last they seemed to skim through the air, hardly touching the ground with their feet, till suddenly, just as Alice was getting quite exhausted, they stopped, and she found herself sitting on the ground, breathless and giddy.

The Queen propped her up against a

"Yet this imaginary chess is easy compared with a game a man has to play against his fellow-men with other fellow-men for his instruments . . ."

Sometimes the players are God and Satan. William James dallies with this theme in his essay on *The Dilemma of Determinism,* and H. G. Wells echoes it in the prologue of his fine novel about education, *The Undying Fire.* Like the Book of Job on which it is modeled, Wells's story opens with a conversation between God and the devil. They are playing chess.

"But the chess they play is not the little ingenious game that originated in India; it is on an altogether different scale. The Ruler of the Universe creates the board, the pieces, and the rules; he makes all the moves; he may make as many moves as he likes whenever he likes; his antagonist, however, is permitted to introduce a slight inexplicable inaccuracy into each move, which necessitates further moves in correction. The Creator determines and conceals the aim of the game, and it is never clear whether the purpose of the adversary is to defeat or assist him in his unfathomable project. Apparently the adversary cannot win, but also he cannot lose so long as he can keep the game going. But he is concerned, it would seem, in preventing the development of any reasoned scheme in the game."

Sometimes the gods themselves are pieces in a higher game, and the players of this game in turn are pieces in an endless hierarchy of larger chessboards. "And there is merriment overhead," says Mother Sereda, after enlarging on this theme, in James Branch Cabell's *Jurgen,* "but it is very far away."

8. Lily, the White Queen's daughter and one of the white pawns, was encountered by Alice in the

previous chapter. In choosing the name "Lily," Carroll may have had in mind his young friend Lilia Scott Macdonald, the eldest daughter of George Macdonald (see Note 2, Chapter 1). Lilia was called "My White Lily" by her father, and Carroll's letters to her (after she passed fifteen) contain many teasing references to her advancing age. The statement here that Lily is too young to play chess may well have been part of this teasing.

There is a record (Collingwood's biography of Carroll, page 427) of a white kitten named Lily ("My imperial kitten" the White Queen calls her child in the previous chapter), which Carroll gave to one of his child-friends. This, however, may have been after the writing of *Through the Looking-Glass*.

9. This has probably been quoted more often (usually in reference to rapidly changing political situations) than any other passage in the *Alice* books.

tree, and said kindly, "You may rest a little, now."

Alice looked round her in great surprise. "Why, I do believe we've been under this tree the whole time! Everything's just as it was!"

"Of course it is," said the Queen. "What would you have it?"

"Well, in *our* country," said Alice, still panting a little, "you'd generally get to somewhere else—if you ran very fast for a long time as we've been doing."

"A slow sort of country!" said the Queen. "Now, *here,* you see, it takes all the running *you* can do, to keep in the same place. If you want to get somewhere else, you must run at least twice as fast as that."**9**

"I'd rather not try, please!" said Alice.

210

"I'm quite content to stay here—only I *am* so hot and thirsty!"

"I know what *you'd* like!" the Queen said good-naturedly, taking a little box out of her pocket. "Have a biscuit?"

Alice thought it would not be civil to say "No," though it wasn't at all what she wanted. So she took it, and ate it as well as she could: and it was *very* dry: and she thought she had never been so nearly choked in all her life.

"While you're refreshing yourself," said the Queen, "I'll just take the measurements." And she took a ribbon out of her pocket, marked in inches, and began measuring the ground, and sticking little pegs in here and there.

"At the end of two yards," she said, putting in a peg to mark the distance, "I shall give you your directions—have another biscuit?"

"No, thank you," said Alice: "one's *quite* enough!"

"Thirst quenched, I hope?" said the Queen.

Alice did not know what to say to this, but luckily the Queen did not wait for an answer, but went on. "At the end of *three* yards I shall repeat them—for fear of your forgetting them. At the end of *four,* I shall say good-bye. And at the end of *five,* I shall go!"

She had got all the pegs put in by this time, and Alice looked on with great interest as she returned to the tree, and then began slowly walking down the row.

At the two-yard peg she faced round, and said "A pawn goes two squares in its first move, you know. So you'll go *very* quickly through the Third Square—by railway, I should think—and you'll find yourself in the Fourth Square in no time. Well, *that* square belongs to Tweedledum and Tweedledee—the Fifth is mostly water—the Sixth belongs to Humpty Dumpty—But you make no remark?"

"I—I didn't know I had to make one— just then," Alice faltered out.

"You *should* have said," the Queen went on in a tone of grave reproof, " 'It's extremely kind of you to tell me all this' —however, we'll suppose it said—the Seventh Square is all forest—however. one of the Knights will show you the way— and in the Eighth Square we shall be Queens together, and it's all feasting and fun!" Alice got up and curtseyed, and sat down again.

At the next peg the Queen turned again, and this time she said "Speak in French when you can't think of the English for a thing — turn out your toes as you walk—and remember who you are!" She did not wait for Alice to curtsey, this time, but walked on quickly to the next peg, where she turned for a moment to say "Good-bye," and then hurried on to the last.

How it happened, Alice never knew, but exactly as she came to the last peg, she was gone.**10** Whether she vanished into the air, or whether she ran quickly into the wood ("and she *can* run very fast!" thought Alice), there was no way of guessing, but she was gone, and Alice began to remember that she was a Pawn, and that it would soon be time for her to move.

10. A glance at the position of the chess pieces, on the diagram in Carroll's preface, shows that Alice (the white pawn) and the Red Queen are side by side on adjacent squares. The first move of the problem now takes place as the Queen moves away to KR4 (the fourth square on the Red King's rook file, counting from the red side of the board. In this notation the squares are always numberéd from the side of the piece that is moved).

CHAPTER III

Looking-Glass Insects

Of course the first thing to do was to make a grand survey of the country she was going to travel through. "It's something very like learning geography," thought Alice, as she stood on tiptoe in hopes of being able to see a little further. "Principal rivers—there *are* none. Principal mountains—I'm on the only one, but I don't think it's got any name. Principal towns—why, what *are* those creatures, making honey down there? They can't be bees—nobody ever saw bees a mile off, you know—" and for some time she stood silent, watching one of them that was bustling about among the flowers, poking its proboscis into them, "just as if it was a regular bee," thought Alice. thought Alice.

However, this was anything but a regular bee: in fact, it was an elephant—as

1. The six little brooks are the six horizontal lines separating Alice from the eighth square on which she is to be queened. Each time she crosses a line, the crossing is marked in the text by three rows of dots. Her first move, P-Q4, is a move of two squares, the only long "journey" permitted a pawn. Here she leaps into the third square, then the train carries her on to the fourth.

Alice soon found out, though the idea quite took her breath away at first. "And what enormous flowers they must be!" was her next idea. "Something like cottages with the roofs taken off, and stalks put to them—and what quantities of honey they must make! I think I'll go down and—no, I won't go *just* yet," she went on, checking herself just as she was beginning to run down the hill, and trying to find some excuse for turning shy so suddenly. "It'll never do to go down among them without a good long branch to brush them away—and what fun it'll be when they ask me how I liked my walk. I shall say 'Oh, I liked it well enough—' (here came the favourite little toss of the head), 'only it *was* so dusty and hot, and the elephants *did* tease so!'

"I think I'll go down the other way," she said after a pause; "and perhaps I may visit the elephants later on. Besides, I *do* so want to get into the Third Square!"

So, with this excuse, she ran down the hill, and jumped over the first of the six little brooks.[1]

"Tickets, please!" said the Guard, putting his head in at the window. In a moment everybody was holding out a ticket: they were about the same size as the people, and quite seemed to fill the carriage.

"Now then! Show your ticket, child!" the Guard went on, looking angrily at Alice. And a great many voices all said together ("like the chorus of a song," thought Alice) "Don't keep him waiting, child! Why, his time is worth a thousand pounds a minute!"

"I'm afraid I haven't got one," Alice said in a frightened tone: "there wasn't a ticket-office where I came from." And again the chorus of voices went on. "There wasn't room for one where she came from. The land there is worth a thousand pounds an inch!"

"Don't make excuses," said the Guard: "you should have bought one from the engine-driver." And once more the chorus of voices went on with "The man that drives the engine. Why, the smoke alone is worth a thousand pounds a puff!"

Alice thought to herself "Then there's no use in speaking." The voices didn't join in, *this* time, as she hadn't spoken, but, to her great surprise, they all *thought* in chorus (I hope you understand what *thinking in chorus* means—for I must confess that *I* don't), "Better say nothing at all. Language is worth a thousand pounds a word!"

2. A comparison of the illustration of the man in white paper with Tenniel's political cartoons in *Punch* leaves little doubt that the face under the folded paper hat is Benjamin Disraeli's. Tenniel and/ or Carroll may have had in mind the "white paper" (official documents) with which such statesmen are surrounded.

"I shall dream about a thousand pounds tonight, I know I shall!" thought Alice.

All this time the Guard was looking at her, first through a telescope, then through a microscope, and then through an opera-glass. At last he said "You're traveling the wrong way," and shut up the window, and went away.

"So young a child," said the gentleman sitting opposite to her, (he was dressed in white paper),**2** "ought to know which way she's going, even if she doesn't know her own name!"

A Goat, that was sitting next to the gentleman in white, shut his eyes and said in a loud voice, "She ought to know her way to the ticket-office, even if she doesn't know her alphabet!"

There was a Beetle sitting next the

Goat (it was a very queer carriage-full of passengers altogether), and, as the rule seemed to be that they should all speak in turn, *he* went on with "She'll have to go back from here as luggage!"

Alice couldn't see who was sitting beyond the Beetle, but a hoarse voice spoke next. "Change engines—" it said, and there it choked and was obliged to leave off.

"It sounds like a horse," Alice thought to herself. And an extremely small voice, close to her ear, said "You might make a joke on that—something about 'horse' and 'hoarse,' you know."

Then a very gentle voice in the distance said, "She must be labeled 'Lass, with care,'**3** you know—"

And after that other voices went on ("What a number of people there are in the carriage!" thought Alice), saying "she must go by post, as she's got a head on her —"**3a** "She must be sent as a message by the telegraph—" "She must draw the train herself the rest of the way—," and so on.

But the gentleman dressed in white paper leaned forwards and whispered in her ear, "Never mind what they all say, my dear, but take a return-ticket every time the train stops."

"Indeed I shan't!" Alice said rather impatiently. "I don't belong to this railway journey at all—I was in a wood just now—and I wish I could get back there!"

3. In England, packages containing glass objects are commonly labeled "Glass, with care."

3a. I am grateful to Martin Burkenroad, of Panama, for pointing out the meaning of this phrase. "Head" was a Victorian slang word for postage stamp. Alice has a head, so she should be posted.

219

"You might make a joke on *that*," said the little voice close to her ear: "something about 'you *would* if you could,' you know."

"Don't tease so," said Alice, looking about in vain to see where the voice came from. "If you're so anxious to have a joke made, why don't you make one yourself?"

The little voice sighed deeply. It was *very* unhappy, evidently, and Alice would have said something pitying to comfort it, "if it would only sigh like other people!" she thought. But this was such a wonderfully small sigh, that she wouldn't have heard it at all, if it hadn't come *quite* close to her ear. The consequence of this was that it tickled her ear very much, and quite took off her thoughts from the unhappiness of the poor little creature.

"I know you are a friend," the little voice went on: "a dear friend, and an old friend. And you wo'n't hurt me, though I *am* an insect."

"What kind of insect?" Alice inquired, a little anxiously. What she really wanted to know was, whether it could sting or not, but she thought this wouldn't be quite a civil question to ask.

"What, then you don't—" the little voice began, when it was drowned by a shrill scream from the engine, and everybody jumped up in alarm, Alice among the rest.

The Horse, who had put his head out of the window, quietly drew it in and said "It's only a brook we have to jump over." Everybody seemed satisfied with this, though Alice felt a little nervous at the idea of trains jumping at all. "However, it'll take us into the Fourth Square, that's some comfort!" she said to herself. In another moment she felt the carriage rise straight up into the air, and in her fright she caught at the thing nearest to her hand, which happened to be the Goat's beard.**4**

*   *   *   *   *
   *   *   *   *
*   *   *   *   *

But the beard seemed to melt away as she touched it, and she found herself sitting quietly under a tree—while the Gnat (for that was the insect she had been talking to) was balancing itself on a twig just over her head, and fanning her with its wings.

It certainly was a *very* large Gnat: "about the size of a chicken," Alice thought. Still, she couldn't feel nervous with it, after they had been talking together so long.

"—then you don't like *all* insects?" the Gnat went on, as quietly as if nothing had happened.

"I like them when they can talk," Alice said. "None of them ever talk, where *I* come from."

"What sort of insects do you rejoice in, where *you* come from?" the Gnat inquired.

"I don't *rejoice* in insects at all," Alice

4. The train's leap completes Alice's move of P-Q4. In Carroll's original manuscript Alice grabbed the hair of an old lady in the carriage, but on June 1, 1870, Tenniel wrote Carroll:

My Dear Dodgson:
I think that when the jump occurs in the railway scene you might very well make Alice lay hold of the goat's *beard* as being the object nearest to her hand—instead of the old lady's hair. The jerk would actually throw them together.
Don't think me brutal, but I am bound to say that the "wasp" chapter does not interest me in the least, and I can't see my way to a picture. If you want to shorten the book, I can't help thinking—with all submission—that *this* is your opportunity.
In an agony of haste,
                    Yours sincerely,
                        J. Tenniel

Carroll adopted both suggestions. The old lady and a thirteenth chapter about the wasp were removed. Alas, nothing of the missing chapter has survived.

221

explained, "because I'm rather afraid of them—at least the large kinds. But I can tell you the names of some of them."

"Of course they answer to their names?" the Gnat remarked carelessly.

"I never knew them do it."

"What's the use of their having names," the Gnat said, "if they won't answer to them?"

"No use to *them*," said Alice; "but it's useful to the people that name them, I suppose. If not, why do things have names at all?"

"I can't say," the Gnat replied. "Further on, in the wood down there, they've got no names—however, go on with your list of insects: you're wasting time."

"Well, there's the Horse-fly," Alice began, counting off the names on her fingers.

"All right," said the Gnat. "Half-way up that bush, you'll see a Rocking-horse-fly, if you look. It's made entirely of wood, and gets about by swinging itself from branch to branch."

"What does it live on?" Alice asked, with great curiosity.

"Sap and sawdust," said the Gnat. "Go on with the list."

Alice looked at the Rocking-horse-fly with great interest, and made up her mind that it must have been just repainted, it looked so bright and sticky; and then she went on.

"And there's the Dragon-fly."

"Look on the branch above your head," said the Gnat, "and there you'll find a Snap-dragon-fly. Its body is made of plum-pudding, its wings of holly-leaves, and its head is a raisin burning in brandy."[4a]

"And what does it live on?" Alice asked, as before.

"Frumenty[5] and mince-pie," the Gnat replied; "and it makes its nest in a Christmas-box."

"And then there's the Butterfly," Alice went on, after she had taken a good look at the insect with its head on fire, and had thought to herself, "I wonder if that's the reason insects are so fond of flying into candles—because they want to turn into Snap-dragon-flies!"

"Crawling at your feet," said the Gnat (Alice drew her feet back in some alarm), "you may observe a Bread-and-butter-fly. Its wings are thin slices of bread-and-butter, its body is a crust, and its head is a lump of sugar."

"And what does *it* live on?"

"Weak tea with cream in it."

A new difficulty came into Alice's head. "Supposing it couldn't find any?" she suggested.

"Then it would die, of course."

"But that must happen very often," Alice remarked thoughtfully.

"It always happens," said the Gnat.

After this, Alice was silent for a minute

4a. Snapdragon (or flapdragon) is the name of a pastime that delighted Victorian children during the Christmas season. A shallow bowl was filled with brandy, raisins were tossed in, and the brandy set on fire. Players tried to snatch raisins from the flickering blue flames and pop them, still blazing, into their mouths. The burning raisins also were called snapdragons.

5. Frumenty is a wheat pudding.

or two, pondering. The Gnat amused itself meanwhile by humming round and
round her head: at last it settled again and
remarked "I suppose you don't want to
lose your name?"

"No, indeed," Alice said, a little anxiously.

"And yet I don't know," the Gnat went
on in a careless tone: "only think how
convenient it would be if you could manage to go home without it! For instance,
if the governess wanted to call you to your
lessons, she would call out 'Come here—,'
and there she would have to leave off,
because there wouldn't be any name for
her to call, and of course, you wouldn't
have to go, you know."

"That would never do, I'm sure," said
Alice: "the governess would never think
of excusing me lessons for that. If she
couldn't remember my name, she'd call
me 'Miss,' as the servants do."

"Well, if she said 'Miss,' and didn't say
anything more," the Gnat remarked, "of
course you'd miss your lessons. That's a
joke. I wish *you* had made it."

"Why do you wish *I* had made it?"
Alice asked. "It's a very bad one."

But the Gnat only sighed deeply, while
two large tears came rolling down its
cheeks.

"You shouldn't make jokes," Alice
said, "if it makes you so unhappy."

Then came another of those mel-

ancholy little sighs, and this time the poor
Gnat really seemed to have sighed itself
away, for, when Alice looked up, there
was nothing whatever to be seen on the
twig, and, as she was getting quite chilly
with sitting still so long, she got up and
walked on.

She very soon came to an open field,
with a wood on the other side of it: it
looked much darker than the last wood,
and Alice felt a *little* timid about going
into it. However, on second thoughts, she
made up her mind to go on: "for I certainly won't go *back*," she thought to herself, and this was the only way to the
Eighth Square.

"This must be the wood," she said
thoughtfully to herself, "where things
have no names. I wonder what'll become
of *my* name when I go in? I shouldn't like
to lose it at all—because they'd have to
give me another, and it would be almost
certain to be an ugly one. But then the fun
would be, trying to find the creature that
had got my old name! That's just like the
advertisements, you know, when people
lose dogs — *'answers to the name of
"Dash": had on a brass collar'*—just fancy
calling everything you met 'Alice,' till
one of them answered! Only they
wouldn't answer at all, if they were wise."

She was rambling on in this way when
she reached the wood: it looked very cool
and shady. "Well, at any rate it's a great

6. Alice is thinking, of course, of "Liddell," her last name. "L" also begins "Lily," the name of the white pawn whose place in the game Alice has taken.

comfort," she said as she stepped under the trees, "after being so hot, to get into the—into the—into *what?*" she went on, rather surprised at not being able to think of the word. "I mean to get under the—under the—under *this,* you know!" putting her hand on the trunk of the tree. "What *does* it call itself, I wonder? I do believe it's got no name—why, to be sure it hasn't!"

She stood silent for a minute, thinking: then she suddenly began again. "Then it really *has* happened, after all! And now, who am I? I *will* remember, if I can! I'm determined to do it!" But being determined didn't help her much, and all she could say, after a great deal of puzzling, was "L, I *know* it begins with L!"**6**

Just then a Fawn came wandering by: it looked at Alice with its large gentle eyes, but didn't seem at all frightened. "Here then! Here then!" Alice said, as she held out her hand and tried to stroke it; but it only started back a little, and then stood looking at her again.

"What do you call yourself?" the Fawn said at last. Such a soft sweet voice it had!

"I wish I knew!" thought poor Alice. She answered, rather sadly, "Nothing, just now."

"Think again," it said: "that won't do."

Alice thought, but nothing came of it. "Please, would you tell me what *you* call

226

yourself?" she said timidly. "I think that might help a little."

"I'll tell you, if you'll come a little further on," the Fawn said. "I can't remember *here*."

So they walked on together through the wood, Alice with her arms clasped lovingly round the soft neck of the Fawn, till they came out into another open field, and here the Fawn gave a sudden bound into the air, and shook itself free from Alice's arm. "I'm a Fawn!" it cried out in a voice of delight.[7] "And, dear me! you're a human child!" A sudden look of alarm came into its beautiful brown eyes, and in another moment it had darted away at full speed.

Alice stood looking after it, almost ready to cry with vexation at having lost her dear little fellow-traveler so suddenly. "However, I know my name now," she said: "that's *some* comfort. Alice—Alice—I won't forget it again. And now, which of these finger-posts ought I to follow, I wonder?"

It was not a very difficult question to answer, as there was only one road through the wood, and the two finger-posts both pointed along it. "I'll settle it," Alice said to herself, "when the road divides and they point different ways."

But this did not seem likely to happen. She went on and on, a long way, but, wherever the road divided, there were

7. The wood in which things have no name is in fact the universe itself, as it is apart from symbol-manipulating creatures who label portions of it because — as Alice earlier remarked with pragmatic wisdom — "it's useful to the people that name them." The realization that the world by itself contains no signs — that there is no connection whatever between things and their names except by way of a mind that finds the tags useful — is by no means a trivial philosophic insight. The fawn's delight in recalling its name reminds one of the old joke about Adam naming the tiger the tiger because it *looked* like a tiger.

sure to be two finger-posts pointing the same way, one marked

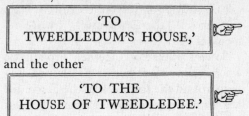

and the other

'TO THE
HOUSE OF TWEEDLEDEE.'

"I do believe," said Alice at last, "that they live in the *same* house! I wonder I never thought of that before—But I can't stay there long. I'll just call and say 'How d'ye do?' and ask them the way out of the wood. If I could only get to the Eighth Square before it gets dark!" So she wandered on, talking to herself as she went, till, on turning a sharp corner, she came upon two fat little men, so suddenly that she could not help starting back, but in another moment she recovered herself, feeling sure that they must be[8]

CHAPTER IV

Tweedledum and Tweedledee

They were standing under a tree, each with an arm round the other's neck, and Alice knew which was which in a moment, because one of them had 'DUM' embroidered on his collar, and the other 'DEE.' "I suppose they've each got 'TWEEDLE' round at the back of the collar," she said to herself.

They stood so still that she quite forgot they were alive, and she was just going round to see if the word 'TWEEDLE' was written at the back of each collar, when she was startled by a voice coming from the one marked 'DUM.'

"If you think we're wax-works," he said, "you ought to pay, you know. Wax-works weren't made to be looked at for nothing. Nohow!"

"Contrariwise," added the one marked

1. In the 1720's there was a bitter rivalry between George Frederick Handel, the German-English composer, and Giovanni Battista Bononcini, an Italian composer. John Byrom, an eighteenth-century hymn writer and teacher of shorthand, described the controversy as follows:

Some say, compared to Bononcini
That Mynheer Handel's but a ninny;
Others aver that he to Handel
Is scarcely fit to hold a candle;
Strange all this difference should be
Twixt tweedle-dum and tweedle-dee.

No one knows whether the nursery rhyme about the Tweedle brothers originally had reference to this famous musical battle, or whether it was an older rhyme from which Byrom borrowed in the last line of his doggerel. (See the Oxford Dictionary of Nursery Rhymes, 1952, edited by Iona and Peter Opie, page 418.)

'DEE,' "if you think we're alive, you ought to speak."

"I'm sure I'm very sorry," was all Alice could say; for the words of the old song kept ringing through her head like the ticking of a clock, and she could hardly help saying them out loud:—**1**

"Tweedledum and Tweedledee
    Agreed to have a battle;
For Tweedledum said Tweedledee
    Had spoiled his nice new rattle.

Just then flew down a monstrous
        crow,
    As black as a tar-barrel;
Which frightened both the heroes so,
    They quite forgot their quarrel."

"I know what you're thinking about,"

said Tweedledum; "but it isn't so, no-how."

"Contrariwise," continued Tweedle-dee, "if it was so, it might be; and if it were so, it would be; but as it isn't, it ain't. That's logic."

"I was thinking," Alice said very po-litely, "which is the best way out of this wood: it's getting so dark. Would you tell me, please?"

But the fat little men only looked at each other and grinned.

They looked so exactly like a couple of great schoolboys, that Alice couldn't help pointing her finger at Tweedledum, and saying "First Boy!"

"Nohow!" Tweedledum cried out briskly, and shut his mouth up again with a snap.

"Next Boy!" said Alice, passing on to Tweedledee, though she felt quite certain he would only shout out "Contrariwise!" and so he did.

"You've begun wrong!" cried Tweedle-dum. "The first thing in a visit is to say 'How d'ye do' and shake hands!" And here the two brothers gave each other a hug, and then they held out the two hands that were free, to shake hands with her.[2]

Alice did not like shaking hands with either of them first, for fear of hurting the other one's feelings; so, as the best way out of the difficulty, she took hold of both hands at once: the next moment

2. Tweedledum and Tweedledee are what geometers call "enantio-morphs," mirror-image forms of each other. That Carroll intended this is strongly suggested by Twee-dledee's favorite word, "contrari-wise," and by the fact that they ex-tend right and left hands for a handshake. Tenniel's picture of the two enantiomorphs arrayed for battle, standing in identical pos-tures, indicates that he looked upon the twins in the same way. Note that the position of the fin-gers of Tweedledum's right hand (or is it Tweedledee's? — the bol-ster was put around the neck of Dee, but the saucepan marks him as Dum) exactly matches the posi-tion of his brother's left fingers.

they were dancing round in a ring. This seemed quite natural (she remembered afterwards), and she was not even surprised to hear music playing: it seemed to come from the tree under which they were dancing, and it was done (as well as she could make it out) by the branches rubbing one across the other, like fiddles and fiddle-sticks.

"But it certainly *was* funny," (Alice said afterwards, when she was telling her sister the history of all this), "to find myself singing '*Here we go round the mulberry bush.*' I don't know when I began it, but somehow I felt as if I'd been singing it a long long time!"

The other two dancers were fat, and very soon out of breath. "Four times round is enough for one dance," Tweedledum panted out, and they left off dancing as suddenly as they had begun: the music stopped at the same moment.

Then they let go of Alice's hands, and stood looking at her for a minute: there was a rather awkward pause, as Alice didn't know how to begin a conversation with people she had just been dancing with. "It would never do to say 'How d'ye do?' *now*," she said to herself: "we seem to have got beyond that, somehow!"

"I hope you're not much tired?" she said at last.

"Nohow. And thank you *very* much for asking," said Tweedledum.

"So *much* obliged!" added Tweedledee. "You like poetry?"

"Ye-es, pretty well—*some* poetry," Alice said doubtfully. "Would you tell me which road leads out of the wood?"

"What shall I repeat to her?" said Tweedledee, looking round at Tweedledum with great solemn eyes, and not noticing Alice's question.

" 'The Walrus and the Carpenter' is the longest," Tweedledum replied, giving his brother an affectionate hug.

Tweedledee began instantly:
  "The sun was shining—"
Here Alice ventured to interrupt him. "If it's *very* long," she said, as politely as she could, "would you please tell me first which road—"

Tweedledee smiled gently, and began again:[3]

"The sun was shining on the sea,
  Shining with all his might:
He did his very best to make
  The billows smooth and bright—
And this was odd, because it was
  The middle of the night.

The moon was shining sulkily,
  Because she thought the sun
Had got no business to be there
  After the day was done—
'It's very rude of him,' she said,
  'To come and spoil the fun!'

The sea was wet as wet could be,
  The sands were dry as dry.

[3.] This masterpiece of nonsense is in the meter of Thomas Hood's *Dream of Eugene Aram,* but only the style of Hood's poem is satirized. As a check against the tendency to find too much intended symbolism in the *Alice* books it is well to remember that, when Carroll gave the manuscript of this poem to Tenniel for illustrating, he offered the artist a choice of drawing a carpenter, butterfly, or baronet. Each word fitted the rhyme scheme, and Carroll had no preference so far as the nonsense was concerned. Tenniel chose the carpenter. The boxlike paper hat that Tenniel placed on the carpenter's head is no longer folded by carpenters. However, these hats are still widely used by operators of newspaper printing presses; they fold them from blank sheets of newsprint and wear them to keep the ink out of their hair.

J. B. Priestley has written an amusing article on "The Walrus and the Carpenter" *(New Statesman,* August 10, 1957, p. 168) in which he interprets the two figures as archetypes of two kinds of politicians.

You could not see a cloud, because
  No cloud was in the sky:
No birds were flying overhead—
  There were no birds to fly.

The Walrus and the Carpenter
  Were walking close at hand:
They wept like anything to see
  Such quantities of sand:
'If this were only cleared away,'
  They said, 'it would be grand!'

'If seven maids with seven mops
  Swept it for half a year,
Do you suppose,' the Walrus said,
  'That they could get it clear?'
'I doubt it,' said the Carpenter,
  And shed a bitter tear.

'O Oysters, come and walk with us!'
  The Walrus did beseech.
'A pleasant walk, a pleasant talk,
  Along the briny beach:
We cannot do with more than four,
  To give a hand to each.'

The eldest Oyster looked at him,
  But never a word he said:
The eldest Oyster winked his eye,
  And shook his heavy head—
Meaning to say he did not choose
  To leave the oyster-bed.

But four young Oysters hurried up,
  All eager for the treat:
Their coats were brushed, their faces
    washed,
  Their shoes were clean and neat—
And this was odd, because, you know,
  They hadn't any feet.

Four other Oysters followed them,
    And yet another four;
And thick and fast they came at last,
    And more, and more, and more—
All hopping through the frothy waves,
    And scrambling to the shore.

The Walrus and the Carpenter
    Walked on a mile or so,
And then they rested on a rock
    Conveniently low:
And all the little Oysters stood
    And waited in a row.

'The time has come,' the Walrus said,
    'To talk of many things:
Of shoes—and ships—and sealing
        wax—
Of cabbages—and kings—4
And why the sea is boiling hot—
    And whether pigs have wings.'

'But wait a bit,' the Oysters cried,
    'Before we have our chat;
For some of us are out of breath,
    And all of us are fat!'
'No hurry!' said the Carpenter.
    They thanked him much for that.

'A loaf of bread,' the Walrus said,
    'Is what we chiefly need:
Pepper and vinegar besides
    Are very good indeed—
Now, if you're ready, Oysters dear,
    We can begin to feed.'

'But not on us!' the Oysters cried,
    Turning a little blue.
'After such kindness, that would be

4. *Cabbages and Kings* was the title of O. Henry's first book. The first four lines of this stanza are the best known and most often quoted lines of the poem. In "The Adventure of the Mad Tea Party," the last story in *The Adventures of Ellery Queen,* these lines are an important element in the detective's curious method of frightening a confession out of a murderer.

5. For Savile Clarke's *Alice* operetta Carroll added an additional
verse:

> The Carpenter he ceased to sob;
>   The Walrus ceased to weep;
> They'd finished all the oysters;
>   And they laid them down to sleep—
> And of their craft and cruelty
>   The punishment to reap.

After the Walrus and Carpenter
have gone to sleep, the ghosts of
two oysters appear on the stage to
sing and dance and punish the
sleepers by stamping on their
chests. Carroll felt, and apparently
audiences agreed with him, that
this provided a more effective ending for the episode and also some-
what mollified oyster sympathizers
among the spectators.

The ghost of the first oyster
dances a mazurka and sings:

> The Carpenter is sleeping, the butter's
>   on his face,
> The vinegar and pepper are all about
>   the place!
> Let oysters rock your cradle and lull
>   you into rest;
> And if that will not do it, we'll sit
>   upon your chest!
>
> We'll sit upon your chest! We'll sit
>   upon your chest!
> The simplest way to do it is to sit
>   upon your chest!

The ghost of the second oyster
dances a horn-pipe and sings:

> O woeful, weeping Walrus, your
>   tears are all a sham!
> You're greedier for Oysters than
>   children are for jam.
> You like to have an Oyster to give
>   the meal a zest—
> Excuse me, wicked Walrus,
>   for stamping on your chest!
> For stamping on your chest!
>   For stamping on your chest!
> Excuse me, wicked Walrus,
>   for stamping on your chest!

(All the above stanzas are quoted
from Roger Green's notes to *The
Diaries of Lewis Carroll*, Vol. II,
pages 446-47.)

A dismal thing to do!'
'The night is fine,' the Walrus said.
   'Do you admire the view?

'It was so kind of you to come!
   And you are very nice!'
The Carpenter said nothing but
   'Cut us another slice.
I wish you were not quite so deaf—
   I've had to ask you twice!'

'It seems a shame,' the Walrus said,
   'To play them such a trick.
After we've brought them out so far,
   And made them trot so quick!'
The Carpenter said nothing but
   'The butter's spread too thick!'

'I weep for you,' the Walrus said:
   'I deeply sympathize.'
With sobs and tears he sorted out
   Those of the largest size,
Holding his pocket-handkerchief
   Before his streaming eyes.

'O Oysters,' said the Carpenter,
   'You've had a pleasant run!
Shall we be trotting home again?'
   But answer came there none—
And this was scarcely odd, because
   They'd eaten every one."[5]

"I like the Walrus best," said Alice:
"because he was a *little* sorry for the poor
oysters."

"He ate more than the Carpenter,
though," said Tweedledee. "You see he
held his hankerchief in front, so that the

Carpenter couldn't count how many he took: contrariwise."

"That was mean!" Alice said indignantly. "Then I like the Carpenter best —if he didn't eat so many as the Walrus."

"But he ate as many as he could get," said Tweedledum.

This was a puzzler.**6** After a pause, Alice began, "Well! They were *both* very unpleasant characters—" Here she checked herself in some alarm, at hearing something that sounded to her like the puffing of a large steam-engine in the wood near them, though she feared it was more likely to be a wild beast. "Are there any lions or tigers about here?" she asked timidly.

"It's only the Red King snoring," said Tweedledee.

"Come and look at him!" the brothers cried, and they each took one of Alice's

6. Alice is puzzled because she faces here the traditional ethical dilemma of having to choose between judging a person in terms of his acts or in terms of his intentions.

237

7. This well-known, much-quoted discussion of the Red King's dream (the monarch is snoring on a square directly east of the square currently occupied by Alice) plunges poor Alice into grim metaphysical waters. The Tweedle brothers defend Bishop Berkeley's view that all material objects, including ourselves, are only "sorts of things" in the mind of God. Alice takes the common-sense position of Samuel Johnson, who supposed that he refuted Berkeley by kicking a large stone. "A very instructive discussion from a philosophical point of view," Bertrand Russell remarked, commenting on the Red King's dream in a radio panel discussion of *Alice*. "But if it were not put humorously, we should find it too painful."

The Berkeleyan theme troubled Carroll as it troubles all Platonists. Both *Alice* adventures are dreams, and in *Sylvie and Bruno* the narrator shuttles back and forth mysteriously between real and dream worlds. "So, either I've been dreaming about Sylvie," he says to himself early in the novel, "and

hands, and led her up to where the King was sleeping.

"Isn't he a *lovely* sight?" said Tweedledum.

Alice couldn't say honestly that he was. He had a tall red night-cap on, with a tassel, and he was lying crumpled up into a sort of untidy heap, and snoring loud—"fit to snore his head off!" as Tweedledum remarked.

"I'm afraid he'll catch cold with lying on the damp grass," said Alice, who was a very thoughtful little girl.

"He's dreaming now," said Tweedledee: "and what do you think he's dreaming about?"

Alice said "Nobody can guess that."

"Why, about *you!*" Tweedledee exclaimed, clapping his hands triumphantly. "And if he left off dreaming about you, where do you suppose you'd be?"

"Where I am now, of course," said Alice.

"Not you!" Tweedledee retorted contemptuously. "You'd be nowhere. Why, you're only a sort of thing in his dream!"[7]

"If that there King was to wake," added Tweedledum, "you'd go out—bang!—just like a candle!"

"I shouldn't!" Alice exclaimed indignantly. "Besides, if *I'm* only a sort of thing in his dream, what are *you*, I should like to know?"

"Ditto," said Tweedledum.

"Ditto, ditto!" cried Tweedledee.

He shouted this so loud that Alice couldn't help saying "Hush! You'll be waking him, I'm afraid, if you make so much noise."

"Well, it's no use *your* talking about waking him," said Tweedledum, "when you're only one of the things in his dream. You know very well you're not real."

"I *am* real!" said Alice, and began to cry.

"You won't make yourself a bit realler by crying," Tweedledee remarked: "there's nothing to cry about."

"If I wasn't real," Alice said—half-laughing through her tears, it all seemed so ridiculous—"I shouldn't be able to cry."

"I hope you don't suppose those are *real* tears?" Tweedledum interrupted in a tone of great contempt.

this is the reality. Or else I've really been with Sylvie, and this is a dream! Is Life itself a dream, I wonder?" In *Through the Looking Glass* Carroll returns to the question in the first paragraph of Chapter 8, in the closing lines of the book, and in the last line of the book's terminal poem.

An odd sort of infinite regress is involved here in the parallel dreams of Alice and the Red King. Alice dreams of the King, who is dreaming of Alice, who is dreaming of the King, and so on, like two mirrors facing each other, or that preposterous cartoon of Saul Steinberg's in which a fat lady paints a picture of a thin lady who is painting a• picture of the fat lady who is painting a picture of the thin lady, and so on deeper into the two canvases. (Cf. *Alice's Adventures in Wonderland,* Chapter 6, Note 8, and Chapter 12, Note 4.)

"I know they're talking nonsense," Alice thought to herself: "and it's foolish to cry about it." So she brushed away her tears, and went on, as cheerfully as she could, "At any rate I'd better be getting out of the wood, for really it's coming on very dark. Do you think it's going to rain?"

Tweedledum spread a large umbrella over himself and his brother, and looked up into it. "No, I don't think it is," he said: "at least—not under *here*. Nohow."

"But it may rain *outside?*"

"It may—if it chooses," said Tweedledee: "we've no objection. Contrariwise."

"Selfish things!" thought Alice, and she was just going to say "Good-night" and leave them, when Tweedledum sprang out from under the umbrella, and seized her by the wrist.

"Do you see *that?*" he said, in a voice choking with passion, and his eyes grew large and yellow all in a moment, as he pointed with a trembling finger at a small white thing lying under the tree.

"It's only a rattle," Alice said, after a careful examination of the little white thing. "Not a rattle-*snake,* you know," she added hastily, thinking that he was frightened: "only an old rattle—quite old and broken."

"I knew it was!" cried Tweedledum, beginning to stamp about wildly and tear his hair. "It's spoilt, of course!" Here he looᴋed at Tweedledee, who immediately sat down on the ground, and tried to hide himself under the umbrella.

Alice laid her hand upon his arm, and said, in a soothing tone, "You needn't be so angry about an old rattle."

"But it *isn't* old!" Tweedledum cried, in a greater fury than ever. "It's *new,* I tell you—I bought it yesterday—my nice NEW RATTLE!" and his voice rose to a perfect scream.

All this time Tweedledee was trying his best to fold up the umbrella, with himself in it: which was such an extraordinary thing to do, that it quite took off Alice's attention from the angry brother. But he couldn't quite succeed, and it ended in his rolling over, bundled up in the umbrella, with only his head out: and there he lay, opening and shutting his mouth and his large eyes—"looking more like a fish than anything else," Alice thought.

"Of course you agree to have a battle?" Tweedledum said in a calmer tone.

"I suppose so," the other sulkily replied, as he crawled out of the umbrella: "only *she* must help us to dress up, you know."

So the two brothers went off hand-in-hand into the wood, and returned in a minute with their arms full of things—such as bolsters, blankets, hearth-rugs, table-cloths, dish-covers, and coal-scuttles.

"I hope you're a good hand at pinning and tying strings?" Tweedledum remarked. "Every one of these things has got to go on, somehow or other."

Alice said afterwards she had never seen such a fuss made about anything in all her life—the way those two bustled about—and the quantity of things they put on—and the trouble they gave her in tying strings and fastening buttons — "Really they'll be more like bundles of old clothes than anything else, by the time they're ready!" she said to herself, as she arranged a bolster round the neck of Tweedledee, "to keep his head from being cut off," as he said.

"You know," he added very gravely, "it's one of the most serious things that can possibly happen to one in a battle— to get one's head cut off."

Alice laughed loud: but she managed to turn it into a cough, for fear of hurting his feelings.

"Do I look very pale?" said Tweedledum, coming up to have his helmet tied on. (He *called* it a helmet, though it certainly looked much more like a saucepan.)

"Well—yes—a *little*," Alice replied gently.

"I'm very brave, generally," he went on in a low voice: "only to-day I happen to have a headache."

"And *I've* got a toothache!" said

Tweedledee, who had overheard the remark. "I'm far worse than you!"

"Then you'd better not fight to-day,"
said Alice, thinking it a good opportunity
to make peace.

"We *must* have a bit of a fight, but I
don't care about going on long," said
Tweedledum, "What's the time now?"

Tweedledee looked at his watch, and
said "Half-past four."

"Let's fight till six, and then have dinner," said Tweedledum.

"Very well," the other said, rather
sadly: "and *she* can watch us—only you'd
better not come *very* close," he added: "I
generally hit every thing I can see—when
I get really excited."

"And *I* hit every thing within reach,"
cried Tweedledum, "whether I can see
it or not!"

Alice laughed. "You must hit the *trees*
pretty often, I should think," she said.

Tweedledum looked round him with
a satisfied smile. "I don't suppose," he
said, "there'll be a tree left standing, for
ever so far round, by the time we've finished!"

"And all about a rattle!" said Alice,
still hoping to make them a *little* ashamed
of fighting for such a trifle.

"I shouldn't have minded it so much,"
said Tweedledum, "if it hadn't been a
new one."

"I wish the monstrous crow would come!" thought Alice.

"There's only one sword, you know," Tweedledum said to his brother: "but *you* can have the umbrella—it's quite as sharp. Only we must begin quick. It's getting as dark as it can."

"And darker," said Tweedledee.

It was getting dark so suddenly that Alice thought there must be a thunderstorm coming on. "What a thick black cloud that is!" she said. "And how fast it comes! Why, I do believe it's got wings!"

"It's the crow!" Tweedledum cried out in a shrill voice of alarm; and the two brothers took to their heels and were out of sight in a moment.

Alice ran a little way into the wood, and stopped under a large tree. "It can never get at me *here*," she thought: "it's far too large to squeeze itself in among the trees. But I wish it wouldn't flap its wings so— it makes quite a hurricane in the wood— here's somebody's shawl being blown away!"

CHAPTER V

Wool and Water

She caught the shawl as she spoke, and looked about for the owner: in another moment the White Queen came running wildly through the wood, with both arms stretched out wide, as if she were flying,[1] and Alice very civilly went to meet her with the shawl.

"I'm very glad I happened to be in the way," Alice said, as she helped her to put on her shawl again.

The White Queen only looked at her in a helpless frightened sort of way, and kept repeating something in a whisper to herself that sounded like "Bread-and-butter, bread-and-butter," and Alice felt that if there was to be any conversation at all, she must manage it herself. So she began rather timidly: "Am I addressing the White Queen?"

"Well, yes, if you call that a-dressing,"

1. By running wildly to QB4, the White Queen arrives on the square directly west of Alice. The fact that queens do a lot of running throughout the story is an allusion to their power of moving an unlimited distance in all directions across the board. With characteristic carelessness the White Queen has just passed up an opportunity to checkmate the Red King by moving to K3. In his article "Alice on the Stage" Carroll writes of the White Queen as follows:

"Lastly, the White Queen seemed, to my dreaming fancy, gentle, stupid, fat and pale; helpless as an infant; and with a slow, maundering, bewildered air about her just *suggesting* imbecility, but never quite passing into it; that would be, I think, fatal to any comic effect she might otherwise produce. There is a character strangely like her in Wilkie Collins' novel *No Name:* by two different converging paths we have somehow reached the same ideal, and Mrs. Wragg and the White Queen might have been twin-sisters."

The role of the White Queen was played by Louise Fazenda in Paramount's film version.

the Queen said. "It isn't *my* notion of the thing, at all."

Alice thought it would never do to have an argument at the very beginning of their conversation, so she smiled and said "If your Majesty will only tell me the right way to begin, I'll do it as well as I can."

"But I don't want it done at all!" groaned the poor Queen. "I've been a-dressing myself for the last two hours."

It would have been all the better, as it seemed to Alice, if she had got some one else to dress her, she was so dreadfully untidy. "Every single thing's crooked," Alice thought to herself, "and she's all over pins!—May I put your shawl straight for you?" she added aloud.

"I don't know what's the matter with it!" the Queen said, in a melancholy voice. "It's out of temper, I think. I've pinned it here, and I've pinned it there, but there's no pleasing it!"

"It *can't* go straight, you know, if you pin it all on one side," Alice said, as she gently put it right for her; "and, dear me, what a state your hair is in!"

"The brush has got entangled in it!" the Queen said with a sigh. "And I lost the comb yesterday."

Alice carefully released the brush, and did her best to get the hair into order. "Come, you look rather better now!" she said, after altering most of the pins. "But really you should have a lady's-maid!"

"I'm sure I'll take *you* with pleasure!" the Queen said. "Twopence a week, and jam every other day."

Alice couldn't help laughing, as she said "I don't want you to hire *me*—and I don't care for jam."

"It's very good jam," said the Queen.

"Well, I don't want any *to-day*, at any rate."

"You couldn't have it if you *did* want it," the Queen said. "The rule is, jam to-morrow and jam yesterday—but never jam *to-day*."

"It *must* come sometimes to 'jam to-day,'" Alice objected.

"No, it can't," said the Queen. "It's jam every *other* day: to-day isn't any *other* day, you know."

"I don't understand you," said Alice. "It's dreadfully confusing!"

That's the effect of living backwards," the Queen said kindly: "it always makes one a little giddy at first—"

"Living backwards!" Alice repeated in great astonishment. "I never heard of such a thing!"[2]

"—but there's one great advantage in it, that one's memory works both ways."

"I'm sure *mine* only works one way," Alice remarked. "I can't remember things before they happen."

2. Since Carroll used it, the gimmick of "backward living" has been the basis of many fantasy and science-fiction tales. The best known is F. Scott Fitzgerald's story, "The Strange Case of Benjamin Button."

3. The King's Messenger, as Tenniel's illustration makes clear and as we shall see in Chapter 7, is none other than the Mad Hatter of the previous book.

"It's a poor sort of memory that only works backwards," the Queen remarked.

"What sort of things do *you* remember best?" Alice ventured to ask.

"Oh, things that happened the week after next," the Queen replied in a careless tone. "For instance, now," she went on, sticking a large piece of plaster on her finger as she spoke, "there's the King's Messenger.**3** He's in prison now, being punished: and the trial doesn't even begin till next Wednesday: and of course the crime comes last of all."

"Suppose he never commits the crime?" said Alice.

"That would be all the better, wouldn't it?" the Queen said, as she bound the plaster round her finger with a bit of ribbon.

Alice felt there was no denying *that*. "Of course it would be all the better," she said: "but it wouldn't be all the better his being punished."

"You're wrong *there,* at any rate," said the Queen. "Were *you* ever punished?"

"Only for faults," said Alice.

"And you were all the better for it, I know!" the Queen said triumphantly.

"Yes, but then I *had* done the things I was punished for," said Alice: "that makes all the difference."

"But if you *hadn't* done them," the Queen said, "that would have been better still; better, and better, and better!"

Her voice went higher with each "better," till it got quite to a squeak at last.

Alice was just beginning to say "There's a mistake somewhere—," when the Queen began screaming, so loud that she had to leave the sentence unfinished. "Oh, oh, oh!" shouted the Queen, shaking her hand about as if she wanted to shake it off. "My finger's bleeding! Oh, oh, oh, oh!"

Her screams were so exactly like the whistle of a steam-engine, that Alice had to hold both her hands over her ears.

"What *is* the matter?" she said, as soon as there was a chance of making herself heard. "Have you pricked your finger?"

"I haven't pricked it *yet,*" the Queen said, "but I soon shall—oh, oh, oh!"

"When do you expect to do it?" Alice asked, feeling very much inclined to laugh.

"When I fasten my shawl again," the poor Queen groaned out: "the brooch will come undone directly. Oh, oh!" As she said the words the brooch flew open, and the Queen clutched wildly at it, and tried to clasp it again.

"Take care!" cried Alice. "You're holding it all crooked!" And she caught at the brooch; but it was too late: the pin had slipped, and the Queen had pricked her finger.

"That accounts for the bleeding, you

see," she said to Alice with a smile. "Now you understand the way things happen here."

"But why don't you scream *now?*" Alice asked, holding her hands ready to put over her ears again.

"Why, I've done all the screaming already," said the Queen. "What would be the good of having it all over again?"

By this time it was getting light. "The crow must have flown away, I think," said Alice: "I'm so glad it's gone. I thought it was the night coming on."

"I wish *I* could manage to be glad!" the Queen said. "Only I never can remember the rule. You must be very happy, living in this wood, and being glad whenever you like!"

"Only it is so *very* lonely here!" Alice said in a melancholy voice; and, at the thought of her loneliness, two large tears came rolling down her cheeks.

"Oh, don't go on like that!" cried the poor Queen, wringing her hands in despair. "Consider what a great girl you are. Consider what a long way you've come to-day. Consider what o'clock it is. Consider anything, only don't cry!"

Alice could not help laughing at this, even in the midst of her tears. "Can *you* keep from crying by considering things?" she asked.

"That's the way it's done," the Queen said with great decision: "nobody can do two things at once, you know.**4** Let's consider your age to begin with—how old are you?"

"I'm seven and a half, exactly."

"You needn't say 'exactually,' " the Queen remarked. "I can believe it without that. Now I'll give *you* something to believe. I'm just one hundred and one, five months and a day."

"I can't believe *that!*" said Alice.

"Can't you?" the Queen said in a pitying tone. "Try again: draw a long breath, and shut your eyes."

Alice laughed. "There's no use trying," she said: "one *can't* believe impossible things."

"I daresay you haven't had much practice," said the Queen. "When I was your age, I always did it for half-an-hour a day. Why, sometimes I've believed as many as six impossible things before breakfast.**5** There goes the shawl again!"

The brooch had come undone as she spoke, and a sudden gust of wind blew the Queen's shawl across a little brook. The Queen spread out her arms again, and went flying after it,**6** and this time she succeeded in catching it for herself. "I've got it!" she cried in a triumphant tone. "Now you shall see me pin it on again, all by myself!"

"Then I hope your finger is better now?" Alice said very politely, as she crossed the little brook after the Queen.**7**

4. Carroll practiced the White Queen's advice. In his introduction to *Pillow Problems* he speaks of working mathematical problems in his head at night, during wakeful hours, as a kind of mental work-therapy to prevent less wholesome thoughts from tormenting him. "There are sceptical thoughts, which seem for the moment to uproot the firmest faith: there are blasphemous thoughts, which dart unbidden into the most reverent souls; there are unholy thoughts, which torture, with their hateful presence, the fancy that would fain be pure. Against all these some real mental work is a most helpful ally."

5. "I believe it," declared Tertullian in an oft-quoted defense of the paradoxical character of certain Christian doctrines, "because it is absurd." In a letter to child-friend Mary Macdonald, 1864, Carroll warned:

> "Don't be in such a hurry to believe next time—I'll tell you why—If you set to work to believe everything, you will tire out the muscles of your mind, and then you'll be so weak you won't be able to believe the simplest true things. Only last week a friend of mine set to work to believe Jack-the-giant-killer. He managed to do it, but he was so exhausted by it that when I told him it was raining (which was true) he *couldn't* believe it, but rushed out into the street without his hat or umbrella, the consequence of which was his hair got seriously damp, and one curl didn't recover its right shape for nearly two days."

6. The White Queen moves forward one square to QB5.

7. Alice likewise advances one square. This carries her to Q5 alongside of the Queen (now a sheep) again.

251

8. Williams and Madan, in their *Handbook of the Literature of the Rev. C. L. Dodgson,* reveal (and they reproduce a photograph to prove it) that Tenniel's two pictures of the shop faithfully copy the window and door of a small grocery shop at 83 Saint Aldgate's Street, Oxford. Tenniel was careful, however, to reverse the positions of door and window as well as the sign giving the price of tea as two shillings. These reversals support the view that Alice is not an anti-Alice (see Note 10, Chapter 1).

* * * * *

* * * * *

"Oh, much better!" cried the Queen, her voice rising into a squeak as she went on. "Much be-etter! Be-etter! Be-e-e-etter! Be-e-ehh!" The last word ended in a long bleat, so like a sheep that Alice quite started.

She looked at the Queen, who seemed to have suddenly wrapped herself up in wool. Alice rubbed her eyes, and looked again. She couldn't make out what had happened at all. Was she in a shop? And was that really—was it really a *sheep* that was sitting on the other side of the counter? Rub as she would, she could make nothing more of it: she was in a little dark shop,[8] leaning with her elbows on the counter, and opposite to her was an old Sheep, sitting in an arm-chair, knitting, and every now and then leaving off to look at her through a great pair of spectacles.

"What is it you want to buy?" the Sheep said at last, looking up for a moment from her knitting.

"I don't *quite* know yet," Alice said very gently. "I should like to look all round me first, if I might."

"You may look in front of you, and on both sides, if you like," said the Sheep; "but you can't look *all* round you—unless

you've got eyes at the back of your head."

But these, as it happened, Alice had *not* got: so she contented herself with turning round, looking at the shelves as she came to them.

The shop seemed to be full of all manner of curious things—but the oddest part of it all was that, whenever she looked hard at any shelf, to make out exactly what it had on it, that particular shelf was always quite empty, though the others round it were crowded as full as they could hold.[9]

"Things flow about so here!" she said at last in a plaintive tone, after she had spent a minute or so in vainly pursuing a large bright thing, that looked sometimes like a doll and sometimes like a work-box, and was always in the shelf next above the one she was looking at. "And this one is the most provoking of all—but I'll tell you what—" she added, as a sudden thought struck her. "I'll follow it up to the very top shelf of all. It'll puzzle it to go through the ceiling, I expect!"

But even this plan failed: the "thing" went through the ceiling as quietly as possible, as if it were quite used to it.

"Are you a child or a teetotum?"[10] the Sheep said, as she took up another pair of needles. "You'll make me giddy soon, if you go on turning round like that." She was now working with fourteen pairs at

9. Alice's difficulty in looking straight at the objects on sale in the shop has been compared by popularizers of quantum theory to the impossible task of pinning down the precise location of an electron in its path around the nucleus of an atom. One thinks also of those minute specks that sometimes appear slightly off the center of one's field of vision, and that can never be seen directly because they move as the eye moves.

10. A teetotum is a small top similar to what in England and the U.S. is now called a "put-and-take top." It was popular in Victorian England as a device used in children's games. The flat sides of the top are labeled with letters or numbers, and when the top comes to rest, the uppermost side indicates what the player is to do in the game. Early forms of the top were square-shaped and marked with letters. The letter T, on one of the sides, stood for the Latin word *totum,* indicating that the player took all.

11. In his prefatory poem to *Alice's Adventures in Wonderland,* Carroll describes the Liddell girls as rowing "with little skill." Perhaps Alice Liddell, on one of Carroll's rowboat excursions, was as mystified as Alice is here by the rowing term "feather." The Sheep is asking Alice to turn her oar blades horizontally as she moves them back for the next "catch" so that the lower edge of the blade will not drag through the water.

12. "Catching a crab" is British rowing slang for two kinds of rowing errors: (1) a failure to lift and feather the oar blade properly on the return stroke, with the result that the blade drags or slaps the water, (2) missing the water altogether in making a stroke. Owing to the motion of the boat, the first mistake can send the oar handle against one's chest with enough force to unseat the rower, an accident that happens to Alice later on.

once, and Alice couldn't help looking at her in great astonishment.

"How *can* she knit with so many?" the puzzled child thought to herself. "She gets more and more like a porcupine every minute!"

"Can you row?" the Sheep asked, handing her a pair of knitting-needles as she spoke.

"Yes, a little—but not on land—and not with needles—" Alice was beginning to say, when suddenly the needles turned into oars in her hands, and she found they were in a little boat, gliding along between banks: so there was nothing for it but to do her best.

"Feather!"**11** cried the Sheep, as she took up another pair of needles.

This didn't sound like a remark that needed any answer: so Alice said nothing, but pulled away. There was something very queer about the water, she thought, as every now and then the oars got fast in it, and would hardly come out again.

"Feather! Feather!" the Sheep cried again, taking more needles. "You'll be catching a crab directly."**12**

"A dear little crab!" thought Alice. "I should like that."

"Didn't you hear me say 'Feather'?" the Sheep cried angrily, taking up quite a bunch of needles.

"Indeed I did," said Alice: "you've said

it very often—and very loud. Please where *are* the crabs?"

"In the water, of course!" said the Sheep, sticking some of the needles into her hair, as her hands were full. "Feather, I say!"

"*Why* do you say 'Feather' so often?" Alice asked at last, rather vexed. "I'm not a bird!"

"You are," said the Sheep: "you're a little goose."

This offended Alice a little, so there was no more conversation for a minute or two, while the boat glided gently on,

sometimes among beds of weeds (which made the oars stick fast in the water, worse than ever), and sometimes under trees, but always with the same tall riverbanks frowning over their heads.

"Oh, please! There are some scented rushes!" Alice cried in a sudden transport of delight. "There really are—and *such* beauties!"

"You needn't say 'please' to *me* about 'em," the Sheep said, without looking up from her knitting: "I didn't put 'em there, and I'm not going to take 'em away."

"No, but I meant—please, may we wait and pick some?" Alice pleaded. "If you don't mind stopping the boat for a minute."

"How am *I* to stop it?" said the Sheep. "If you leave off rowing, it'll stop of itself."

So the boat was left to drift down the stream as it would, till it glided gently in among the waving rushes. And then the little sleeves were carefully rolled up, and the little arms were plunged in elbow-deep, to get hold of the rushes a good long way down before breaking them off—and for a while Alice forgot all about the Sheep and the knitting, as she bent over the side of the boat, with just the ends of her tangled hair dipping into the water—while with bright eager eyes she caught at one bunch after another of the darling scented rushes.

"I only hope the boat won't tipple over!" she said to herself. "Oh, *what* a lovely one! Only I couldn't quite reach it." And it certainly *did* seem a little provoking ("almost as if it happened on purpose," she thought) that, though she managed to pick plenty of beautiful rushes as the boat glided by, there was always a more lovely one that she couldn't reach.

"The prettiest are always further!" she said at last, with a sigh at the obstinacy of the rushes in growing so far off, as, with flushed cheeks and dripping hair and hands, she scrambled back into her place, and began to arrange her new-found treasures.

What mattered it to her just then that the rushes had begun to fade, and to lose all their scent and beauty, from the very moment that she picked them?[13] Even real scented rushes, you know, last only a very little while—and these, being dream-rushes, melted away almost like snow, as they lay in heaps at her feet—but Alice hardly noticed this, there were so many other curious things to think about.

They hadn't gone much farther before the blade of one of the oars got fast in the water and *wouldn't* come out again (so Alice explained it afterwards), and the consequence was that the handle of it caught her under the chin, and, in spite of a series of little shrieks of "Oh, oh, oh!" from poor Alice, it swept her straight off

13. It is possible that Carroll thought of these dream-rushes as symbols of his child-friends. The loveliest seem to be the most distant, just out of reach, and, once picked, they quickly fade and lose their scent and beauty. They are, of course, consciously intended symbols of the fleeting, short-lived, hard-to-keep quality of all beauty.

the seat, and down among the heap of rushes.

However, she wasn't a bit hurt, and was soon up again: the Sheep went on with her knitting all the while, just as if nothing had happened. "That was a nice crab you caught!" she remarked, as Alice got back into her place, very much relieved to find herself still in the boat.

"Was it? I didn't see it," said Alice, peeping cautiously over the side of the boat into the dark water. "I wish it hadn't let go—I should so like a little crab to take home with me!" But the Sheep only laughed scornfully, and went on with her knitting.

"Are there many crabs here?" said Alice.

"Crabs, and all sorts of things," said the Sheep: "plenty of choice, only make up your mind. Now, what *do* you want to buy?"

"To buy!" Alice echoed in a tone that was half astonished and half frightened—for the oars, and the boat, and the river, had vanished all in a moment, and she was back again in the little dark shop.

"I should like to buy an egg, please," she said timidly. "How do you sell them?"

"Fivepence farthing for one—twopence for two," the Sheep replied.

"Then two are cheaper than one?" Alice said in a surprised tone, taking out her purse.

"Only you *must* eat them both, if you buy two," said the Sheep.

"Then I'll have *one,* please," said Alice, as she put the money down on the counter. For she thought to herself, "They mightn't be at all nice, you know."[14]

The Sheep took the money, and put it away in a box: then she said "I never put things into people's hands—that would never do—you must get it for yourself." And so saying, she went off to the other end of the shop,[15] and set the egg upright on a shelf.

"I wonder *why* it wouldn't do?" thought Alice, as she groped her way among the tables and chairs, for the shop was very dark towards the end. "The egg seems to get further away the more I walk towards it. Let me see, is this a chair? Why, it's got branches, I declare! How very odd to find trees growing here! And actually here's a little brook! Well, this is the very queerest shop I ever saw!"[16]

* * * * *
* * * * *
* * * * *

So she went on, wondering more and more at every step, as everything turned into a tree the moment she came up to it, and she quite expected the egg to do the same.

14. Undergraduates at Christ Church, in Carroll's day, insisted that if you ordered one boiled egg for breakfast you usually received two, one good and one bad. (See *The Diaries of Lewis Carroll*, Vol. I, page 176.)

15. The Sheep's movement to the other end of the shop is indicated on the chessboard by a move of the White Queen to KB8.

16. The dots show that Alice has crossed the brook by advancing to Q6. She is now on the square to the right of the White King, although she does not meet him until after the Humpty Dumpty episode of the next chapter.

CHAPTER VI

Humpty Dumpty

However, the egg only got larger and larger, and more and more human: when she had come within a few yards of it, she saw that it had eyes and a nose and mouth; and, when she had come close to it, she saw clearly that it was HUMPTY DUMPTY himself. "It can't be anybody else!" she said to herself. "I'm as certain of it, as if his name were written all over his face!"

It might have been written a hundred times, easily, on that enormous face. Humpty Dumpty was sitting, with his legs crossed like a Turk, on the top of a high wall—such a narrow one that Alice quite wondered how he could keep his balance —and, as his eyes were steadily fixed in the opposite direction, and he didn't take the least notice of her, she thought he must be a stuffed figure, after all.

1. The Humpty Dumpty episode, like the episodes about the Jack of Hearts, the Tweedle twins, and the Lion and the Unicorn, elaborates on the incidents related in the familiar nursery rhyme. Another and quite different elaboration will be found in L. Frank Baum's first book for children, *Mother Goose in Prose,* 1897. In recent years Mr. Dumpty has been editing a children's magazine *(Humpty Dumpty's Magazine,* published by Parents Institute). I have had the privilege of working under him since the first issue, October 1952, as chronicler of the adventures of his son, Humpty Dumpty Junior. A high point in Paramount's film version of Alice was the portrayal of Humpty by W. C. Fields.

"And how exactly like an egg he is!" she said aloud, standing with her hands ready to catch him, for she was every moment expecting him to fall.

"It's *very* provoking," Humpty Dumpty said after a long silence, looking away from Alice as he spoke, "to be called an egg,—*very!*"

"I said you *looked* like an egg, Sir," Alice gently explained. "And some eggs are very pretty, you know," she added, hoping to turn her remark into a sort of compliment.

"Some people," said Humpty Dumpty, looking away from her as usual, "have no more sense than a baby!"

Alice didn't know what to say to this: it wasn't at all like conversation, she thought, as he never said anything to *her;* in fact, his last remark was evidently addressed to a tree—so she stood and softly repeated to herself:—1

> "Humpty Dumpty sat on a wall:
> Humpty Dumpty had a great fall.
> All the King's horses and all the King's men
> Couldn't put Humpty Dumpty in his place again."

"That last line is much too long for the poetry," she added, almost out loud, forgetting that Humpty Dumpty would hear her.

"Don't stand chattering to yourself like

that," Humpty Dumpty said, looking at her for the first time, "but tell me your name and your business."

"My *name* is Alice, but—"

"It's a stupid name enough!" Humpty Dumpty interrupted impatiently. "What does it mean?"

"Must a name mean something?" Alice asked doubtfully.

"Of course it must," Humpty Dumpty said with a short laugh: *"my* name means the shape I am—and a good handsome shape it is, too. With a name like yours, you might be any shape, almost."**2**

"Why do you sit out here all alone?" said Alice, not wishing to begin an argument.

"Why, because there's nobody with me!" cried Humpty Dumpty. "Did you think I didn't know the answer to *that?* Ask another."

"Don't you think you'd be safer down on the ground?" Alice went on, not with any idea of making another riddle, but simply in her good-natured anxiety for the queer creature. "That wall is so *very* narrow!"

"What tremendously easy riddles you ask!" Humpty Dumpty growled out. "Of course I don't think so! Why, if ever I *did* fall off—which there's no chance of— but *if* I did—" Here he pursed up his lips, and looked so solemn and grand that Alice could hardly help laughing. *"If* I

2. Peter Alexander, in his excellent paper "Logic and the Humor of Lewis Carroll" *(Proceedings of the Leeds Philosophical Society,* Vol. 6, May 1951, pages 551–66), calls attention to a Carrollian inversion here that is easily overlooked. In real life proper names seldom have a meaning other than the fact that they denote an individual object, whereas other words have general, universal meanings. In Humpty Dumpty's realm, the reverse is true. Ordinary words mean whatever Humpty wants them to mean, whereas proper names like "Alice" and "Humpty Dumpty" are supposed to have general significance. Mr. Alexander's thesis, with which one must heartily concur, is that Carroll's humor is strongly colored by his interest in formal logic.

did fall," he went on, *"the King has prom-ised me*—ah, you may turn pale, if you like! You didn't think I was going to say that, did you? *The King has promised me —with his very own mouth—*to—to—"

"To send all his horses and all his men," Alice interrupted, rather unwisely.

"Now I declare that's too bad!" Humpty Dumpty cried, breaking into a sudden passion. "You've been listening at doors—and behind trees—and down chimneys—or you couldn't have known it!"

"I haven't, indeed!" Alice said very gently. "It's in a book."

"Ah, well! They may write such things in a *book,*" Humpty Dumpty said in a calmer tone. "That's what you call a His-tory of England, that is. Now, take a good look at me! I'm one that has spoken to a King, *I* am: mayhap you'll never see such another: and, to show you I'm not proud, you may shake hands with me!"**3** And he

3. These remarks of Humpty (note also his frequent use of the word "proud" in the rest of his conversa-tion with Alice) reveal the pride that goeth before his fall.

grinned almost from ear to ear, as he leant forwards (and as nearly as possible fell off the wall in doing so) and offered Alice his hand. She watched him a little anxiously as she took it. "If he smiled much more the ends of his mouth might meet behind," she thought: "and then I don't know *what* would happen to his head! I'm afraid it would come off!"

"Yes, all his horses and all his men," Humpty Dumpty went on. "They'd pick me up again in a minute, *they* would! However, this conversation is going on a little too fast: let's go back to the last remark but one."

"I'm afraid I can't quite remember it," Alice said, very politely.

"In that case we start afresh," said Humpty Dumpty, "and it's my turn to choose a subject—" ("He talks about it just as if it was a game!" thought Alice.) "So here's a question for you. How old did you say you were?"

Alice made a short calculation, and said "Seven years and six months."

"Wrong!" Humpty Dumpty exclaimed triumphantly. "You never said a word like it!"

"I thought you meant 'How old *are* you?'" Alice explained.

"If I'd meant that, I'd have said it," said Humpty Dumpty.

Alice didn't want to begin another argument, so she said nothing.

4. As others have noted, this is the subtlest, grimmest, easiest-to-miss quip in the *Alice* books. No wonder that Alice, quick to catch an implication, changes the subject.

"Seven years and six months!" Humpty Dumpty repeated thoughtfully. "An uncomfortable sort of age. Now if you'd asked *my* advice, I'd have said 'Leave off at seven'—but it's too late now."

"I never ask advice about growing," Alice said indignantly.

"Too proud?" the other enquired.

Alice felt even more indignant at this suggestion. "I mean," she said, "that one can't help growing older."

"*One* can't, perhaps," said Humpty Dumpty; "but *two* can. With proper assistance, you might have left off at seven."**4**

"What a beautiful belt you've got on!" Alice suddenly remarked. (They had had quite enough of the subject of age, she thought: and, if they really were to take turns in choosing subjects, it was *her* turn now.) "At least," she corrected herself on second thoughts, "a beautiful cravat, I should have said—no, a belt, I mean—I beg your pardon!" she added in dismay, for Humpty Dumpty looked thoroughly offended, and she began to wish she hadn't chosen that subject. "If only I knew," she thought to herself, "which was neck and which was waist!"

Evidently Humpty Dumpty was very angry, though he said nothing for a minute or two. When he *did* speak again, it was in a deep growl.

"It is a—*most*—*provoking*—thing," he

said at last, "when a person doesn't know a cravat from a belt!"

"I know it's very ignorant of me," Alice said, in so humble a tone that Humpty Dumpty relented.

"It's a cravat, child, and a beautiful one, as you say. It's a present from the White King and Queen. There now!"

"Is it really?" said Alice, quite pleased to find that she *had* chosen a good subject, after all.

"They gave it me," Humpty Dumpty continued thoughtfully, as he crossed one knee over the other and clasped his hands round it, "they gave it me—for an un-birthday present."

"I beg your pardon?" Alice said with a puzzled air.

"I'm not offended," said Humpty Dumpty.

"I mean, what *is* an un-birthday present?"

"A present given when it isn't your birthday, of course."

Alice considered a little. "I like birthday presents best," she said at last.

"You don't know what you're talking about!" cried Humpty Dumpty. "How many days are there in a year?"

"Three hundred and sixty-five," said Alice.

"And how many birthdays have you?"

"One."

"And if you take one from three hun-

5. Humpty Dumpty is a philologist and philosopher skilled primarily in linguistic matters. Perhaps Carroll is suggesting here that such types, exceedingly plentiful both then and now in the Oxford area, are seldom gifted mathematically.

6. Lewis Carroll was fully aware of the profundity in Humpty Dumpty's whimsical discourse on semantics. Humpty takes the point of view known in the Middle Ages as nominalism; the view that universal terms do not refer to objective existences but are nothing more than *flatus vocis*, verbal utterances. The view was skillfully defended by William of Occam and is now held by almost all contemporary logical empiricists.

Even in logic and mathematics, where terms are usually more precise than in other subject matters, enormous confusion often results from a failure to realize that words mean "neither more nor less" than what they are intended to mean. In Carroll's time a lively controversy in formal logic concerned the "existential import" of Aristotle's four basic propositions. Do the universal statements "All A is B" and "No A is B" imply that A is a set that actually contains members? Is it implied in the particular statements "Some A is B" and "Some A is not B"?

Carroll answers these questions at some length on page 165 of his *Symbolic Logic*. The passage is worth quoting, for it is straight from the broad mouth of Humpty Dumpty.

The writers, and editors, of the Logical text-books which run in the ordinary grooves — to whom I shall hereafter refer by the (I hope inoffensive) title "The Logicians" — take, on this subject, what seems to me to be a more humble position than is at all necessary. They speak of the Copula of a Proposition "with bated breath"; almost as if it were a

dred and sixty-five, what remains?"

"Three hundred and sixty-four, of course."

Humpty Dumpty looked doubtful. "I'd rather see that done on paper," he said.[5]

Alice couldn't help smiling as she took out her memorandum-book, and worked the sum for him:

$$\frac{\begin{array}{r}365\\1\end{array}}{364}$$

Humpty Dumpty took the book, and looked at it carefully. "That seems to be done right—" he began.

"You're holding it upside down!" Alice interrupted.

"To be sure I was!" Humpty Dumpty said gaily, as she turned it round for him. "I thought it looked a little queer. As I was saying, that *seems* to be done right—though I haven't time to look it over thoroughly just now—and that shows that there are three hundred and sixty-four days when you might get un-birthday presents—"

"Certainly," said Alice.

"And only *one* for birthday presents, you know. There's glory for you!"

"I don't know what you mean by 'glory,'" Alice said.

Humpty Dumpty smiled contemptuously. "Of course you don't—till I tell you. I meant 'there's a nice knock-down argument for you!' "

"But 'glory' doesn't mean 'a nice knock-down argument,' " Alice objected.

"When *I* use a word," Humpty Dumpty said, in rather a scornful tone, "it means just what I choose it to mean—neither more nor less."

"The question is," said Alice, "whether you *can* make words mean so many different things."

"The question is," said Humpty Dumpty, "which is to be master—that's all."**6**

Alice was too much puzzled to say anything; so after a minute Humpty Dumpty began again. "They've a temper, some of them—particularly verbs: they're the proudest—adjectives you can do anything with, but not verbs—however, *I* can manage the whole lot of them! Impenetrability! That's what *I* say!"

"Would you tell me, please," said Alice, "what that means?"

"Now you talk like a reasonable child," said Humpty Dumpty, looking very much pleased. "I meant by 'impenetrability' that we've had enough of that subject, and it would be just as well if you'd mention what you mean to do next, as I suppose you don't mean to stop here all the rest of your life."

"That's a great deal to make one word mean," Alice said in a thoughtful tone.

living, conscious Entity, capable of declaring for itself what it chose to mean, and that we, poor human creatures, had nothing to do but to ascertain *what* was its sovereign will and pleasure, and submit to it.

In opposition to this view, I maintain that any writer of a book is fully authorised in attaching any meaning he likes to any word or phrase he intends to use. If I find an author saying, at the beginning of his book, "Let it be understood that by the word '*black*' I shall always mean '*white*', and that by the word '*white*' I shall always mean '*black*'," I meekly accept his ruling, however injudicious I may think it.

And so, with regard to the question whether a Proposition is or is not to be understood as asserting the existence of its Subject, I maintain that every writer may adopt his own rule, provided of course that it is consistent with itself and with the accepted facts of Logic.

Let us consider certain views that may *logically* be held, and thus settle which of them may *conveniently* be held; after which I shall hold myself free to declare which of them *I* intend to hold.

The view adopted by Carroll (that both "all" and "some" imply existence but that "no" leaves the question open) did not finally win out. In modern logic only the "some" propositions are taken to imply that a class is not a null class. This does not, of course, invalidate the nominalistic attitude of Carroll and his egg. The current point of view was adopted solely because logicians believed it to be the most useful.

When logicians shifted their interest from the class logic of Aristotle to the propositional or truth-value calculus, another furious and funny debate (though mostly among non-logicians) raged over the meaning of "material implication." Most of the confusion sprang from a failure to realize that "implies" in the statement "A implies B" has a restricted meaning peculiar to the calculus and does not refer to any causal relation between A and B. A similar confusion still persists in regard to the multivalued logics in which terms such as "and," "not," and "implies" have no common-sense or intuitive meaning; in fact, they have no meaning whatever other than that which is exactly defined by the matrix tables, which generate these "connective" terms. Once this is fully understood, most of the mystery surrounding these queer logics evaporates.

In mathematics equal amounts of energy have been dissipated in useless argumentation over the "meaning" of such phrases as "imaginary number," "transfinite number," and so on; useless because such words mean precisely what they are defined to mean; no more, no less.

On the other hand, if we wish to communicate accurately we are under a kind of moral obligation to avoid Humpty's practice of giving private meanings to commonly used words. "*May* we . . . make our words mean whatever we choose them to mean?" asks Roger W. Holmes in his article, "The Philosopher's Alice in Wonderland," *Antioch Review*, Summer 1959. "One thinks of a Soviet delegate using 'democracy' in a UN debate. May we pay our words extra, or is this the stuff that propaganda is made of? Do we have an obligation to past usage? In one sense words are our masters, or communication would be impossible. In another we are the masters; otherwise there could be no poetry."

"When I make a word do a lot of work like that," said Humpty Dumpty, "I always pay it extra."

"Oh!" said Alice. She was too much puzzled to make any other remark.

"Ah, you should see 'em come round me of a Saturday night," Humpty Dumpty went on, wagging his head gravely from side to side, "for to get their wages, you know."

(Alice didn't venture to ask what he paid them with; and so you see I can't tell *you*.)

"You seem very clever at explaining words, Sir," said Alice. "Would you kindly tell me the meaning of the poem called 'Jabberwocky'?"

"Let's hear it," said Humpty Dumpty. "I can explain all the poems that ever were invented—and a good many that haven't been invented just yet."

This sounded very hopeful, so Alice repeated the first verse:—

> " 'Twas brillig, and the slithy toves
>   Did gyre and gimble in the wabe:
> All mimsy were the borogoves,
>   And the mome raths outgrabe."

"That's enough to begin with," Humpty Dumpty interrupted: "there are plenty of hard words there. *'Brillig'* means four o'clock in the afternoon—the time when you begin *broiling* things for dinner."

"That'll do very well," said Alice: "and *'slithy'*?"

"Well, *slithy* means 'lithe and slimy.' 'Lithe' is the same as 'active.' You see it's like a portmanteau—there are two meanings packed up into one word."**7**

"I see it now," Alice remarked thoughtfully: "and what are *'toves'*?" .. ..

"Well, *'toves'* are something like badgers—they're something like lizards—and they're something like corkscrews."

"They must be very curious-looking creatures."

"They are that," said Humpty Dumpty: "also they make their nests under sundials—also they live on cheese."

7. "Portmanteau word" will be found in many modern dictionaries. It has become a common phrase for words that are packed, like a suitcase, with more than one meaning. In English literature, the great master of the portmanteau word is, of course, James Joyce. *Finnegans Wake* (like the *Alice* books, a dream) contains them by the tens of thousands. This includes those ten hundred-letter thunderclaps that symbolize, among other things, the mighty fall from his ladder of Tim Finnegan, the Irish hod carrier. Humpty Dumpty himself is packed up in the seventh thunderclap:

Bothallchoractorschumminaroundgansumuminarumdrumstrumtruminahumptadumpwaultopoofoolooderamaunsturnup!

8. Some readers may not be as quick as Alice to catch Humpty's point here: each of the three "ways" is followed by a word beginning with "be."

9. "From home," spoken with a dropped "h," produces the "mome" sound.

"And what's to *'gyre'* and to *"gimble'*?"

"To *'gyre'* is to go round and round like a gyroscope. To *'gimble'* is to make holes like a gimlet."

"And *'the wabe'* is the grass-plot round a sun-dial, I suppose?" said Alice, surprised at her own ingenuity.

"Of course it is. It's called *'wabe,'* you know, because it goes a long way before it, and a long way behind it—"

"And a long way beyond it on each side,"**8** Alice added.

"Exactly so. Well then, *'mimsy'* is 'flimsy and miserable' (there's another portmanteau for you). And a *'borogove'* is a thin shabby-looking bird with its feathers sticking out all round—something like a live mop."

"And then *'mome raths'*?" said Alice. "I'm afraid I'm giving you a great deal of trouble."

"Well, a *'rath'* is a sort of green pig: but *'mome'* I'm not certain about. I think it's short for 'from home'—meaning that they'd lost their way, you know."**9**

"And what does *'outgrabe'* mean?"

"Well, *'outgribing'* is something between bellowing and whistling, with a kind of sneeze in the middle: however, you'll hear it done, maybe—down in the wood yonder—and, when you've once heard it, you'll be *quite* content. Who's been repeating all that hard stuff to you?"

"I read it in a book," said Alice. "But

I *had* some poetry repeated to me much easier than that, by—Tweedledee, I think it was."

"As to poetry, you know," said Humpty Dumpty, stretching out one of his great hands, "*I* can repeat poetry as well as other folk, if it comes to that—"

"Oh, it needn't come to that!" Alice hastily said, hoping to keep him from beginning.

"The piece I'm going to repeat," he went on without noticing her remark, "was written entirely for your amusement."

Alice felt that in that case she really *ought* to listen to it; so she sat down, and said "Thank you" rather sadly.

> "In winter, when the fields are white,
> I sing this song for your delight—

only I don't sing it," he added, as an explanation.

"I see you don't," said Alice.

"If you can *see* whether I'm singing or not, you've sharper eyes than most," Humpty Dumpty remarked severely. Alice was silent.

> "In spring, when woods are getting green,
> I'll try and tell you what I mean:"

"Thank you very much," said Alice.

> "In summer, when the days are long,
> Perhaps you'll understand the song:

> In autumn, when the leaves are
>   brown,
>
> Take pen and ink, and write it
>   down."

"I will, if I can remember it so long,"
said Alice.

"You needn't go on making remarks
like that," Humpty Dumpty said: "they're
not sensible, and they put me out."

> "I sent a message to the fish:
> I told them 'This is what I wish.'
>
> The little fishes of the sea,
> They sent an answer back to me.
>
> The little fishes' answer was
> 'We cannot do it, Sir, because—' "

"I'm afraid I don't quite understand,"
said Alice.

"It gets easier further on," Humpty
Dumpty replied.

> "I sent to them again to say
> 'It will be better to obey.'
>
> The fishes answered, with a grin,
> 'Why, what a temper you are in!'
>
> I told them once, I told them twice:
> They would not listen to advice.
>
> I took a kettle large and new,
> Fit for the deed I had to do.
>
> My heart went hop, my heart went
>   thump:
> I filled the kettle at the pump.
>
> Then some one came to me and said
> 'The little fishes are in bed.'

I said to him, I said it plain,
'Then you must wake them up again.'

I said it very loud and clear:
I went and shouted in his ear."

Humpty Dumpty raised his voice almost to a scream as he repeated this verse, and Alice thought, with a shudder, "I wouldn't have been the messenger for *anything!*"

"But he was very stiff and proud:
He said 'You needn't shout so loud!'"

And he was very proud and stiff:
He said 'I'd go and wake them, if—'

I took a corkscrew from the shelf:
I went to wake them up myself.

And when I found the door was
locked,
I pulled and pushed and kicked and
knocked.

And when I found the door was shut,
I tried to turn the handle, but—"

There was a long pause.
"Is that all?" Alice timidly asked.
"That's all," said Humpty Dumpty. "Good-bye."

This was rather sudden, Alice thought: but, after such a *very* strong hint that she ought to be going, she felt that it would hardly be civil to stay. So she got up, and held out her hand. "Good-bye, till we meet again!" she said as cheerfully as she could.

10. Students of *Finnegans Wake* do not have to be reminded that Humpty Dumpty is one of that book's basic symbols: the great cosmic egg whose fall, like the drunken fall of Finnegan, suggests the fall of Lucifer and the fall of man.

"I shouldn't know you again if we *did* meet," Humpty Dumpty replied in a discontented tone, giving her one of his fingers to shake: "you're so exactly like other people."

"The face is what one goes by, generally," Alice remarked in a thoughtful tone.

"That's just what I complain of," said Humpty Dumpty. "Your face is the same as everybody has—the two eyes, so—" (marking their places in the air with his thumb) "nose in the middle, mouth under. It's always the same. Now if you had the two eyes on the same side of the nose, for instance—or the mouth at the top— that would be *some* help."

"It wouldn't look nice," Alice objected. But Humpty Dumpty only shut his eyes, and said "Wait till you've tried."

Alice waited a minute to see if he would speak again, but, as he never opened his eyes or took any further notice of her, she said "Good-bye!" once more, and, getting no answer to this, she quietly walked away: but she couldn't help saying to herself, as she went, "Of all the unsatisfactory—" (she repeated this aloud, as it was a great comfort to have such a long word to say) "of all the unsatisfactory people I *ever* met—" She never finished the sentence, for at this moment a heavy crash shook the forest from end to end.[10]

CHAPTER VII

The Lion and the Unicorn

The next moment soldiers came running through the wood, at first in twos and threes, then ten or twenty together, and at last in such crowds that they seemed to fill the whole forest. Alice got behind a tree, for fear of being run over, and watched them go by.

She thought that in all her life she had never seen soldiers so uncertain on their feet: they were always tripping over something or other, and whenever one went down, several more always fell over him, so that the ground was soon covered with little heaps of men.

Then came the horses. Having four feet, these managed rather better than the foot-soldiers; but even *they* stumbled now and then; and it seemed to be a regular rule that, whenever a horse stumbled, the rider fell off instantly. The confusion

got worse every moment, and Alice was
very glad to get out of the wood into an
open place, where she found the White
King seated on the ground, busily writing
in his memorandum-book.

"I've sent them all!" the King cried in
a tone of delight, on seeing Alice. "Did
you happen to meet any soldiers, my dear,
as you came through the wood?"

"Yes, I did," said Alice: "several thousand, I should think."

"Four thousand two hundred and
seven, that's the exact number," the King
said, referring to his book. "I couldn't

278

send all the horses, you know, because two of them are wanted in the game.[1] And I haven't sent the two Messengers, either. They're both gone to the town. Just look along the road, and tell me if you can see either of them."

"I see nobody on the road," said Alice.

"I only wish *I* had such eyes," the King remarked in a fretful tone. "To be able to see Nobody! And at that distance too! Why, it's as much as *I* can do to see real people, by this light!"

All this was lost on Alice, who was still looking intently along the road, shading her eyes with one hand. "I see somebody now!" she exclaimed at last. "But he's coming very slowly—and what curious attitudes he goes into!" (For the Messenger kept skipping up and down, and wriggling like an eel, as he came along, with his great hands spread out like fans on each side.)

"Not at all," said the King. "He's an Anglo-Saxon Messenger—and those are Anglo-Saxon attitudes.[2] He only does them when he's happy. His name is Haigha.[3] (He pronounced it so as to rhyme with 'mayor.')

"I love my love with an H,"[4] Alice couldn't help beginning, "because he is Happy. I hate him with an H because he is Hideous. I fed him with—with—with Ham-sandwiches and Hay. His name is Haigha, and he lives—"

1. The two horses are needed in the chess game to provide steeds for the two white knights.

2. In his references to Anglo-Saxon attitudes Carroll is spoofing the Anglo-Saxon scholarship fashionable in his day. Harry Morgan Ayres, in his book *Carroll's Alice*, reproduces some drawings of Anglo-Saxons in various costumes and attitudes, from the Caedmon Manuscript of the Junian codex (owned by Oxford's Bodleian Library), and suggests that they may have been used as a source by both Carroll and Tenniel. A recent novel by Angus Wilson, *Anglo-Saxon Attitudes,* quotes this passage of Carroll's on the title page.

3. Haigha, as the illustrations make clear, is our old friend the March Hare. It has already been noted (Chapter 5) that Hatta, the other messenger, is the Mad Hatter, just released from the prison to which he was confined at the close of the previous book.

4. "I love my love with an A" was a popular parlor game in Victorian England. The first player recited:

> I love my love with an A because
> he's ———.
> I hate him because he's ———.
> He took me to the Sign of
> the ———
> And treated me with———.
> His name's ———
> And he lives at ———.

In each blank space the player used a suitable word beginning with "A." The second player then repeated the same lines, using "B" instead of "A," and the game continued in this fashion through the alphabet. Players unable to supply an acceptable word dropped out of the game. The wording of the recitation varied; the lines quoted above are taken from James Orchard Halliwell's *The Nursery*

Rhymes of England, a book popular in Carroll's day. It was clever of Alice to start the game with "H" instead of "A," for the Anglo-Saxon Messengers undoubtedly dropped their "H's."

5. Taking phrases literally instead of as they are commonly understood is characteristic of the creatures behind the looking-glass, and a basis for much of Carroll's humor. Another good example occurs in Chapter 9, when the Red Queen tells Alice that she couldn't deny something if she tried with both hands.

One of Carroll's most amusing hoaxes furnishes still another instance of his fondness for this variety of nonsense. In 1873, when Ella Monier - Williams (a child-friend) let him borrow her travel diary, he returned the book with the following letter:

MY DEAR ELLA,
I return your book with many thanks; you will be wondering why I kept it so long. I understand, from what you said about it, that you have no idea

"He lives on the Hill," the King remarked simply, without the least idea that he was joining in the game, while Alice was still hesitating for the name of a town beginning with H. "The other Messenger's called Hatta. I must have *two,* you know—to come and go. One to come, and one to go."

"I beg your pardon?" said Alice.

"It isn't respectable to beg," said the King.

"I only meant that I didn't understand," said Alice. "Why one to come and one to go?"

"Don't I tell you?" the King repeated impatiently. "I must have *two*—to fetch and carry. One to fetch, and one to carry."

At this moment the Messenger arrived: he was far too much out of breath to say a

word, and could only wave his hands about, and make the most fearful faces at the poor King.

"This young lady loves you with an H," the King said, introducing Alice in the hope of turning off the Messenger's attention from himself—but it was of no use—the Anglo-Saxon attitudes only got more extraordinary every moment, while the great eyes rolled wildly from side to side.

"You alarm me!" said the King. "I feel faint—Give me a ham sandwich!"

On which the Messenger, to Alice's great amusement, opened a bag that hung round his neck, and handed a sandwich to the King, who devoured it greedily.

"Another sandwich!" said the King.

"There's nothing but hay left now," the Messenger said, peeping into the bag.

"Hay, then," the King murmured in a faint whisper.

Alice was glad to see that it revived him a good deal. "There's nothing like eating hay when you're faint," he remarked to her, as he munched away.

"I should think throwing cold water over you would be better," Alice suggested: "—or some sal-volatile."

"I didn't say there was nothing *better*," the King replied. "I said there was nothing *like* it." Which Alice did not venture to deny.**5**

"Who did you pass on the road?" the

of publishing any of it yourself, and hope you will not be annoyed at my sending three short chapters of extracts from it, to be published in *The Monthly Packet*. I have not given any names in full, nor put any more definite title to it than simply "Ella's Diary, or The Experiences of an Oxford Professor's Daughter, during a' Month of Foreign Travel."
I will faithfully hand over to you any money I may receive on account of it, from Miss Yonge, the editor of *The Monthly Packet*.
　　　Your affect. friend,
　　　　　　C. L. Dodgson.

Ella suspected that he was joking, but began to take him seriously when she received a second letter containing the following passage:

I grieve to tell you that *every word of my letter was strictly true*. I will now tell you more—that Miss Yonge *has not declined* the MS., but she will not give more than a guinea a chapter. Will that be enough?

Carroll's third letter cleared up the hoax:

My dear Ella,
I'm afraid I have hoaxed you too much. But it really was true. I "hoped you wouldn't be annoyed at my etc.," for the very good reason that I hadn't done it. And I gave no *other* title than "Ella's Diary," nor did I give *that* title. Miss Yonge hasn't declined it—because she hasn't seen it. And I need hardly explain that she hasn't given more than three guineas!
Not for three hundred guineas would I have shown it to *any* one—after I had promised you I wouldn't.
In haste,
　　　Yours affectionately,
　　　　　　C. L. D.

King went on, holding out his hand to the Messenger for some more hay.

"Nobody," said the Messenger.

"Quite right," said the King: "this young lady saw him too. So of course Nobody walks slower than you."

"I do my best," the Messenger said in a sullen tone. "I'm sure nobody walks much faster than I do!"

"He can't do that," said the King, "or else he'd have been here first. However, now you've got your breath, you may tell us what's happened in the town."

"I'll whisper it," said the Messenger, putting his hands to his mouth in the shape of a trumpet and stooping so as to get close to the King's ear. Alice was sorry for this, as she wanted to hear the news too. However, instead of whispering, he simply shouted, at the top of his voice, "They're at it again!"

"Do you call *that* a whisper?" cried the poor King, jumping up and shaking himself. "If you do such a thing again, I'll have you buttered! It went through and through my head like an earthquake!"

"It would have to be a very tiny earthquake!" thought Alice. "Who are at it again?" she ventured to ask.

"Why, the Lion and the Unicorn, of course," said the King.

"Fighting for the crown?"

"Yes, to be sure," said the King: "and the best of the joke is, that it's *my* crown

all the while! Let's run and see them."
And they trotted off, Alice repeating to
herself, as she ran, the words of the old
song:6

"The Lion and the Unicorn were fighting for
the crown:
The Lion beat the Unicorn all round the
town.
Some gave them white bread, some gave them
brown:
Some gave them plum-cake and drummed
them out of town."

"Does—the one—that wins—get the
crown?" she asked, as well as she could,
for the run was putting her quite out of
breath.

"Dear me, no!" said the King. "What
an idea!"7

"Would you—be good enough—"
Alice panted out, after running a little
further, "to stop a minute—just to get
—one's breath again?"

"I'm *good* enough," the King said,
"only I'm not *strong* enough. You see, a
minute goes by so fearfully quick. You
might as well try to stop a Bandersnatch!"

Alice had no more breath for talking;
so they trotted on in silence, till they
came into sight of a great crowd, in the
middle of which the Lion and Unicorn
were fighting. They were in such a cloud
of dust, that at first Alice could not make
out which was which; but she soon man-

6. According to the Oxford Dictionary of Nursery Rhymes, rivalry between the lion and unicorn goes back for thousands of years. The nursery rhyme is popularly supposed to have arisen in the early seventeenth century when the union of Scotland and England resulted in a new British coat of arms on which the Scottish unicorn and the British lion appear, as they do today, as the two supporters of the royal arms.

7. If Carroll intended his Lion and Unicorn to represent Gladstone and Disraeli (see Note 10 below), then this dialogue takes on an obvious meaning. Carroll, who was conservative in his political views and did not care for Gladstone, composed two remarkable anagrams on the full name, William Ewart Gladstone. They are: "Wilt tear down *all* images?" and "Wild agitator! Means well." (See *The Diaries of Lewis Carroll*, Vol. II, page 277.)

aged to distinguish the Unicorn by his horn.

They placed themselves close to where Hatta, the other Messenger, was standing watching the fight, with a cup of tea in one hand and a piece of bread-and-butter in the other.

"He's only just out of prison, and he hadn't finished his tea when he was sent in," Haigha whispered to Alice: "and they only give them oyster-shells in there —so you see he's very hungry and thirsty. How are you, dear child?" he went on, putting his arm affectionately round Hatta's neck.

Hatta looked round and nodded, and went on with his bread-and-butter.

"Were you happy in prison, dear child?" said Haigha.

Hatta looked round once more, and this time a tear or two trickled down his cheek; but not a word would he say.

"Speak, can't you!" Haigha cried impatiently. But Hatta only munched away, and drank some more tea.

"Speak, won't you!" cried the King. "How are they getting on with the fight?"

Hatta made a desperate effort, and swallowed a large piece of bread-and-butter. "They're getting on very well," he said in a choking voice: "each of them has been down about eighty-seven times."

"Then I suppose they'll soon bring the

white bread and the brown?" Alice ventured to remark.

"It's waiting for 'em now," said Hatta; "this is a bit of it as I'm eating."

There was a pause in the fight just then, and the Lion and the Unicorn sat down, panting, while the King called out "Ten minutes allowed for refreshments!" Haigha and Hatta set to work at once, carrying round trays of white and brown bread. Alice took a piece to taste, but it was *very* dry.

"I don't think they'll fight any more to-day," the King said to Hatta: "go and order the drums to begin." And Hatta went bounding away like a grasshopper.

For a minute or two Alice stood silent, watching him. Suddenly she brightened

8. The White Queen is moving from a square due west of the Red Knight to QB8. She really doesn't have to flee — the Knight could not have taken her, whereas she could have taken him — but the move is characteristic of her stupidity.

up. "Look, look!" she cried, pointing eagerly. "There's the White Queen running across the country![8] She came flying out of the wood over yonder—How fast those Queens *can* run!"

"There's some enemy after her, no doubt," the King said, without even looking round. "That wood's full of them."

"But aren't you going to run and help her?" Alice asked, very much surprised at his taking it so quietly.

"No use, no use!" said the King. "She runs so fearfully quick. You might as well try to catch a Bandersnatch! But I'll make a memorandum about her, if you like— She's a dear good creature," he repeated softly to himself, as he opened his memorandum-book. "Do you spell 'creature' with a double 'e'?"

At this moment the Unicorn sauntered by them, with his hands in his pockets. "I had the best of it this time?" he said to the King, just glancing at him as he passed.

"A little—a little," the King replied, rather nervously. "You shouldn't have run him through with your horn, you know."

"It didn't hurt him," the Unicorn said carelessly, and he was going on, when his eye happened to fall upon Alice: he turned round instantly, and stood for some time looking at her with an air of the deepest disgust.

"What—is—this?" he said at last.

"This is a child!" Haigha replied eagerly, coming in front of Alice to introduce her, and spreading out both his hands towards her in an Anglo-Saxon attitude. "We only found it to-day. It's as large as life, and twice as natural!"**9**

"I always thought they were fabulous monsters!" said the Unicorn. "Is it alive?"

"It can talk," said Haigha solemnly.

The Unicorn looked dreamily at Alice, and said "Talk, child."

Alice could not help her lips curling up into a smile as she began: "Do you know, I always thought Unicorns were fabulous monsters, too? I never saw one alive before!"

"Well, now that we *have* seen each other," said the Unicorn, "if you'll believe in me, I'll believe in you. Is that a bargain?"

"Yes, if you like," said Alice.

"Come, fetch out the plum-cake, old man!" the Unicorn went on, turning from her to the King. "None of your brown bread for me!"

"Certainly—certainly!" the King muttered, and beckoned to Haigha. "Open the bag!" he whispered. "Quick! Not that one—that's full of hay!"

Haigha took a large cake out of the bag, and gave it to Alice to hold, while he got out a dish and carving-knife. How they all came out of it Alice couldn't guess.

9. "As large as life and *quite* as natural" was a common phrase in Carroll's time (the Oxford English Dictionary quotes it from an 1853 source); but apparently Carroll was the first to substitute "twice" for "quite." This is now the usual phrasing in both England and the U.S.

10. It was widely believed in England that Tenniel's lion and unicorn, in the illustration for this scene, were intended as caricatures of Gladstone and Disraeli respectively. There is no proof of this; but they do resemble Tenniel's *Punch* cartoons of the two political figures who often sparred with each other.

It was just like a conjuring-trick, she thought.

The Lion had joined them while this was going on: he looked very tired and sleepy, and his eyes were half shut. "What's this!" he said, blinking lazily at Alice, and speaking in a deep hollow tone that sounded like the tolling of a great bell.**10**

"Ah, what *is* it, now?" the Unicorn cried eagerly. "You'll never guess! *I* couldn't."

The Lion looked at Alice wearily. "Are you animal—or vegetable—or mineral?" he said, yawning at every other word.

"It's a fabulous monster!" the Unicorn cried out, before Alice could reply.

"Then hand round the plum-cake,

Monster," the Lion said, lying down and putting his chin on his paws. "And sit down, both of you," (to the King and the Unicorn): "fair play with the cake, you know!"

The King was evidently very uncomfortable at having to sit down between the two great creatures; but there was no other place for him.

"What a fight we might have for the crown, *now!*" the Unicorn said, looking slyly up at the crown, which the poor King was nearly shaking off his head, he trembled so much.

"I should win easy," said the Lion.

"I'm not so sure of that," said the Unicorn.

"Why, I beat you all round the town, you chicken!" the Lion replied angrily, half getting up as he spoke.

Here the King interrupted, to prevent the quarrel going on: he was very nervous, and his voice quite quivered. "All round the town?" he said. "That's a good long way. Did you go by the old bridge, or the market-place? You get the best view by the old bridge."

"I'm sure I don't know," the Lion growled out as he lay down again. "There was too much dust to see anything. What a time the Monster is, cutting up that cake!"

Alice had seated herself on the bank of a little brook, with the great dish on her

10a. That is, a "lion's share." The phrase comes from a fable of Aesop's that tells how a group of beasts divided the spoils of a hunt. The lion demanded one-fourth in virtue of his rank, another fourth for his superior courage, a third quarter for his wife and children. As for the remaining fourth, the lion adds, anyone who wishes to dispute it with him is free to do so.

11. Alice advances to Q7.

knees, and was sawing away diligently with the knife. "It's very provoking!" she said, in reply to the Lion (she was getting quite used to being called 'the Monster'). "I've cut several slices already, but they always join on again!"

"You don't know how to manage Looking-glass cakes," the Unicorn remarked. "Hand it round first, and cut it afterwards."

This sounded nonsense, but Alice very obediently got up, and carried the dish round, and the cake divided itself into three pieces as she did so. "*Now* cut it up," said the Lion, as she returned to her place with the empty dish.

"I say, this isn't fair!" cried the Unicorn, as Alice sat with the knife in her hand, very much puzzled how to begin. "The Monster has given the Lion twice as much as me!"**10a**

"She's kept none for herself, anyhow," said the Lion. "Do you like plum-cake, Monster?"

But before Alice could answer him, the drums began.

Where the noise came from, she couldn't make out: the air seemed full of it, and it rang through and through her head till she felt quite deafened. She started to her feet and sprang across the little brook in her terror,**11** and had just

* * * * * *
* * * * * *

time to see the Lion and the Unicorn rise
to their feet, with angry looks at being interrupted in their feast, before she
dropped to her knees, and put her hands
over her ears, vainly trying to shut out
the dreadful uproar.

"If *that* doesn't 'drum them out of
town,' " she thought to herself, "nothing
ever will!"

CHAPTER VIII

"It's My Own Invention"

After a while the noise seemed gradually to die away, till all was dead silence, and Alice lifted up her head in some alarm. There was no one to be seen, and her first thought was that she must have been dreaming about the Lion and the Unicorn and those queer Anglo-Saxon Messengers. However, there was the great dish still lying at her feet, on which she had tried to cut the plum-cake, "So I wasn't dreaming, after all," she said to herself, "unless—unless we're all part of the same dream. Only I do hope it's *my* dream, and not the Red King's! I don't like belonging to another person's dream," she went on in a rather complaining tone: "I've a great mind to go and wake him, and see what happens!"

At this moment her thoughts were interrupted by a loud shouting of "Ahoy!

1. The Red Knight has moved to
K2; a powerful move in a conventional chess game, for he simultaneously checks the White King
and attacks the White Queen. The
Queen is lost unless the Red
Knight can be removed from the
board.

2. The White Knight, landing on
the square occupied by the Red
Knight (the square adjacent to
Alice on her east side), absentmindedly shouts, "Check!"; actually he checks only his own King.
The defeat of the Red Knight indicates a move of Kt. X Kt. in the
chess game.

Ahoy! Check!" and a Knight, dressed in
crimson armour, came galloping down
upon her, brandishing a great club.[1] Just
as he reached her, the horse stopped suddenly: "You're my prisoner!" the Knight
cried, as he tumbled off his horse.

Startled as she was, Alice was more
frightened for him than for herself at the
moment, and watched him with some
anxiety as he mounted again. As soon as
he was comfortably in the saddle, he began once more. "You're my—" but here
another voice broke in "Ahoy! Ahoy!
Check!" and Alice looked round in some
surprise for the new enemy.

This time it was a White Knight.[2] He
drew up at Alice's side, and tumbled off
his horse just as the Red Knight had done:
then he got on again, and the two Knights
sat and looked at each other for some
time without speaking. Alice looked from
one to the other in some bewilderment.

"She's *my* prisoner, you know!" the
Red Knight said at last.

"Yes, but then *I* came and rescued her!"
the White Knight replied.

"Well, we must fight for her, then,"
said the Red Knight, as he took up his
helmet (which hung from the saddle, and
was something the shape of a horse's
head) and put it on.

"You will observe the Rules of Battle,
of course?" the White Knight remarked,
putting on his helmet too.

"I always do," said the Red Knight, and they began banging away at each other with such fury that Alice got behind a tree to be out of the way of the blows.

"I wonder, now, what the Rules of Battle are," she said to herself, as she watched the fight, timidly peeping out from her hiding-place. "One Rule seems to be, that if one Knight hits the other, he knocks him off his horse; and, if he misses, he tumbles off himself—and another Rule seems to be that they hold their clubs with their arms, as if they were Punch and Judy—3 What a noise they make when they tumble! Just like a whole set of fire-irons falling into the fender! And how

3. Carroll may be suggesting here that the knights, like Punch and Judy, are merely puppets moved by the hands of the invisible players of the game. Note that Tenniel, unlike modern illustrators in his scrupulous following of the text, shows the knights holding their clubs in traditional Punch-and-Judy fashion.

4. Many Carrollian scholars have surmised, and with good reason, that Carroll intended the White Knight to be a caricature of himself. Like the knight, Carroll had shaggy hair, mild blue eyes, a kind and gentle face. Like the knight, his mind seemed to function best when it saw things in topsy-turvy fashion. Like the knight, he was fond of curious gadgets and a "great hand at inventing things." He was forever "thinking of a way" to do this or that a bit differently. Many of his inventions, like the knight's blotting-paper pudding, were very clever but unlikely ever to be made (though some turned out to be not so useless when others reinvented them decades later).

Carroll's inventions include a chess set for travelers, with holes to hold pegged pieces; a cardboard grill (he called it a Nyctograph) to assist one in writing in the dark; a postage-stamp case with two "pictorial surprises" (see Chapter 6, Note 4, of *Alice's Adventures in Wonderland*). His diary contains such entries as: "The idea occurred to me that a game might be made of letters, to be moved about on a chess-board till they form words" (Dec. 19, 1880); "Concocted a new 'Proportional Representation' scheme, far the best I have yet devised. . . . Also invented rules for testing Divisibility of a number by 17 and by 19. An inventive day!" (June 3, 1884); "Invented a substitute for gum, for fastening envelopes . . . , mounting small things in books, etc. — viz: paper with gum on *both* sides." (June 18, 1896); "Thought of a plan for simplifying money-orders, by making the sender fill up two duplicate papers, one of which he hands in to be transmitted by the postmaster — it contains a key-number, which the receiver has to supply in order to get the money. I think of

quiet the horses are! They let them get on and off them just as if they were tables!"

Another Rule of Battle, that Alice had not noticed, seemed to be that they always fell on their heads; and the battle ended with their both falling off in this way, side by side. When they got up again, they shook hands, and then the Red Knight mounted and galloped off.

"It was a glorious victory, wasn't it?" said the White Knight, as he came up panting.

"I don't know," Alice said doubtfully. "I don't want to be anybody's prisoner. I want to be a Queen."

"So you will, when you've crossed the next brook," said the White Knight. "I'll see you safe to the end of the wood—and then I must go back, you know. That's the end of my move."

"Thank you very much," said Alice. "May I help you off with your helmet?" It was evidently more than he could manage by himself: however she managed to shake him out of it at last.

"Now one can breathe more easily," said the Knight, putting back his shaggy hair with both hands, and turning his gentle face and large mild eyes to Alice. She thought she had never seen such a strange-looking soldier in all her life.[4]

He was dressed in tin armour, which seemed to fit him very badly, and he had a queer-shaped little deal box[5] fastened across his shoulders, upside-down, and with the lid hanging open. Alice looked at it with great curiosity.

"I see you're admiring my little box," the Knight said in a friendly tone. "It's my own invention—to keep clothes and sandwiches in. You see I carry it upside-down, so that the rain can't get in."

"But the things can get *out*," Alice gently remarked. "Do you know the lid's open?"

"I didn't know it," the Knight said, a shade of vexation passing over his face. "Then all the things must have fallen out! And the box is no use without them." He unfastened it as he spoke, and was just going to throw it into the bushes, when a sudden thought seemed to strike him, and he hung it carefully on a tree. "Can you guess why I did that?" he said to Alice.

Alice shook her head.

"In hopes some bees may make a nest in it—then I should get the honey."

"But you've got a bee-hive—or something like one—fastened to the saddle," said Alice.

"Yes, it's a very good bee-hive," the Knight said in a discontented tone, "one of the best kind. But not a single bee has come near it yet. And the other thing is a mouse-trap. I suppose the mice keep the bees out—or the bees keep the mice out, I don't know which."

suggesting this, and my plan for double postage on Sunday, to the Government" (Nov. 16, 1880).

Carroll's rooms contained a variety of toys for the amusement of his child-guests: music boxes, dolls, windup animals (including a walking bear and one called "Bob the Bat," which flew around the room), games, an "American orguinette" that played when you cranked a strip of punched paper through it. When he went on a journey, Stuart Collingwood tells us in his biography, "each separate article used to be carefully wrapped up in a piece of paper all to itself, so that his trunks contained nearly as much paper as of the more useful things."

It is noteworthy also that, of all the characters Alice meets on her two dream adventures, only the White Knight seems to be genuinely fond of her and to offer her special assistance. He is almost alone in speaking to her with respect and courtesy, and we are told that Alice remembered him better than anyone else whom she met behind the mirror. His melancholy farewell may be Carroll's farewell to Alice when she grew up (became a queen) and abandoned him. At any rate, we hear loudest in this episode that "shadow of a sigh" that Carroll tells us in his prefatory poem will "tremble through the story."

The role of White Knight was taken by Gary Cooper in Paramount's 1933 film, *Alice in Wonderland*.

5. A deal box is a box made of fir or pine wood.

"I was wondering what the mouse-trap was for," said Alice. "It isn't very likely there would be any mice on the horse's back."

"Not very likely, perhaps," said the Knight; "but, if they *do* come, I don't choose to have them running all about."

"You see," he went on after a pause, "it's as well to be provided for *everything*. That's the reason the horse has all those anklets round his feet."

"But what are they for?" Alice asked in a tone of great curiosity.

"To guard against the bites of sharks," the Knight replied. "It's an invention of my own. And now help me on. I'll go with you to the end of the wood—What's that dish for?"

"It's meant for plum-cake," said Alice.

"We'd better take it with us," the Knight said. "It'll come in handy if we find any plum-cake. Help me to get it into this bag."

This took a long time to manage, though Alice held the bag open very carefully, because the Knight was so *very* awkward in putting in the dish: the first two or three times that he tried he fell in himself instead. "It's rather a tight fit, you see," he said, as they got it in at last; "there are so many candlesticks in the bag." And he hung it to the saddle, which was already loaded with bunches of carrots, and fire-irons, and many other things.

"I hope you've got your hair well fastened on?" he continued, as they set off.

"Only in the usual way," Alice said, smiling.

"That's hardly enough," he said, anxiously. "You see the wind is so *very* strong here. It's as strong as soup."

"Have you invented a plan for keeping the hair from being blown off?" Alice enquired.

"Not yet," said the Knight. "But I've got a plan for keeping it from *falling* off."

"I should like to hear it, very much."

"First you take an upright stick," said the Knight. "Then you make your hair creep up it, like a fruit-tree. Now the reason hair falls off is because it hangs *down* —things never fall *upwards,* you know. It's a plan of my own invention. You may try it if you like."

It didn't sound a comfortable plan, Alice thought, and for a few minutes she walked on in silence, puzzling over the idea, and every now and then stopping to help the poor Knight, who certainly was *not* a good rider.

Whenever the horse stopped (which it did very often), he fell off in front; and, whenever it went on again (which it generally did rather suddenly), he fell off behind. Otherwise he kept on pretty well, except that he had a habit of now and then falling off sideways; and, as he generally did this on the side on which Alice

was walking, she soon found that it was
the best plan not to walk *quite* close to
the horse.

"I'm afraid you've not had much practice in riding," she ventured to say, as she
was helping him up from his fifth tumble.

The Knight looked very much surprised, and a little offended at the remark.
"What makes you say that?" he asked, as
he scrambled back into the saddle, keeping hold of Alice's hair with one hand, to
save himself from falling over on the
other side.

"Because people don't fall off quite so
often, when they've had much practice."

"I've had plenty of practice," the
Knight said very gravely: "plenty of practice!"

Alice could think of nothing better to
say than "Indeed?" but she said it as heartily as she could. They went on a little
way in silence after this, the Knight with
his eyes shut, muttering to himself, and
Alice watching anxiously for the next
tumble.

"The great art of riding," the Knight
suddenly began in a loud voice, waving
his right arm as he spoke, "is to keep—"
Here the sentence ended as suddenly as
it had begun, as the Knight fell heavily
on the top of his head exactly in the path
where Alice was walking. She was quite
frightened this time, and said in an

anxious tone, as she picked him up, "I hope no bones are broken?"

"None to speak of," the Knight said, as if he didn't mind breaking two or three of them. "The great art of riding, as I was saying, is—to keep your balance properly. Like this, you know—"

He let go the bridle, and stretched out both his arms to show Alice what he meant, and this time he fell flat on his back, right under the horse's feet.

"Plenty of practice!" he went on repeating, all the time that Alice was getting him on his feet again. "Plenty of practice!"

"It's too ridiculous!" cried Alice, losing all her patience this time. "You ought to have a wooden horse on wheels, that you ought!"

"Does that kind go smoothly?" the Knight asked in a tone of great interest, clasping his arms round the horse's neck as he spoke, just in time to save himself from tumbling off again.

"Much more smoothly than a live horse," Alice said, with a little scream of laughter, in spite of all she could do to prevent it.

"I'll get one," the Knight said thoughtfully to himself. "One or two—several."

There was a short silence after this, and then the Knight went on again. "I'm a great hand at inventing things. Now, I

301

6. In Carroll's day refined sugar was formed into conical chunks called sugar loaves. The term "sugar loaf" is commonly applied to cone-shaped hats and hills.

daresay you noticed, the last time you picked me up, that I was looking rather thoughtful?"

"You *were* a little grave," said Alice.

"Well, just then I was inventing a new way of getting over a gate—would you like to hear it?"

"Very much indeed," Alice said politely.

"I'll tell you how I came to think of it," said the Knight. "You see, I said to myself 'The only difficulty is with the feet: the *head* is high enough already.' Now, first I put my head on the top of the gate —then the head's high enough—then I stand on my head—then the feet are high enough, you see—then I'm over, you see."

"Yes, I suppose you'd be over when that was done," Alice said thoughfully: "but don't you think it would be rather hard?"

"I haven't tried it yet," the Knight said, gravely; "so I can't tell for certain—but I'm afraid it *would* be a little hard."

He looked so vexed at the idea, that Alice changed the subject hastily. "What a curious helmet you've got!" she said cheerfully. "Is that your invention too?"

The Knight looked down proudly at his helmet, which hung from the saddle. "Yes," he said; "but I've invented a better one than that—like a sugar-loaf.**6** When I used to wear it, if I fell off the horse, it always touched the ground directly. So I

had a *very* little way to fall, you see—But
there *was* the danger of falling *into* it, to
be sure. That happened to me once—and
the worst of it was, before I could get out
again, the other White Knight came and
put it on. He thought it was his own
helmet."

The Knight looked so solemn about it
that Alice did not dare to laugh. "I'm
afraid you must have hurt him," she said
in a trembling voice, "being on the top
of his head."

"I had to kick him, of course," the
Knight said, very seriously. "And then he
took the helmet off again—but it took
hours and hours to get me out. I was as
fast as—as lightning, you know."

"But that's a different kind of fastness,"
Alice objected.

The Knight shook his head. "It was all
kinds of fastness with me, I can assure
you!" he said. He raised his hands in some
excitement as he said this, and instantly
rolled out of the saddle, and fell headlong
into a deep ditch.

Alice ran to the side of the ditch to
look for him. She was rather startled by
the fall, as for some time he had kept on
very well, and she was afraid that he really
was hurt this time. However, though she
could see nothing but the soles of his feet,
she was much relieved to hear that he was
talking on in his usual tone. "All kinds of
fastness," he repeated: "but it was care-

less of him to put another man's helmet on—with the man in it, too."

"How *can* you go on talking so quietly, head downwards?" Alice asked, as she dragged him out by the feet, and laid him in a heap on the bank.

The Knight looked surprised at the question. "What does it matter where my body happens to be?" he said. "My mind goes on working all the same. In fact, the more head downwards I am, the more I keep inventing new things.

"Now the cleverest thing of the sort that I ever did," he went on after a pause, "was inventing a new pudding during the meat-course."

"In time to have it cooked for the next course?" said Alice. "Well, that *was* quick work, certainly!"

"Well, not the *next* course," the Knight

said in a slow thoughtful tone: "no, certainly not the next *course*."

"Then it would have to be the next day. I suppose you wouldn't have two pudding-courses in one dinner?"

"Well, not the *next* day," the Knight repeated as before: "not the next *day*. In fact," he went on, holding his head down, and his voice getting lower and lower, "I don't believe that pudding ever *was* cooked! In fact, I don't believe that pudding ever *will* be cooked! And yet it was a very clever pudding to invent."

"What did you mean it to be made of?" Alice asked, hoping to cheer him up, for the poor Knight seemed quite low-spirited about it.

"It began with blotting-paper," the Knight answered with a groan.

"That wouldn't be very nice, I'm afraid—"

"Not very nice *alone*," he interrupted, quite eagerly: "but you've no idea what a difference it makes, mixing it with other things—such as gunpowder and sealing wax. And here I must leave you." They had just come to the end of the wood.

Alice could only look puzzled: she was thinking of the pudding.

"You are sad," the Knight said in an anxious tone: "let me sing you a song to comfort you."

"Is it very long?" Alice asked, for she had heard a good deal of poetry that day.

7. In two-valued logic this would be called an example of the law of excluded middle: a statement is either true or false, with no third alternative. The law is the basis of a number of old nonsense rhymes: e.g., There was an old woman who lived on the hill,/ And if she's not gone, she is living there still.

8. To a student of logic and semantics all this is perfectly sensible. The song *is* "A-Sitting on a Gate"; it is *called* "Ways and Means"; the *name* of the song is "The Aged Aged Man"; and the name is *called* "Haddocks'. Eyes." Carroll is distinguishing here among things, the names of things, and the names of names of things. "Haddocks' Eyes," the name of a name, belongs to what logicians now call a "metalanguage." By adopting the convention of a hierarchy of metalanguages logicians manage to side-step certain paradoxes that have plagued them since the time of the Greeks. For Earnest Nagel's amusing translation of the White Knight's remarks into symbolic notation, see his article "Symbolic Notation, Haddocks' Eyes and the Dog-Walking Ordinance," in Vol. III of James R. Newman's anthology, *The World of Mathematics*, 1956.

A less technical but equally sound and delightful analysis of this passage is included in Roger W. Holmes' article, "The philosopher's Alice in Wonderland," *Antioch Review*, Summer 1959. Professor Holmes (he is chairman of the philosophy department at Mount Holyoke College) thinks that Carroll was pulling our leg when he has the White Knight say that the song *is* "A-sitting on a Gate." Clearly this cannot be the song itself, but only another name. "To be consistent," Holmes concludes, "the White Knight, when he had said that the song *is* . . . ,

"It's long," said the Knight, "but it's very, *very* beautiful. Everybody that hears me sing it—either it brings the *tears* into their eyes, or else—"

"Or else what?" said Alice, for the Knight had made a sudden pause.

"Or else it doesn't, you know.[7] The name of the song is called '*Haddocks' Eyes.*'"

"Oh, that's the name of the song, is it?" Alice said, trying to feel interested.

"No, you don't understand," the Knight said, looking a little vexed. "That's what the name is *called*. The name really *is 'The Aged Aged Man.*'"

"Then I ought to have said 'That's what the *song* is called'?" Alice corrected herself.

"No, you oughtn't: that's quite another thing! The *song* is called '*Ways And Means*': but that's only what it's *called*, you know!"

"Well, what *is* the song, then?" said Alice, who was by this time completely bewildered.

"I was coming to that," the Knight said. "The song really *is 'A-sitting On A Gate*': and the tune's my own invention."[8]

So saying, he stopped his horse and let the reins fall on its neck: then, slowly beating time with one hand, and with a faint smile lighting up his gentle foolish face, as if he enjoyed the music of his song, he began.

Of all the strange things that Alice saw in her journey Through The Looking-Glass, this was the one that she always remembered most clearly. Years afterwards she could bring the whole scene back again, as if it had been only yesterday—the mild blue eyes and kindly smile of the Knight—the setting sun gleaming through his hair, and shining on his armour in a blaze of light that quite dazzled her—the horse quietly moving about, with the reins hanging loose on his neck, cropping the grass at her feet—and the black shadows of the forest behind—all this she took in like a picture, as, with one hand shading her eyes, she leant against a tree, watching the strange pair, and listening, in a half-dream, to the melancholy music of the song.**9**

"But the tune *isn't* his own invention," she said to herself: "it's '*I give thee all, I can no more.*' " She stood and listened very attentively, but no tears came into her eyes.

"I'll tell thee everything I can:
There's little to relate.
I saw an aged aged man,
A-sitting on a gate.
'Who are you, aged man?' I said.
'And how is it you live?'

(Continued on Page 311)

could only have burst into the song itself. Whether consistent or not, the White Knight is Lewis Carroll's cherished gift to logicians."

The White Knight's song also exhibits a kind of hierarchy, like a mirror reflection of a mirror reflection of an object. Carroll's eccentric White Knight, whom Alice couldn't forget, is also unable to forget another eccentric with traits that suggest that he too may be a caricature of Carroll; perhaps Carroll's vision of himself as a lonely, unloved old man.

9. The White Knight's song is a revised, expanded version of this earlier poem by Carroll, which appeared anonymously in 1856 in a magazine called *The Train*.

UPON THE LONELY MOOR

*I met an aged, aged man
Upon the lonely moor:
I knew I was a gentleman,
And he was but a boor.
So I stopped and roughly questioned him,
"Come, tell me how you live!"
But his words impressed my ear no more
Than if it were a sieve.*

*He said, "I look for soap-bubbles,
That lie among the wheat,
And bake them into mutton-pies,
And sell them in the street.
I sell them unto men," he said,
"Who sail on stormy seas;
And that's the way I get my bread—
A trifle, if you please."*

*But I was thinking of a way
To multiply by ten,
And always, in the answer, get
The question back again.
I did not hear a word he said,
But kicked that old man calm,
And said, "Come, tell me how you live!"
And pinched him in the arm.*

His accents mild took up the tale:
    He said, "I go my ways,
And when I find a mountain-rill,
    I set it in a blaze.
And thence they make a stuff they call
    Rowland's Macassar Oil;
But fourpence-halfpenny is all
    They give me for my toil."

But I was thinking of a plan
    To paint one's gaiters green,
So much the colour of the grass
    That they could ne'er be seen.
I gave his ear a sudden box,
    And questioned him again,
And tweaked his grey and reverend locks,
    And put him into pain.

He said, "I hunt for haddocks' eyes
    Among the heather bright,
And work them into waistcoat-buttons
    In the silent night.
And these I do not sell for gold,
    Or coin of silver-mine,
But for a copper-halfpenny,
    And that will purchase nine.

"I sometimes dig for buttered rolls,
    Or set limed twigs for crabs;
I sometimes search the flowery knolls
    For wheels of hansom cabs.
And that's the way" (he gave a wink)
    "I get my living here,
And very gladly will I drink
    Your Honour's health in beer."

I heard him then, for I had just
    Completed my design
To keep the Menai bridge from rust
    By boiling it in wine.
I duly thanked him, ere I went,
    For all his stories queer,
But chiefly for his kind intent
    To drink my health in beer.

And now if e'er by chance I put
    My fingers into glue,
Or madly squeeze a right-hand foot
    Into a left-hand shoe;
Or if a statement I aver
    Of which I am not sure,
I think of that strange wanderer
    Upon the lonely moor.

    The poem is a travesty on the subject matter of Wordsworth's poem about the aged leech-gatherer, *Resolution and Independence.*

Wordsworth's poem is here reproduced in its entirety so that one may see exactly where and how Carroll borrowed from it. On the whole it is a fine poem, and I say this with awareness of the fact that a portion of it is included in *The Stuffed Owl,* that hilarious anthology of bad verse compiled by D. B. Wyndham Lewis and Charles Lee. The "Him" in stanza 7 is Robert Burns.

THERE was a roaring in the wind all night;
The rain came heavily and fell in floods;
But now the sun is rising calm and bright;
The birds are singing in the distant woods;
Over his own sweet voice the Stock-dove broods;
The Jay makes answer as the Magpie chatters;
And all the air is filled with pleasant noise of waters.

All things that love the sun are out of doors;
The sky rejoices in the morning's birth;
The grass is bright with rain-drops;
    —on the moors
The hare is running races in her mirth;
And with her feet she from the plashy earth
Raises a mist; that, glittering in the sun,
Runs with her all the way, wherever she doth run.

I was a Traveller then upon the moor;
I saw the hare that raced about with joy;
I heard the woods and distant waters roar;
Or heard them not, as happy as a boy:
The pleasant season did my heart employ:
My old remembrances went from me wholly;
And all the ways of men, so vain and melancholy.

But, as it sometimes chanceth, from the might

308

Of joy in minds that can no
     further go,
As high as we have mounted in
     delight
In our dejection do we sink as low;
To me that morning did it
     happen so;
And fears and fancies thick upon me
     came;
Dim sadness—and blind thoughts, I
     knew not, nor could name.

I heard the sky-lark warbling in
     the sky;
And I bethought me of the playful
     hare:
Even such a happy Child of earth
     am I;
Even as these blissful creatures do I
     fare;
Far from the world I walk, and from
     all care;
But there may come another day
     to me—
Solitude, pain of heart, distress, and
     poverty.

My whole life I have lived in
     pleasant thought,
As if life's business were a summer
     mood;
As if all needful things would come
     unsought
To genial faith, still rich in genial
     good;
But how can He expect that others
     should
Build for him, sow for him, and at
     his call
Love him, who for himself will take
     no heed at all?

I thought of Chatterton, the
     marvellous Boy,
The sleepless Soul that perished in
     his pride;
Of Him who walked in glory and
     in joy
Following his plough, along the
     mountain-side:
By our own spirits are we deified:
We Poets in our youth begin in
     gladness;
But thereof come in the end
     despondency and madness.

Now, whether it were by peculiar
     grace,
A leading from above, a something
     given,
Yet it befell that, in this lonely place,

When I with these untoward thoughts
     had striven,
Beside a pool bare to the eye of
     heaven
I saw a Man before me unawares:
The oldest man he seemed that ever
     wore grey hairs.

As a huge stone is sometimes seen
     to lie
Couched on the bald top of an
     eminence;
Wonder to all who do the same espy,
By what means it could thither come,
     and whence;
So that it seems a thing endued with
     sense:
Like a sea-beast crawled forth, that
     on a shelf
Of rock or sand reposeth, there to
     sun itself;

Such seemed this Man, not all alive
     nor dead,
Nor all asleep—in his extreme old
     age:
His body was bent double, feet and
     head
Coming together in life's pilgrimage;
As if some dire constraint of pain,
     or rage
Of sickness felt by him in times long
     past,
A more than human weight upon his
     frame had cast.

Himself he propped, limbs, body,
     and pale face,
Upon a long grey staff of shaven
     wood:
And, still as I drew near with gentle
     pace,
Upon the margin of that moorish
     flood
Motionless as a cloud the old Man
     stood,
That heareth not the loud winds
     when they call;
And moveth all together, if it move
     at all.

At length, himself unsettling, he the
     pond
Stirred with his staff, and fixedly did
     look
Upon the muddy water, which he
     conned,
As if he had been reading in a book:
And now a stranger's privilege I took;
And, drawing to his side, to him
     did say,

"This morning gives us promise of a
glorious day."

A gentle answer did the old Man
make,
In courteous speech which forth he
slowly drew:
And him with further words I thus
bespake,
"What occupation do you there
pursue?
This is a lonesome place for one
like you."
Ere he replied, a flash of mild
surprise
Broke from the sable orbs of his
yet-vivid eyes.

His words came feebly, from a
feeble chest,
But each in solemn order followed
each,
With something of a lofty utterance
drest—
Choice word and measured phrase,
above the reach
Of ordinary men; a stately speech;
Such as grave Livers do in Scotland
use,
Religious men, who give to God and
man their dues.

He told, that to these waters he had
come
To gather leeches, being old and
poor:
Employment hazardous and
wearisome!
And he had many hardships to
endure:
From pond to pond he roamed, from
moor to moor;
Housing, with God's good help, by
choice or chance;
And in this way he gained an honest
maintenance.

The old Man still stood talking by
my side;
But now his voice to me was like a
stream
Scarce heard; nor word from word
could I divide;
And the whole body of the Man did
seem
Like one whom I had met with in a
dream;
Or like a man from some far region
sent,
To give me human strength, by apt
admonishment.

My former thoughts returned: the
fear that kills;
And hope that is unwilling to be fed;
Cold, pain, and labour, and all
fleshly ills;
And mighty Poets in their misery
dead.
—Perplexed, and longing to be
comforted,
My question eagerly did I renew,
"How is it that you live, and what is
it you do?"

He with a smile did then his words
repeat;
And said that, gathering leeches, far
and wide
He travelled; stirring thus about his
feet
The waters of the pools where they
abide.
"Once I could meet with them on
every side;
But they have dwindled long by slow
decay;
Yet still I persevere, and find them
where I may."

While he was talking thus the lonely
place,
The old Man's shape, and speech—
all troubled me:
In my mind's eye I seemed to see him
pace
About the weary moors continually,
Wandering about alone and silently.
While I these thoughts within
myself pursued,
He, having made a pause, the same
discourse renewed.

And soon with this he other matter
blended,
Cheerfully uttered, with demeanour
kind,
But stately in the main; and, when
he ended,
I could have laughed myself to scorn
to find
In that decrepit Man so firm a mind.
"God," said I, "be my help and stay
secure;
I'll think of the Leech-gatherer on
the lonely moor!"

The opening lines of the White
Knight's song burlesque Wordsworth's lines "I'll tell you everything I know" and "I'll give you all
the help I can," from the original

310

And his answer trickled through my
    head,
  Like water through a sieve.

He said 'I look for butterflies
  That sleep among the wheat:
I make them into mutton-pies,
  And sell them in the street.
I sell them unto men,' he said,
  'Who sail on stormy seas;
And that's the way I get my bread—
  A trifle, if you please.'

But I was thinking of a plan
  To dye one's whiskers green,
And always use so large a fan
  That they could not be seen.[10]
So, having no reply to give
  To what the old man said,
I cried 'Come, tell me how you live!'
  And thumped him on the head.

His accents mild took up the tale:
  He said 'I go my ways,
And when I find a mountain-rill,
  I set it in a blaze;
And thence they make a stuff they call
  Rowland's Macassar-Oil—[11]
Yet twopence-halfpenny is all
  They give me for my toil.'

But I was thinking of a way
  To feed oneself on batter,
And so go on from day to day
  Getting a little fatter.
I shook him well from side to side,
  Until his face was blue:
'Come, tell me how you live,' I cried,
  'And what it is you do!'

version of one of the poet's less happy efforts called *The Thorn.* The line also reflects the title of the song, "I give thee all, I can no more," to the tune of which the White Knight sings about the aged aged man. This song is Thomas Moore's lyric, *My Heart and Lute,* which was set to music by the English composer Sir Henry Rowley Bishop. Carroll's song follows the metrical pattern and rhyme scheme of Moore's poem.

"The character of the White Knight," Carroll wrote in a letter, "was meant to suit the speaker in the poem." That the speaker is Carroll himself is suggested by his thoughts on multiplying by ten in the third stanza of the earlier version. It is quite possible that Carroll regarded Moore's love lyric as the song that he, the White Knight, would have liked to sing to Alice but dared not. The full text of Moore's poem follows.

I give thee all—I can no more—
  Though poor the off'ring be;
My heart and lute are all the store
  That I can bring to thee.
A lute whose gentle song reveals
  The soul of love full well;
And, better far, a heart that feels
  Much more than lute could tell.

Though love and song may fail, alas!
  To keep life's clouds away,
At least 'twill make them lighter pass
  Or gild them if they stay.
And ev'n if Care, at moments, flings
  A discord o'er life's happy strain,
Let love but gently touch the strings,
  'Twill all be sweet again!

10. Bertrand Russell, in *The ABC of Relativity,* Chapter 3, applies these four lines to the Lorentz-Fitzgerald contraction hypothesis, an early attempt to account for the failure of the Michelson-Morley experiment to detect an influence of the earth's motion on the speed of light. According to this hypothesis, objects shrink in the direction of their motion, but since all measuring rods are similarly shortened, they serve, like the White Knight's fan, to prevent us from detecting any change in the length of objects. The same lines are quoted by Arthur Stanley Eddington in chapter 2 of *The Nature of the Physical World*, but with a larger metaphorical meaning: the apparent habit nature has of forever concealing from us her basic structural plan.

11. The Oxford English Dictionary describes this oil as "an unguent for the hair, grandiloquently advertised in the early part of the nineteenth century, and represented by the makers (Rowland and Son) to consist of ingredients obtained from Macassar." In the first canto, stanza 17, of *Don Juan*, Byron writes:

> *In virtues nothing earthly could*
> *surpass her,*
> *Save thine "incomparable oil,"*
> *Macassar!*

The term "antimacassar," for the piece of cloth put on the backs of chairs and sofas to prevent soiling of the fabric by hair oil, had its origin in the popularity of this oil.

12. Limed twigs are twigs that have been smeared with birdlime (or any sticky substance) for the purpose of catching birds.

He said 'I hunt for haddocks' eyes
   Among the heather bright,
And work them into waistcoat-
     buttons
   In the silent night.
And these I do not sell for gold
   Or coin of silvery shine,
But for a copper halfpenny,
   And that will purchase nine.

'I sometimes dig for buttered rolls,
   Or set limed twigs[12] for crabs:
I sometimes search the grassy knolls
   For wheels of Hansom-cabs.
And that's the way' (he gave a wink)
   'By which I get my wealth —
And very gladly will I drink
   Your Honour's noble health.'

I heard him then, for I had just
  Completed my design
To keep the Menai[13] bridge from
    rust
  By boiling it in wine.
I thanked him much for telling me
  The way he got his wealth,
But chiefly for his wish that he
  Might drink my noble health.

And now, if e'er by chance I put
  My fingers into glue,
Or madly squeeze a right-hand foot
  Into a left-hand shoe,
Or if I drop upon my toe
  A very heavy weight,
I weep, for it reminds me so
Of that old man I used to know —
Whose look was mild, whose speech
    was slow,
Whose hair was whiter than the snow,
Whose face was very like a crow,
With eyes, like cinders, all aglow,
Who seemed distracted with his woe,
Who rocked his body to and fro,
And muttered mumblingly and low,
As if his mouth were full of dough,
Who snorted like a buffalo —
That summer evening long ago,
  A-sitting on a gate."

13. The Menai Bridge is a famous suspension bridge across the Menai Straits in North Wales. It was completed in 1826. As a child, Carroll had crossed the bridge on a long holiday trip with his family.

As the Knight sang the last words of the ballad, he gathered up the reins, and turned his horse's head along the road by which they had come. "You've only a few yards to go," he said, "down the hill and over that little brook, and then you'll be

14. The White Knight has returned to KB5, the square he occupied before capturing the Red Knight.

a Queen—But you'll stay and see me off first?" he added as Alice turned with an eager look in the direction to which he pointed. "I shan't be long. You'll wait and wave your handkerchief when I get to that turn in the road! I think it'll encourage me, you see."

"Of course I'll wait," said Alice: "and thank you very much for coming so far—and for the song—I liked it very much."

"I hope so," the Knight said doubtfully: "but you didn't cry so much as I thought you would."

So they shook hands, and then the Knight rode slowly away into the forest. "It won't take long to see him *off,* I expect," Alice said to herself, as she stood watching him. "There he goes! Right on his head as usual! However, he gets on again pretty easily—that comes of having so many things hung round the horse—" So she went on talking to herself, as she watched the horse walking leisurely along the road, and the Knight tumbling off, first on one side and then on the other. After the fourth or fifth tumble he reached the turn, and then she waved her handkerchief to him, and waited till he was out of sight.**14**

"I hope it encouraged him," she said, as she turned to run down the hill: "and now for the last brook, and to be a Queen! How grand it sounds!" A very few steps brought her to the edge of the brook.

"The Eighth Square at last!" she cried as she bounded across, and threw herself

*   *   *   *   *

*   *   *   *   *

*   *   *   *   *

15. Alice has leaped the one remaining brook and is now on Q8, the last square of the queen's file. For readers unfamiliar with chess it should be said that when a pawn reaches the last row of the chessboard it may become any piece the player desires. He usually chooses a queen, the most powerful of the chess pieces.

down to rest on a lawn as soft as moss, with little flower-beds dotted about it here and there. "Oh, how glad I am to get here! And what *is* this on my head?" she exclaimed in a tone of dismay, as she put her hands up to something very heavy, that fitted tight all round her head.

"But how *can* it have got there without my knowing it?" she said to herself, as she lifted it off, and set it on her lap to make out what it could possibly be.

It was a golden crown.15

CHAPTER IX

Queen Alice

"Well, this *is* grand!" said Alice. "I never expected I should be a Queen so soon— and I'll tell you what it is, your Majesty," she went on, in a severe tone (she was always rather fond of scolding herself), "it'll never do for you to be lolling about on the grass like that! Queens have to be dignified, you know!"

So she got up and walked about— rather stiffly just at first, as she was afraid that the crown might come off: but she comforted herself with the thought that there was nobody to see her, "and if I really am a Queen," she said as she sat down again, "I shall be able to manage it quite well in time."

Everything was happening so oddly that she didn't feel a bit surprised at finding the Red Queen and the White Queen sitting close to her, one on each side:**1** she

1. The Red Queen has just moved to the King's square so that Alice now has a queen on each side of her. The White King is placed in check by this move, but neither side seems to notice it.

317

would have liked very much to ask them how they came there, but she feared it would not be quite civil. However, there would be no harm, she thought, in asking if the game was over. "Please, would you tell me——" she began, looking timidly at the Red Queen.

"Speak when you're spoken to!" the Queen sharply interrupted her.

"But if everybody obeyed that rule," said Alice, who was always ready for a little argument, "and if you only spoke when you were spoken to, and the other person always waited for *you* to begin, you see nobody would ever say anything, so that——"

"Ridiculous!" cried the Queen. "Why, don't you see, child——" here she broke off with a frown, and, after thinking for a minute, suddenly changed the subject of the conversation. "What do you mean by 'If you really are a Queen'? What right have you to call yourself so? You can't be a Queen, you know, till you've passed the proper examination. And the sooner we begin it, the better."

"I only said 'if'!" poor Alice pleaded in a piteous tone.

The two Queens looked at each other, and the Red Queen remarked, with a little shudder, "She *says* she only said 'if'——"

"But she said a great deal more than that!" the White Queen moaned, wringing her hands, "Oh, ever so much more than that!"

"So you did, you know," the Red Queen said to Alice. "Always speak the truth—think before you speak—and write it down afterwards."

"I'm sure I didn't mean—" Alice was beginning, but the Red Queen interrupted her impatiently.

"That's just what I complain of! You *should* have meant! What do you suppose is the use of a child without any meaning? Even a joke should have some meaning—and a child's more important than a joke, I hope. You couldn't deny that, even if you tried with both hands."

"I don't deny things with my *hands*," Alice objected.

"Nobody said you did," said the Red Queen. "I said you couldn't if you tried."

"She's in that state of mind," said the White Queen, "that she wants to deny *something*—only she doesn't know what to deny!"

"A nasty, vicious temper," the Red Queen remarked; and then there was an uncomfortable silence for a minute or two.

The Red Queen broke the silence by saying, to the White Queen, "I invite you to Alice's dinner-party this afternoon."

The White Queen smiled feebly, and said "And I invite *you*."

"I didn't know I was to have a party at all," said Alice; "but, if there *is* to be one, I think *I* ought to invite the guests."

"We gave you the opportunity of doing it," the Red Queen remarked: "but I daresay you've not had many lessons in manners yet?"

"Manners are not taught in lessons," said Alice. "Lessons teach you to do sums, and things of that sort."

"Can you do Addition?" the White Queen asked. "What's one and one and one and one and one and one and one and one and one and one?"

"I don't know," said Alice. "I lost count."

"She can't do Addition," the Red Queen interrupted. "Can you do Subtraction? Take nine from eight."

"Nine from eight I can't, you know," Alice replied very readily: "but—"

"She can't do Substraction," said the White Queen. "Can you do Division? Divide a loaf by a knife—what's the answer to *that?*"

"I suppose—" Alice was beginning, but the Red Queen answered for her. "Bread-and-butter, of course. Try another Subtraction sum. Take a bone from a dog: what remains?"

Alice considered. "The bone wouldn't remain, of course, if I took it—and the dog wouldn't remain: it would come to bite me—and I'm sure *I* shouldn't remain!"

"Then you think nothing would remain?" said the Red Queen.

"I think that's the answer."

"Wrong, as usual," said the Red Queen: "the dog's temper would remain."

"But I don't see how—"

"Why, look here!" the Red Queen cried. "The dog would lose its temper, wouldn't it?"

"Perhaps it would," Alice replied cautiously.

"Then if the dog went away, its temper would remain!" the Queen exclaimed triumphantly.

Alice said, as gravely as she could, "They might go different ways." But she couldn't help thinking to herself "What dreadful nonsense we *are* talking!"

"She can't do sums a *bit!*" the Queens said together, with great emphasis.

"Can *you* do sums?" Alice said, turning suddenly on the White Queen, for she didn't like being found fault with so much.

The Queen gasped and shut her eyes. "I can do Addition," she said, "if you give me time—but I can't do Substraction under *any* circumstances!"

"Of course you know your A B C?" said the Red Queen.

"To be sure I do," said Alice.

"So do I," the White Queen whispered: "we'll often say it over together, dear. And I'll tell you a secret—I can read words of one letter! Isn't *that* grand? However, don't be discouraged. You'll come to it in time."

Here the Red Queen began again. "Can you answer useful questions?" she said. "How is bread made?"

"I know *that!*" Alice cried eagerly. "You take some flour—"

"Where do you pick the flower?" the White Queen asked. "In a garden or in the hedges?"

"Well, it isn't *picked* at all," Alice explained: "it's *ground*—"

"How many acres of ground?" said the White Queen. "You mustn't leave out so many things."

"Fan her head!" the Red Queen anxiously interrupted. "She'll be feverish after so much thinking." So they set to work and fanned her with bunches of leaves, till she had to beg them to leave off, it blew her hair about so.

"She's all right again now," said the Red Queen. "Do you know Languages? What's the French for fiddle-de-dee?"

"Fiddle-de-dee's not English," Alice replied gravely.

"Who ever said it was?" said the Red Queen.

Alice thought she saw a way out of the difficulty, this time. "If you'll tell me what language 'fiddle-de-dee' is, I'll tell you the French for it!" she exclaimed triumphantly.

But the Red Queen drew herself up rather stiffly, and said "Queens never make bargains."

"I wish Queens never asked questions," Alice thought to herself.

"Don't let us quarrel," the White Queen said in an anxious tone. "What is the cause of lightning?"

"The cause of lightning," Alice said very decidedly, for she felt quite certain about this, "is the thunder—no, no!" she hastily corrected herself. "I meant the other way."

"It's too late to correct it," said the Red Queen: "when you've once said a thing, that fixes it, and you must take the consequences."

"Which reminds me—" the White Queen said, looking down and nervously clasping and unclasping her hands, "we

2. Carroll was particularly fond of Tuesdays. "Spent the day in London," he wrote in his diary on Tuesday, April 10, 1877. "It was (like so many Tuesdays in my life) a very enjoyable day." The joy on this occasion was his meeting of a modest little girl "who is about the most gloriously beautiful child (both face and figure) that I ever saw. One would like to do 100 photographs of her."

3. It is easy to miss the Red Queen's implication here that "rich" and "clever" are opposites, like "warm" and "cold."

had *such* a thunder-storm last Tuesday—I mean one of the last set of Tuesdays, you know."**2**

Alice was puzzled. "In *our* country," she remarked, "there's only one day at a time."

The Red Queen said "That's a poor thin way of doing things. Now *here,* we mostly have days and nights two or three at a time, and sometimes in the winter we take as many as five nights together—for warmth, you know."

"Are five nights warmer than one night, then?" Alice ventured to ask.

"Five times as warm, of course."

"But they should be five times as *cold,* by the same rule—"

"Just so!" cried the Red Queen. "Five times as warm, *and* five times as cold—just as I'm five times as rich as you are, *and* five times as clever!"**3**

Alice sighed and gave it up. "It's exactly like a riddle with no answer!" she thought.

"Humpty Dumpty saw it too," the White Queen went on in a low voice, more as if she were talking to herself. "He came to the door with a corkscrew in his hand—"

"What did he want?" said the Red Queen.

"He said he *would* come in," the White Queen went on, "because he was looking for a hippopotamus. Now, as it happened, there wasn't such a thing in the house, that morning."

"Is there generally?" Alice asked in an astonished tone.

"Well, only on Thursdays," said the Queen.

"I know what he came for," said Alice: "he wanted to punish the fish, because—"**4**

Here the White Queen began again. "It was *such* a thunderstorm, you can't think!" ("She *never* could, you know," said the Red Queen.) "And part of the roof came off, and ever so much thunder got in—and it went rolling round the room in great lumps—and knocking over the tables and things—till I was so frightened, I couldn't remember my own name!"

Alice thought to herself "I never should *try* to remember my name in the middle of an accident! Where would be the use of it?" but she did not say this aloud, for fear of hurting the poor Queen's feelings.

"Your Majesty must excuse her," the Red Queen said to Alice, taking one of the White Queen's hands in her own, and gently stroking it: "she means well, but she can't help saying foolish things, as a general rule."

The White Queen looked timidly at Alice, who felt she *ought* to say something kind, but really couldn't think of anything at the moment.

4. Alice is recalling Humpty's song (Chapter 6) in which he tells of taking a corkscrew and going to wake up the fish to punish them for not obeying him.

325

"She never was really well brought up," the Red Queen went on: "but it's amazing how good-tempered she is! Pat her on the head, and see how pleased she'll be!" But this was more than Alice had courage to do.

"A little kindness—and putting her hair in papers—would do wonders with her—"

The White Queen gave a deep sigh, and laid her head on Alice's shoulder. "I *am* so sleepy!" she moaned.

"She's tired, poor thing!" said the Red Queen. "Smooth her hair—lend her your nightcap—and sing her a soothing lullaby."

"I haven't got a nightcap with me," said Alice, as she tried to obey the first direction: "and I don't know any soothing lullabies."

"I must do it myself, then," said the Red Queen, and she began:—**5**

"Hush-a-by lady, in Alice's lap!
 Till the feast's ready, we've time for a nap.
 When the feast's over, we'll go to the ball —
 Red Queen, and White Queen, and Alice,
     and all!

"And now you know the words," she added, as she put her head down on Alice's other shoulder, "just sing it through to *me*. I'm getting sleepy, too." In another moment both Queens were fast asleep, and snoring loud.

"What *am* I to do?" exclaimed Alice, looking about in great perplexity, as first one round head, and then the other, rolled down from her shoulder, and lay like a heavy lump in her lap. "I don't think it *ever* happened before, that any one had to take care of two Queens asleep at once! No, not in all the History of England—it couldn't, you know, because there never was more than one Queen at a time. Do wake up, you heavy things!" she went on in an impatient tone; but there was no answer but a gentle snoring.

The snoring got more distinct every minute, and sounded more like a tune: at last she could even make out words, and she listened so eagerly that, when the two great heads suddenly vanished from her lap, she hardly missed them.

She was standing before an arched doorway, over which were the words "QUEEN ALICE" in large letters, and on each side of the arch there was a bell-handle; one was marked "Visitors' Bell," and the other "Servants' Bell."

"I'll wait till the song's over," thought Alice, "and then I'll ring the—the— *which* bell must I ring?" she went on, very much puzzled by the names. "I'm not a visitor, and I'm not a servant. There *ought* to be one marked 'Queen,' you know—"

Just then the door opened a little way, and a creature with a long beak put its head out for a moment and said "No admittance till the week after next!" and shut the door again with a bang.

Alice knocked and rang in vain for a long time; but at last a very old Frog, who was sitting under a tree, got up and hobbled slowly towards her: he was dressed in bright yellow, and had enormous boots on.

"What is it, now?" the Frog said in a deep hoarse whisper.

Alice turned round, ready to find fault with anybody. "Where's the servant whose business it is to answer the door?" she began angrily.

"Which door?" said the Frog.

Alice almost stamped with irritation at the slow drawl in which he spoke. *"This* door, of course!"

The Frog looked at the door with his large dull eyes for a minute: then he went nearer and rubbed it with his thumb, as if he were trying whether the paint would come off: then he looked at Alice.

"To answer the door?" he said. "What's it been asking of?" He was so hoarse that Alice could scarcely hear him.

"I don't know what you mean," she said.

"I speaks English, doesn't I?" the Frog went on. "Or are you deaf? What did it ask you?"

"Nothing!" Alice said impatiently. "I've been knocking at it!"

"Shouldn't do that—shouldn't do that —" the Frog muttered. "Wexes[6] it, you know." Then he went up and gave the door a kick with one of his great feet. "You let *it* alone," he panted out, as he hobbled back to his tree, "and it'll let *you* alone, you know."

At this moment the door was flung open, and a shrill voice was heard singing:—[7]

"To the Looking-Glass world it was Alice that said
'I've a sceptre in hand, I've a crown on my head.
Let the Looking-Glass creatures, whatever they be
Come and dine with the Red Queen, the White Queen and me!' "

And hundreds of voices joined in the chorus:—

"Then fill up the glasses as quick as you can,
And sprinkle the table with buttons and bran:
Put cats in the coffee, and mice in the tea —
And welcome Queen Alice with thirty-times-three!"

Then followed a confused noise of cheering, and Alice thought to herself "Thirty times three makes ninety. I wonder if any one's counting?" In a minute there was silence again, and the same shrill voice sang another verse:—

6. A common pronunciation of "vexes" by uneducated classes in England.

7. This is a parody of Sir Walter Scott's song, "Bonny Dundee," from his play *The Doom of Devorgoil*.

BONNY DUNDEE

To the Lords of Convention 'twas Claver'se who spoke,
'Ere the King's crown shall fall there are crowns to be broke;
So let each Cavalier who loves honour and me,
Come follow the bonnet of Bonny Dundee.

'Come fill up my cup, come fill up my can,
Come saddle your horses, and call up your men;
Come open the West Port, and let me gang free,
And it's room for the bonnets of Bonny Dundee!'

Dundee he is mounted; he rides up the street,
The bells are rung backward, the drums they are beat;
But the Provost, douce man, said, 'Just e'en let him be,
The Gude Town is weel quit of that Deil of Dundee.'

Come fill up my cup, &c.

As he rode down the sanctified bends of the Bow,
Ilk carline was flyting and shaking her pow;
But the young plants of grace they look'd couthie and slee,
Thinking, 'Luck to thy bonnet, thou Bonny Dundee!'

Come fill up my cup, &c.

With sour-featured Whigs the Grassmarket was cramm'd
As if half the West had set tryst to be hang'd;
There was spite in each look, there was fear in each e'e,
As they watch'd for the bonnets of Bonny Dundee.

Come fill up my cup, &c.

*These cowls of Kilmarnock had spits
    and had spears,
And lang-hafted gullies to kill
    Cavaliers;
But they shrunk to close-heads, and
    the causeway was free,
At the toss of the bonnet of Bonny
    Dundee.*

    Come fill up my cup, &c.

*He spurr'd to the foot of the proud
    Castle rock,
And with the gay Gordon he gallantly
    spoke;
'Let Mons Meg and her marrows
    speak twa words or three,
For the love of the bonnet of Bonny
    Dundee.'*

    Come fill up my cup, &c.

*The Gordon demands of him which
    way he goes—
'Where'er shall direct me the shade
    of Montrose!
Your Grace in short space shall hear
    tidings of me,
Or that low lies the bonnet of Bonny
    Dundee.*

    Come fill up my cup, &c.

*'There are hills beyond Pentland, and
    lands beyond Forth,
If there's lords in the Lowlands,
    there's chiefs in the North;
There are wild Duniewassals, three
    thousand times three,
Will cry hoigh! for the bonnet of
    Bonny Dundee.*

    Come fill up my cup, &c.

*'There's brass on the target of
    barken'd bull-hide;
There's steel in the scabbard that
    dangles beside;
The brass shall be burnish'd, the steel
    shall flash free,
At a toss of the bonnet of Bonny
    Dundee.*

    Come fill up my cup, &c.

*'Away to the hills, to the caves, to
    the rocks—
Ere I own an usurper, I'll couch with
    the fox;
And tremble, false Whigs, in the
    midst of your glee,
You have not seen the last of my
    bonnet and me!'*

" 'O Looking-Glass creatures,' quoth Alice,
    'draw near!
'Tis an honour to see me, a favour to hear:
'Tis a privilege high to have dinner and tea
Along with the Red Queen, the White
    Queen, and me!' "

Then came the chorus again:—

"Then fill up the glasses with treacle and ink,
    Or anything else that is pleasant to drink:
Mix sand with the cider, and wool with the
        wine —
And welcome Queen Alice with
        ninety-times-nine!"

"Ninety times nine!" Alice repeated in despair. "Oh, that'll never be done! I'd better go in at once—" and in she went, and there was a dead silence the moment she appeared.

Alice glanced nervously along the table, as she walked up the large hall, and noticed that there were abouty fifty guests, of all kinds: some were animals, some birds, and there were even a few flowers among them. "I'm glad they've come without waiting to be asked," she thought: "I should never have known who were the right people to invite!"

There were three chairs at the head of the table: the Red and White Queens had already taken two of them, but the middle one was empty. Alice sat down in it, rather uncomfortable at the silence, and longing for some one to speak.

330

At last the Red Queen began. "You've missed the soup and fish," she said. "Put on the joint!" And the waiters set a leg of mutton before Alice, who looked at it rather anxiously, as she had never had to carve a joint before.

"You look a little shy: let me introduce you to that leg of mutton," said the Red Queen. "Alice — Mutton: Mutton — Alice." The leg of mutton got up in the dish and made a little bow to Alice; and Alice returned the bow, not knowing whether to be frightened or amused.

"May I give you a slice?" she said, taking up the knife and fork, and looking from one Queen to the other.

"Certainly not," the Red Queen said, very decidedly: "it isn't etiquette to cut any one you've been introduced to. Remove the joint!" And the waiters carried it off, and brought a large plum-pudding in its place.

"I won't be introduced to the pudding, please," Alice said rather hastily, "or we shall get no dinner at all. May I give you some?"

But the Red Queen looked sulky, and growled "Pudding—Alice: Alice—Pudding. Remove the pudding!" and the waiters took it away so quickly that Alice couldn't return its bow.

However, she didn't see why the Red Queen should be the only one to give orders; so, as an experiment, she called

Come fill up my cup, &c.

He waved his proud hand, and the trumpets were blown,
The kettle-drums clash'd, and the horsemen rode on,
Till on Ravelston's cliffs and on Clermiston's lee,
Died away the wild war-notes of Bonny Dundee.

Come fill up my cup, come fill up my can,
Come saddle the horses and call up the men,
Come open your gates, and let me gae free,
For it's up with the bonnets of Bonny Dundee!

out "Waiter! Bring back the pudding!"
and there it was again in a moment, like
a conjuring-trick. It was so large that she
couldn't help feeling a *little* shy with it,
as she had been with the mutton: however, she conquered her shyness by a
great effort, and cut a slice and handed it
to the Red Queen.

"What impertinence!" said the Pudding. "I wonder how you'd like it, if I
were to cut a slice out of *you*, you creature!"

It spoke in a thick, suety sort of voice,
and Alice hadn't a word to say in reply:
she could only sit and look at it and gasp.

"Make a remark," said the Red Queen:
"it's ridiculous to leave all the conversation to the pudding!"

"Do you know, I've had such a quantity of poetry repeated to me to-day,"
Alice began, a little frightened at finding
that, the moment she opened her lips,
there was dead silence, and all eyes were
fixed upon her; "and it's a very curious
thing, I think—every poem was about
fishes in some way. Do you know why
they're so fond of fishes, all about here?"

She spoke to the Red Queen, whose
answer was a little wide of the mark. "As
to fishes," she said, very slowly and solemnly, putting her mouth close to Alice's
ear, "her White Majesty knows a lovely
riddle—all in poetry—all about fishes.
Shall she repeat it?"

"Her Red Majesty's very kind to mention it," the White Queen murmured into Alice's other ear, in a voice like the cooing of a pigeon. "It would be *such* a treat! May I?" "Please do," Alice said very politely.

The White Queen laughed with delight, and stroked Alice's cheek. Then she began:

" 'First, the fish must be caught.'
That is easy: a baby, I think, could have
caught it.
'Next, the fish must be bought.'
That is easy: a penny, I think, would have
bought it.

'Now cook me the fish!'
That is easy, and will not take more than a
minute.
'Let it lie in a dish!'
That is easy, because it already is in it.

'Bring it here! Let me sup!'
It is easy to set such a dish on the table.
'Take the dish-cover up!'
Ah, *that* is so hard that I fear I'm unable!

For it holds it like glue —
Holds the lid to the dish, while it lies in the
middle:
Which is easiest to do,
Un-dish-cover the fish, or dishcover the
riddle?"**8**

"Take a minute to think about it, and then guess," said the Red Queen. "Meanwhile, we'll drink your health—Queen

8. The answer: an oyster. *The Lewis Carroll Handbook*, 1962, reveals (p. 95) that a four-stanza answer to the White Queen's riddle, in the same meter as the riddle, appeared in the English periodical *Fun*, October 30, 1878, p. 175. The answer had been previously submitted to Carroll, who polished up the meter for the anonymous author. The answer's final stanza, as quoted in the *Handbook*, is:

Get an oyster-knife strong,
Insert it 'twixt cover and dish in
the middle;
Then you shall before long
Un-dish-cover the OYSTERS—dish-
cover the riddle!

9. The reference is to candle extinguishers, small hollow cones used for snuffing out candles to prevent the smoke fumes from circulating around the room.

Alice's health!" she screamed at the top of her voice, and all the guests began drinking it directly, and very queerly they managed it: some of them put their glasses upon their heads like extinguishers,[9] and drank all that trickled down their faces—others upset the decanters, and drank the wine as it ran off the edges of the table—and three of them (who looked like kangaroos) scrambled into the dish of roast mutton, and began eagerly lapping up the gravy, "just like pigs in a trough!" thought Alice.

"You ought to return thanks in a neat speech," the Red Queen said, frowning at Alice as she spoke.

"We must support you, you know," the White Queen whispered, as Alice got up to do it, very obediently, but a little frightened.

"Thank you very much," she whispered in reply, "but I can do quite well without."

"That wouldn't be at all the thing," the Red Queen said very decidedly: so Alice tried to submit to it with a good grace.

("And they *did* push so!" she said afterwards, when she was telling her sister the history of the feast. "You would have thought they wanted to squeeze me flat!")

In fact it was rather difficult for her to keep in her place while she made her speech: the two Queens pushed her so, one on each side, that they nearly lifted her up into the air. "I rise to return thanks—" Alice began: and she really *did* rise as she spoke, several inches; but she got hold of the edge of the table, and managed to pull herself down again.

"Take care of yourself!" screamed the White Queen, seizing Alice's hair with both her hands. "Something's going to happen!"

And then (as Alice afterwards described it) all sorts of things happened in a moment. The candles all grew up to the ceiling, looking something like a bed of rushes with fire works at the top. As to the bottles, they each took a pair of plates, which they hastily fitted on as wings, and so, with forks for legs, went fluttering about in all directions: "and very like birds they look," Alice thought to herself, as well as she could in the dreadful confusion that was beginning.

At this moment she heard a hoarse laugh at her side, and turned to see what was the matter with the White Queen; but, instead of the Queen, there was the leg of mutton sitting in the chair. "Here I am!" cried a voice from the soup-tureen, and Alice turned again, just in time to see the Queen's broad good-natured face grinning at her for a moment over the edge of the tureen, before she disappeared into the soup.[10]

There was not a moment to be lost.

10. The White Queen has moved away from Alice to QR6; an illegal move in an orthodox chess game because it does not take the White King out of check.

11. This is Alice's capture of the
Red Queen. It results in a legiti-
mate checkmate of the Red King,
who has slept throughout the entire chess problem without moving.
Alice's victory gives a faint moral
to the story, for the white pieces
are good and gentle characters in
contrast to the fierce vindictive
temperaments of the red pieces.
The checkmate ends the dream
but leaves open the question of
whether the dream was Alice's or
the Red King's.

Already several of the guests were lying
down in the dishes, and the soup-ladle
was walking up the table towards Alice's
chair, and beckoning to her impatiently
to get out of its way.

"I can't stand this any longer!" she
cried, as she jumped up and seized the
tablecloth with both hands: one good
pull, and plates, dishes, guests, and
candles came crashing down together in
a heap on the floor.

"And as for *you*," she went on, turning
fiercely upon the Red Queen, whom she
considered as the cause of all the mischief—but the Queen was no longer at
her side—she had suddenly dwindled
down to the size of a little doll, and was
now on the table, merrily running round
and round after her own shawl, which was
trailing behind her.

At any other time, Alice would have
felt surprised at this, but she was far too
much excited to be
surprised at anything
now. "As for *you*," she
repeated, catching
hold of the little crea-
ture in the very act of
jumping over a bottle
which had just lighted
upon the table, "I'll
shake you into a kit-
ten, that I will!"**11**

CHAPTER X

Shaking

She took her off the table as she spoke, and shook her backwards and forwards with all her might.

The Red Queen made no resistance whatever: only her face grew very small, and her eyes got large and green: and still, as Alice went on shaking her, she kept on growing shorter—and fatter—and softer—and rounder—and—

CHAPTER XI

Waking

—and it really *was* a kitten, after all.

CHAPTER XII

Which Dreamed It?

"Your Red Majesty shouldn't purr so loud," Alice said, rubbing her eyes, and addressing the kitten, respectfully, yet with some severity. "You woke me out of oh! such a nice dream! And you've been along with me, Kitty—all through the Looking-Glass world. Did you know it, dear?"

It is a very inconvenient habit of kittens (Alice had once made the remark) that, whatever you say to them, they *always* purr. "If they would only purr for 'yes,' and mew for 'no,' or any rule of that sort," she had said, "so that one could keep up a conversation! But how *can* you talk with a person if they *always* say the same thing?"

On this occasion the kitten only purred: and it was impossible to guess whether it meant 'yes' or 'no.'

So Alice hunted among the chessmen on the table till she had found the Red Queen: then she went down on her knees on the hearthrug, and put the kitten and the Queen to look at each other. "Now, Kitty!" she cried, clapping her hands triumphantly. "Confess that was what you turned into!"

("But it wouldn't look at it," she said, when she was explaining the thing afterwards to her sister: "it turned away its head, and pretended not to see it: but it looked a *little* ashamed of itself, so I think it *must* have been the Red Queen.")

"Sit up a little more stiffly, dear!" Alice cried with a merry laugh. "And curtsey while you're thinking what to—what to purr. It saves time, remember!" And she caught it up and gave it one little kiss, "just in honour of its having been a Red Queen."

"Snowdrop, my pet!" she went on, looking over her shoulder at the White Kitten, which was still patiently undergoing its toilet, "when *will* Dinah have finished with your White Majesty, I wonder? That must be the reason you were so untidy in my dream.—Dinah! Do you know that you're scrubbing a White Queen? Really, it's most disrespectful of you!

"And what did *Dinah* turn to, I wonder?" she prattled on, as she settled comfortably down, with one elbow on the rug, and her chin in her hand to watch the kittens. "Tell me, Dinah, did you turn to Humpty Dumpty? I *think* you did —however, you'd better not mention it to your friends just yet, for I'm not sure.

"By the way, Kitty, if only you'd been really with me in my dream, there was one thing you *would* have enjoyed—I had such a quantity of poetry said to me, all about fishes! To-morrow morning you shall have a real treat. All the time you're eating your breakfast, I'll repeat 'The Walrus and the Carpenter' to you; and then you can make believe it's oysters, dear!

"Now, Kitty, let's consider who it was that dreamed it all. This is a serious question, my dear, and you should *not* go on licking your paw like that—as if Dinah hadn't washed you this morning! You see, Kitty, it *must* have been either me or the Red King. He was part of my dream, of course—but then I was part of his dream, too! *Was* it the Red King, Kitty? You were his wife, my dear, so you ought to know—Oh, Kitty, *do* help to settle it! I'm sure your paw can wait!" But the provoking kitten only began on the other paw, and pretended it hadn't heard the question.

Which do *you* think it was?

A boat, beneath a sunny sky
Lingering onward dreamily
In an evening of July —

Children three that nestle near,
Eager eye and willing ear,
Pleased a simple tale to hear —

Long has paled that sunny sky:
Echoes fade and memories die:
Autumn frosts have slain July.

Still she haunts me, phantomwise,
Alice moving under skies
Never seen by waking eyes.

Children yet, the tale to hear,
Eager eye and willing ear,
Lovingly shall nestle near.

In a Wonderland they lie,
Dreaming as the days go by,
Dreaming as the summers die:

Ever drifting down the stream —
Lingering in the golden gleam —
Life, what is it but a dream?[1]

1. In this terminal poem, one of Carroll's best, he recalls that July 4 boating expedition up the Thames on which he first told the story of *Alice's Adventures in Wonderland* to the three Liddell girls. The poem echoes the themes of winter and death that run through the prefatory poem of *Through the Looking-Glass*. It is the song of the White Knight, remembering Alice as she was before she turned away, with tearless and eager eyes, to run down the hill and leap the last brook into womanhood. The poem is an acrostic, the initial letters of the lines spelling Alice's full name.

Bibliography

The following bibliography is highly selective but includes all the major references to which I am indebted for most of the material contained in this volume's annotations. (The biography by Florence Becker Lennon was an unusually rich source.) For a collector's bibliography of works by the Reverend Dodgson, including his numerous leaflets and pamphlets, one must consult A *Handbook of the Literature of the Rev. C. L. Dodgson,* by Sidney Herbert Williams and Falconer Madan, 1931. An excellent check list of books and articles about Dodgson will be found in Mrs. Lennon's book.

BY LEWIS CARROLL

ALICE'S ADVENTURES IN WONDERLAND, *Macmillan,* 1865.
Carroll arranged for the first edition of two thousand copies to be published on July 4 to commemorate the date of the boating trip, three years earlier, on which he first told the story of Alice. This edition was recalled by Carroll and Tenniel because they did not like the quality of the printing. Unbound sheets were then sold to the New York firm of Appleton, who issued a thousand copies with a new title page printed at Oxford and dated 1866. This was the second issue of the first edition. The third issue was the remaining batch of 952 copies, carrying a title page printed in the U.S. Carroll had little interest in the quality of his U.S. printings. "I fear it is true that there are no children in America," he wrote in his diary (Sept. 3, 1880) after meeting an eight-year-old New York girl whose behavior he did not approve.

THROUGH THE LOOKING-GLASS, AND WHAT ALICE FOUND THERE,
Macmillan, 1871.

THE HUNTING OF THE SNARK, AN AGONY IN EIGHT FITS, *Macmillan*, 1876.

ALICE'S ADVENTURES UNDERGROUND, *Macmillan*, 1886.
A facsimile of the original manuscript, which Carroll hand-lettered and crudely illustrated as a gift for Alice Liddell. It is a little more than half the length of *Alice's Adventures in Wonderland*.

SYLVIE AND BRUNO, *Macmillan*, 1889.

THE NURSERY "ALICE," *Macmillan*, 1889.
A rewritten and shortened version of the first *Alice* book, for very young readers "from Nought to Five." The illustrations are Tenniel's, enlarged and colored.

SYLVIE AND BRUNO CONCLUDED, *Macmillan*, 1893.

THE LEWIS CARROLL PICTURE BOOK *edited by Stuart Dodgson Collingwood, Unwin*, 1899.
A valuable collection of miscellaneous short pieces by Carroll, including many of his original games, puzzles, and other mathematical recreations.

A SELECTION FROM THE LETTERS OF LEWIS CARROLL TO HIS CHILD-FRIENDS, *edited by Evelyn M. Hatch, Macmillan*, 1933.

THE RUSSIAN JOURNAL AND OTHER SELECTIONS FROM THE WORKS OF LEWIS CARROLL, *edited by John Francis McDermott, Dutton*, 1935.
Includes Carroll's diary record of his trip to Russia in 1867 with Canon Henry Liddon.

THE COMPLETE WORKS OF LEWIS CARROLL, *introduction by Alexander Woollcott, Random House*, 1937, *Nonesuch Press*, 1939.
The title is something of a fraud for the book is far from complete even when one excludes (as this book does) the many books published under the name of Charles Dodgson. It continues, however, (as a Modern Library book), to be the most easily obtained collection of Carroll's prose and verse.

THE DIARIES OF LEWIS CARROLL, *two volumes, edited by Roger Lancelyn Green, Cassell*, 1953.
Indispensable for any student of Carroll, though one regrets that Green's excisions include "mathematical and logical formulae and

minor problems," and "long accounts of how he [Carroll] saw children on the shore at Eastbourne, but failed to cultivate their friendship." An excellent review by W. H. Auden appeared in the *New York Times Book Review*, February 28, 1954.

SYMBOLIC LOGIC AND THE GAME OF LOGIC, *Dover*, 1958.
Single-volume reprint of Carroll's two books on logic, both intended for children.

PILLOW PROBLEMS AND A TANGLED TALE, *Dover*, 1958.
Single-volume reprint of Carroll's two books of problems in recreational mathematics.

ABOUT CARROLL

THE LIFE AND LETTERS OF LEWIS CARROLL, *Stuart Dodgson Collingwood*, 1898.
A biography by Carroll's nephew; the primary source of information about Carroll's life.

THE STORY OF LEWIS CARROLL, *Isa Bowman*, 1899.
Recollections of Carroll by one of the actresses who played Alice in Savile Clarke's stage musical and who became one of Carroll's leading child-friends.

LEWIS CARROLL, *Walter de laMare*, 1930.

THE LIFE OF LEWIS CARROLL, *Langford Reed*, 1932.

CARROLL'S ALICE, *Harry Morgan Ayres*, 1936.

VICTORIA THROUGH THE LOOKING-GLASS, *Florence Becker Lennon*, 1945.
(This is the U.S. edition. It later appeared in England under the title: *Lewis Carroll.*)

THE STORY OF LEWIS CARROLL, *Roger Lancelyn Green*, 1949.

LEWIS CARROLL: PHOTOGRAPHER, *Helmut Gernsheim*, 1949.
Includes excellent reproductions of sixty-four photographs by Carroll.

THE WHITE KNIGHT, *Alexander L. Taylor,* 1952.

LEWIS CARROLL, *Derek Hudson,* 1954.

"LEWIS CARROLL," a radio panel discussion by Bertrand Russell, Katherine Anne Porter, and Mark Van Doren. *The New Invitation to Learning,* 1942.

ON NONSENSE

"A Defence of Nonsense," Gilbert Chesterton in THE DEFENDANT, 1901.

"Lewis Carroll" and "How Pleasant to Know Mr. Lear," Gilbert Chesterton in A HANDFUL OF AUTHORS, 1953.

THE POETRY OF NONSENSE, Emile Cammaerts, 1925.

"Nonsense Poetry," George Orwell in SHOOTING AN ELEPHANT, 1945.

THE FIELD OF NONSENSE, *Elizabeth Sewell,* 1952.

ON CARROLL AS LOGICIAN AND MATHEMATICIAN

"Lewis Carroll as Logician," R. B. Braithwaite in THE MATHEMATICAL GAZETTE, Vol. 16, July 1932, pages 174-178.

"Lewis Carroll, Mathematician," D. B. Eperson in THE MATHEMATICAL GAZETTE, Vol. 17, May 1933, pages 92-100.

"Lewis Carroll and a Geometrical Paradox," Warren Weaver in THE AMERICAN MATHEMATICAL MONTHLY, Vol. 45, April 1938, pages 234-36.

"The Mathematical Manuscripts of Lewis Carroll," Warren Weaver in the PROCEEDINGS OF THE AMERICAN PHILOSOPHICAL SOCIETY, Vol. 98, October 15, 1954, pages 377-381.

"Lewis Carroll: Mathematician," Warren Weaver in SCIENTIFIC AMERICAN, April 1956.

"Mathematical Games," Martin Gardner in SCIENTIFIC AMERICAN, March 1960, pages 172-176. A discussion of Carroll's games and puzzles.

PSYCHOANALYTIC INTERPRETATIONS OF CARROLL

"Alice in Wonderland: the Child as Swain," William Empson in SOME VERSIONS OF PASTORAL, Chatto and Windus, 1935. The U.S. edition is titled ENGLISH PASTORAL POETRY. Reprinted in ART AND PSYCHOANALYSIS, edited by William Phillips, Criterion Books, 1957.

"Alice in Wonderland Psycho-Analyzed," A. M. E. Goldschmidt in NEW OXFORD OUTLOOK, May 1933.

"Psychoanalyzing Alice," Joseph Wood Krutch in THE NATION, Vol. 144, Jan. 30, 1937, pages 129-30.

"Psychoanalytic Remarks on 'Alice in Wonderland' and Lewis Carroll," Paul Schilder in THE JOURNAL OF NERVOUS AND MENTAL DISEASES, Vol. 87, 1938, pages 159-68.

"About the Symbolization of Alice's Adventures in Wonderland," Martin Grotjahn in AMERICAN IMAGO, Vol. 4, 1947, pages 32-41.

"Lewis Carroll's Adventures in Wonderland," John Skinner in AMERICAN IMAGO, Vol. 4, 1947, pages 3-31.

SWIFT AND CARROLL, Phyllis Greenacre, International Universities Press, 1955.

"All on a Golden Afternoon," Robert Bloch in FANTASY AND SCIENCE FICTION, June 1956. A short story burlesquing the analytic approach to Alice.

ON TENNIEL

> *Enchanting Alice! Black-and-white*
> *Has made your charm perennial;*
> *And nought save "Chaos and old Night"*
> *Can part you now from Tenniel.*

> — from a poem by Austin Dobson

CREATORS OF WONDERLAND, *Marguerite Mespoulet*, 1934.

The book argues that Tenniel was influenced by the French artist J. J. Grandville.

SIR JOHN TENNIEL, *Frances Sarzano*, 1948.

"The Life and Works of Sir John Tenniel," W. C. Monkhouse in the ART JOURNAL, Easter Number, 1901.